EFFECTS OF CONSERVATIVE RELIGION *on* LESBIAN *and* GAY CLIENTS *and* PRACTITIONERS: PRACTICE IMPLICATIONS

NASW PRESS

National Association of Social Workers
Washington, DC

James J. Kelly, PhD, ACSW, LCSW, *President*
Elizabeth J. Clark, PhD, ACSW, MPH, *Executive Director*

Cheryl Y. Bradley, *Publisher*
Lisa M. O'Hearn, *Managing Editor*
John Cassels, *Project Manager and Staff Editor*
Amanda Morgan, *Copyeditor*
Lori J. Holtzinger, *Proofreader*
Tom Fish, *Indexer*

Cover by Blue House
Interior design and composition by Rick Soldin
Printed and bound by Hamilton Printing Company

Library of Congress Cataloging-in-Publication Data

Hunter, Ski.
Effects of conservative religion on lesbian and gay clients and practitioners: practice implications / Ski Hunter.
    p. cm.
  ISBN 978-0-87101-400-9
 1. Social work with gays—United States. 2. Social work with lesbians— United States. 3. Gays—Religious life—United States. 4. Lesbians—Religious life—United States. 5. Homosexuality—Religious aspects. I. Title.
  HV1449.H8654 2010
  362.8—dc22

                                                              2010009819

Printed in the United States of America

I dedicate this book to lesbian and gay people who are in conflict with their religion. I hope a resolution develops for you.

Contents

About the Author

Ski Hunter, PhD, LMSW, MSW, MA, is a professor in the School of Social Work, University of Texas at Arlington. She has written a number of books on LGBT people and done many workshops on the topic. She also teaches a course on this topic.

Part I

Heterosexism and Religion

One

Religious Views of Same-Sex Attraction

dvances for lesbian and gay people have occurred in the United States in the form of antidiscrimination laws, elimination of all sodomy laws, making hate crimes against lesbian and gay people a crime, and legalization of civil unions and marriage in some states. But this secular progress is not matched in heterosexist religious arenas. As stated by Yip (2007), lesbian and gay issues are still contentious.

Heterosexism pervades our culture and beliefs. Herek (1995) defined it as "the ideological system that denies, denigrates, and stigmatizes any nonheterosexual form of behavior, identity, relationship, or community" (p. 321). It dismisses and stigmatizes anyone who does not comply with heterosexual norms. Heterosexism operates at two levels: cultural and individual. Cultural heterosexism is so pervasive that we may not notice it until something comes along like the gay marriage issue. Many people have risen up against gay marriage and called for the passing of laws to prevent it or, in some states, overturning of laws that support it. They believe that marriage can only happen between a woman and a man. Almost any time a legal move takes place that is favorable to lesbian and gay people, a backlash of negative commentary develops and moves start up to have the favorable laws overturned. So progress is made but also upended by those who oppose this progress. Another example of cultural heterosexism took place when, in 2005, an Alabama state representative proposed a bill to strip public libraries of books by lesbian or gay authors, promising to dig a hole in the ground, dump the books in it, and bury them (Burr, 2009). The bill failed to pass.

Because of the pervasiveness of cultural heterosexism, it is not surprising to see it also manifested at the individual level in feelings and behaviors. This can range from jokes and derogatory language to violence (Herek, 1995). At this level, lesbian and gay people have to contend with stigma, prejudice, discrimination, and sometimes violence and death. It also affects the coming-out process and decisions about whether or not to disclose one's sexual identity to others. As an example, in 1999, gay partners ages 50 and 40 were brutally murdered while asleep in their bed by two white supremacist brothers in Redding, California. They claimed they were carrying out God's will (Kaiser Family Foundation, 2001; Violence Against LGBT People, n.d.). This is just one example of many murders of lesbian and gay people.

Yep (2002) described four categories of heterosexism, based on whether the prejudice is interior or exterior and individual or collective. *Interior-individual* or internalized heterosexism occurs when people learn at a young age that being lesbian or gay is considered shameful and is stigmatized as deviant, immoral, and deficient, that lesbian and gay people are outcasts, and that something is wrong with them. The stigmatization, which can be learned from many sources such as family, friends, teachers, and the mass media, becomes internalized.

Exterior-individual or externalized heterosexism happens when lesbian and gay people are subjected to verbal abuse, avoidance, discrimination, and physical violence.

Interior-collective heterosexism, or discursive violence, occurs when lesbian and gay people are treated and talked about differently from heterosexuals in order to degrade and pathologize them. This can include not only words but also tones and gestures. People sometimes ask questions that would hardly ever be asked of heterosexuals, such as: What do lesbians do in bed? Are you the man or the woman in your relationship?

Exterior-collective heterosexism can also be thought of as institutional violence. Heterosexist thinking is deeply ingrained in our social and collective consciousness. Heterosexuals are normalized while lesbian and gay people are disadvantaged and disempowered. Few employers, for example, provide benefits to domestic partners, while their availability for heterosexual couples is taken for granted. All four types of heterosexism are psychological violence or, as Yep (2002) put it, soul murder.

Interior-individual heterosexism affects everyone, as heterosexism is internalized in all of us. A strong religious commitment has been shown to predict internalized heterosexism in both heterosexuals and lesbian and gay people (Herek, 1987). Research studies have overwhelmingly found that people with conservative or fundamentalist religious beliefs are especially likely to hold anti-gay attitudes (Altemeyer, 2003b; Altemeyer & Hunsberger, 1992; Batson, Floyd, Meyer, & Winner, 1999; Burdette, Ellison, & Hill, 2005; Duck & Hunsberger, 1999; R. D. Fisher, Derison, Polley, Cadman, & Johnston, 1994; Herek, 1987; Hunsberger, 1996; Hunsberger & Jackson, 2005; Veenvliet & Esses, 2007; Wilkinson, 2004; Wilkinson & Roys, 2005). Heterosexist messages are often delivered in churches (Ream, 2001). The outcome is that people develop negative attitudes about same-sex attractions and the people who experience them.

Lesbian and gay people internalize heterosexism and develop negative attitudes about themselves (Meyer & Dean, 1998; Otis and Skinner, 1996; Ross and Rosser, 1996; Wagner, Brandolo, & Rabkhi, 1996). High levels of internalized heterosexism have negative outcomes for lesbian and gay people. They experience decreased levels of self-acceptance and self-esteem along with shame and self-hatred (Purcell, Camos, & Perrilla, 1996). They can also experience depression, demoralization, guilt, fear, suicidal ideation and behavior, sexual dysfunction, lessening of involvement in intimate relationships, expectations of rejection by others, isolation, lack of connection to the lesbian and gay community, drug or alcohol abuse, and limited aspirations (Boatwright, Gilbert, Forrest, & Ketzenberger, 1996; Harris, Cook, & Kashubeck-West, 2008; Kus, 1992; Meyer and Dean, 1998; Otis and Skinner, 1996; Shidlo & Schroeder, 2002; Wagner et al., 1996). In addition, they accept negative myths about themselves (Boatwright et al., 1996; Meyer and Dean, 1998; Otis and Skinner, 1996; Wagner et al., 1996), such as that they are abnormal, pathological, perverted, shameful, and evil.

Internalized heterosexism in lesbian and gay people can be overt or covert. Overt expression includes depreciation of oneself as inferior or deviant. People may not seek support because they think they do not deserve it. Covert forms are more common. People may appear to accept themselves and their sexual identity but act in ways that sabotage themselves. For example, they may abandon educational or career plans, or they may tolerate abusive behavior from others. They may also set themselves up for rejection with impulsive disclosures in situations in which people are likely to react with hostility (Gonsiorek, 1993).

Religious Views of Same-Sex Attractions

An interchange exists between heterosexism and conservative religion. Heterosexist religions create the sin of being lesbian or gay. Judgmental words they associate with sin include *damnation*, *penance*, *iniquity*, and *transgression* (Burr, 2009). Nugent and Gramick (1989) identified various religious views about lesbian and gay people, and several of these views are tied to sin. The views presented here range from the most negative to the most positive, but few are positive. The religious views are categorized as rejecting–punitive, rejecting–nonpunitive, qualified acceptance, and full acceptance.

Rejecting-Punitive

The majority of mainline Protestant, Catholic, Islamic, and Judaic traditions strictly prohibit same-sex relations and consider them sinful, immoral, and evil (Clark, Brown, & Hochstein, 1990; Melton, 1991). This view is one of the strongest sources of heterosexist rhetoric in the United States and around the world. In Christian churches, it relies heavily on Biblical texts that are thought to condemn same-sex relations. Some fundamentalists with this view endorse the death penalty for lesbian and gay people. The author heard the president of a U.S. fundamentalist college say on a radio program that lesbian and gay people should be stoned to death and for no other reason than their sexual orientation. The response of this religious view to lesbian and gay people throughout history included, as punishment or cures for same-sex relations, stoning, burning, imprisonment, banishment, torture, and sexual mutilation (Nugent & Gramick, 1989). In more modern times, refusal to be cured or turned into a heterosexual can result in being expelled from one's church and often from one's family. In this view, the only way lesbian and gay people can be saved is to renounce their same-sex relations and experience a religious conversion to heterosexuality. This is based on the assumption that being lesbian or gay is a choice and that one can change one's sexual orientation. This view also teaches that God does not love same-sex-attracted people who cannot or will not change. Added as a motivator is the threat that being lesbian or gay is punishable by an eternity in hell (Greenberg & Bystryn, 1982).

Rejecting-Nonpunitive

This view rejects same-sex attractions and behavior but not the person. It advocates the position "love the sinner, hate the sin" (Lease, Horne, & Noffsinger-Frazier, 2005). This was the view taught by Saint Augustine. Conservative religious people follow this principle when they claim that they accept lesbian and gay people but not their sexual behavior. But can one distinguish between a behavior and the person who carries it out (Batson et al., 1999)? Wilkinson and Roys (2005) conducted a study with 171 college students (58 men, 113 women) to determine if they could distinguish between same-sex behavior, fantasies, and emotions. They found that lesbian and gay people were rated more negatively when they were described as engaging in sexual behavior than when they were described as only having sexual fantasies or feelings. The behavior of having sex was viewed as sinful.

This view entails a negative prejudicial judgment against lesbian and gay people (Bassett et al., 2001). Those with this view are attempting to be affirmative while at the same time they are prejudiced. They say they accept lesbian and gay people but not one of the core parts of their sexual orientation, having sex with a person of the same sex (A. R. Fisher & DeBord, 2007). Churches that hold this view tell gay and lesbian people to go through a conversion or reorientation to heterosexuality or live a life of sexual abstinence (Bassett et al., 2001).

Qualified Acceptance

This view considers heterosexual identity to be the ideal and same-sex sexual identity to be inferior. Same-sex behavior is considered imperfect and incomplete, but lesbian and gay people are not seen as immoral, sinful, or evil. This position also asserts that lesbian and gay people do not choose their sexual orientation and cannot change it (Nugent & Gramick, 1989). Same-sex relations are not forbidden by this view, but they are also not embraced (Barret & Barzan, 1966; Dworkin, 1997).

Full Acceptance

This view proclaims that same-sex attractions are equal to heterosexual attractions, natural, and part of the divine plan of creation. Sexuality is to be evaluated by the quality of the relationships of those involved, regardless of their genders (Nugent & Gramick, 1989).

The Predominant Rejecting-Punitive Religious View

All of the views identified above, except full acceptance, can be troubling to lesbian and gay people. But the rejecting–punitive view is the most difficult one to cope with and is central in this book. Many believe that this religious view contributes strongly to internalized heterosexism and rejection of oneself as lesbian or gay (Gage Davidson, 2000; Haldeman, 1998; Wood, 2000).

The rejecting–punitive view is represented by most major religious denominations. Those who identify as lesbian and gay have been rejected by nearly every major religious denomination in the United States. Only a few of the more than 2,500 religious denominations in the United States affirm lesbian and gay people (Sherkat, 2002).

Evangelical and fundamentalist groups also hold the rejecting-punitive religious view. Evangelicalism developed out of the Protestant revivals that took place in the United States in the eighteenth and nineteenth centuries. Groups such as Southern Baptists, Catholic charismatics, Pentecostals, and Mennonites are examples of evangelical religions. Evangelicals hold that the Bible is the sole source of religious authority. They believe in the inerrancy of the Bible, the authenticity of Jesus's miracles, and the virgin birth of Jesus. Fundamentalists are a subsect of evangelicalism (Kahn, 2006). Fundamentalism today is traceable to the 1840s with the local growth of revivalism. It holds that only one religion, evangelicalism, has the inerrant truth (Hunsberger, 1996). Those high in strong religious fundamentalism had strong early training in identifying with their religion. The early emphasis on family religion may be accompanied with "us versus them" mentality that leads to discrimination (Altemeyer, 2003b).

The rise of American fundamentalism was associated with rejection of Darwinian ideas of evolution and historical and critical studies of Biblical texts at the end of the nineteenth century. The intellectual advances of Western culture were shut out of their churches, and this has not changed. Fundamentalists believe that every word in the Bible came directly from God. Inerrancy was a code word (Marsden, 2006) for their belief that the Bible is literally true: "God cannot make any mistakes" (Houts, 2009, p. 284). In addition to being antimodern, other aspects of fundamentalism include opposition to progressive liberal political reform, communism, and foreign policy involvement. They oppose psychology because of its acceptance of sexual freedom and "homosexuals." They also think that individual believers can understand Biblical truths (Houts, 2009).

The author knows of a conservative Baptist school of theology in which the staff rewrote the NASW *Code of Ethics* to conform to their orthodoxy. Statements they thought were too progressive, including everything related to same-sex sexual orientation, were deleted. These statements did not fit with their view of religious truth.

Authority for the rejection-punitive view is external, derived from scripture, religious leaders, creeds, and canons (Buchanan, Dzelme, Harris, & Hecker, 2001). Religious truths must be followed, and church members must comply with unchangeable religious practices (Altemeyer and Hunsberger, 1992; Paloutzian, 1996). Evangelical and fundamentalist Christians rely on the Bible as a guide to living (Noll, 1992). Religion is looked to for decision making (Deutsch, Coleman, & Marcus, 2006) and directions in life. Religious leaders and congregations also give instructions on everything including appropriate sexual activity (D. L. Levy, 2008). Instruction to lesbian and gay people typically includes three choices: repentance and conversion, celibacy, or heterosexual marriage (Ritter & O'Neill, 1998).

Those holding the rejecting-punitive view, including evangelical and fundamentalist Christians, believe that one set of religious teachings contains the fundamental, essential, and inerrant truth about humanity and the deity (Parga-ment, 1997). They also believe that the Bible is a literal transcription of ultimate truth or the word of God (Hogge & Friedman, 1967). Taylor (2000) found that the belief that the Bible should be taken literally was the strongest predictor of negative attitudes toward lesbian and gay people.

Duck and Hunsberger (1999) found that authoritarianism (rigid traditional attitudes) and intrinsic religiosity (internally motivated) had the strongest rela-tionships with prejudice. Religious fundamentalism has in its structure authori-tarianism, discrimination, and hostility toward lesbian and gay people (Duck & Hunsberger, 1999; Hunsberger, 1996).

Religious fundamentalists have been characterized as closed-minded and unwilling to question their beliefs or consider other points of view (English, 1996; Hunsberger, Pratt, & Prancer, 1994; Schwartz & Lindley, 2005). The reject-ing-punitive view brings with it lowered levels of understanding and acceptance of beliefs and values that are different from its perceived morally superior view (Friedman & Downey, 1994). Religious groups that interpret scripture with a greater emphasis on historical context and that allow for variations in interpre-tation report less prejudice and discrimination against lesbian and gay people (Nelson, 1982; Nungesser, 1983).

Rejecting-punitive religious teachings and doctrines have also been used to discriminate against other groups. Churches with this view support a patriarchal culture in which women occupy second-class status. The Bible and other reli-gious texts have also been used to support miscegenation laws, racial segregation, the Holocaust, slavery, and genocide among Native Americans. Every group that has practiced genocide against another group did so out of a valuative frame-work, often religiously based (Greene, 2007). Most of the groups justified their behavior as coming from a religious mandate, and they often received popular support. This continues to be true for lesbian and gay people. Believers hold to the view that they are upholding a moral order sanctioned by religious tradition and divine authority, and they rationalize their treatment of lesbian and gay people in these moralistic terms (Yip, 2003).

The rejecting-punitive view finds support in several Bible verses (quota-tions that follow are from the King James version). The most often quoted is the story of Sodom and Gomorrah (Genesis 19:1–8, 10–13). Two angels arrived at Sodom in the evening. Lot, who was sitting in the gateway of the city, saw them. He got up to meet them and bowed down. "My lords," he said, "please turn aside to your servant's house. You can wash your feet and spend the night and then go on your way early in the morning." "No," they answered, "we will spend the night in the square." But he insisted so strongly that they went with him and entered his house. He prepared a meal for them.

Before they went to bed, all the men from every part of the city of Sodom—both young and old—surrounded the house. They called to Lot, "Where are the men who came to you tonight? Bring them out to us so that we can have sex with them." Lot went outside to meet them and shut the door behind him and said, "No, my friends. Don't do this wicked thing. Look, I have two daughters who have never slept with a man. Let me bring them out to you, and you can do what you like with them. But don't do anything to these men, for they have come under the protection of my room." The men inside reached out and pulled Lot back into the house and shut the door. Then they struck the men who were at the door of the house with blindness so that they could not find the door. The two men said to Lot, "Do you have anyone else here—sons-in-law, sons, or daughters, or anyone else in the city who belongs to you? Get them out of here, because we are going to destroy this place. The outcry to the Lord against its people in this city is so great that He has sent us to destroy it."

Many Christians believe that God destroyed the city of Sodom due to the sin of "homosexuality." However, other verses in the Bible referring to this story (Ezekiel 16:49; Luke 10:10–12, 17:28–29; and Mathew 10:14–15) explain that the sins of the city were actually inhospitality, haughtiness and arrogance, and lack of concern for the poor (Boswell, 1980).

Leviticus 18:22 instructs men: "Do not lie with a man as one lies with a woman; that is detestable." Leviticus 20:13 says that "if a man lies with a man as one lies with a woman, both of them have done what is detestable. They must be put to death; their blood will be on their own heads." These two verses are part of the Levitical Code or rules for living. But many view this code as outdated. In addition to prohibiting male-to-male sexual contact, it includes other prohibitions such as the following:

- Leviticus 11:6–10: One is forbidden to eat rabbit, pork, lobster, shrimp, or clams.

- Leviticus 12:2: If a woman bears a son, she is unclean for seven days; after bearing a daughter, she is unclean for 14 days.

- Leviticus 20:18: Any husband who sees his naked wife during the time she is menstruating must be ostracized.

While most of these prohibitions are no longer considered relevant, many religious leaders still speak about the prohibition against same-sex acts. This is a manifestation of heterosexism (D. R. Morrow & Tyson, 2006). Most Christians do not follow any of the other Levitical laws, so it is hypocritical to apply one of these laws to gay people (Wilcox, 2003).

First Corinthians 6:9–10 states, "Do you not know that the wicked will not inherit the kingdom of God? Do not be deceived: Neither the sexually immoral nor idolaters nor adulterers nor male prostitutes nor homosexual offenders…will inherit the kingdom of God." And Timothy 1:9–10 says, "We also know that law is made not for the righteous but for lawbreakers and rebels, the ungodly and sinful, the unholy and irreligious…homosexuals."

Most books of the New Testament, including the Gospels, do not address same-sex acts. Paul is the only New Testament writer to do so. The two passages above were written by Paul.

> **Romans 1:26-27 states:**
> God gave them over to shameful lusts. Even their women
> exchanged natural relations for unnatural ones. In the same way
> the men also abandoned natural relations with women and were
> inflamed with lust for one another. Men committed indecent acts
> with other men, and received in themselves the due penalty for
> their perversion.

This is another passage written by Paul. The problem here is that we only have Paul's answer and do not know the question or situation. He may have responded to idolatry and pagan rites that honor false gods. Since no one studied "homosexuals" as a distinct group until the twentieth century, it may have been that Paul was not discussing sexual minorities but same-sex acts carried out by heterosexuals with temple prostitutes (Burr, 2009).

Burr (2009) identified seven issues to consider when thinking about a Biblical view of "homosexuality":

1. There are no teachings on "homosexuality" in the Bible. Jesus never mentioned it in the four gospels.

2. "Homosexual" behavior is never the main focus of a text. It is mentioned in a discussion of something else such as attempted rape, idolatry, or purity codes. The meaning and context of these texts is difficult to discern.

3. Biblical authors did not understand "homosexual" orientation. Social science did not understand sexual orientation until midway through the 20th century.

4. Jesus embraced two sexual minorities. He welcomed prostitutes and eunuchs, men who could not perform sexually or had been castrated, and said they would enter the Kingdom of Heaven and attain full salvation.

5. Literal application of scriptures to contemporary moral issues can lead to terrible consequences. Slavery is an example.

6. Jesus and the writings of the early church condemn being judgmental (Matthew 7:1–5; Romans 2:1, 14:4–13). The church and society are judgmental of lesbian and gay people and cruel to them. Jesus advocated love.

7. There is no single sexual ethic in the Bible.

The Bible as we know it today did not come into existence until the fourth century. In 1546 at the Council of Trent, Catholic Church leaders voted to accept the 66 books of the Old and New Testaments as authoritative. The list of scriptures that the church considered to be inspired came to be called the canon. Its selection was the result of a long process of deciding which of the books that had been circulating for a long time were to be regarded as authoritative and inspired. Books were chosen by general consensus of church leaders (Houts, 2009). The Bible, however, is confusing. Many fragments of manuscripts canonized by the Roman Catholic Church and many English translations as well as translations into other languages add to the confusion. There is no literal translation; only approximations to literal translations. The multitude of English translations renders claims of a single literal meaning of English-language Bibles impossible (Burr, 2009). Genesis 1–19 is an example. Traditional interpretations cite the creation story as evidence that God intended women and men to come together to propagate the Earth and say that this is the literal meaning of this story. Newer interpretations assert that the creation story is not meant to present a paradigm for all human relationships but to answer the question: Where do we come from? Also the creation story does not mention the varieties of human experience (Bennett, 1998).

Most Christians are not able to identify the particular verses of the Bible that are used to justify discrimination against lesbian and gay people. Nor do they know that Jesus said nothing on this topic. Nevertheless, they have the notion that same-sex relations are wrong (Walton, 2006). The Biblical references, whether one can identify them or not, suggest to those who hold the rejecting-punitive view that they are not only justified in hating and denigrating lesbian and gay people but are required to do so by their church. They are insulated from other views. They and their churches give no consideration to alternate views (Burr, 2009).

In addition to putting great emphasis on particular Bible passages, the rejecting-punitive view also fosters righteousness and morality by pointing to sin as a contrast. Morality stands in stark contrast to the depravity of immorality and sin. Lesbian and gay people are an acceptable target for vilification as they are viewed as depraved and immoral (Yakushko, 2005). Much of our society overlooks social sins like poverty, crime, and exploitation of the earth. They are too overwhelming to handle, so people shift their attention to an enemy who seems easier to attack (Brown-Taylor, 2000).

Rejecting-punitive churches do not only rely on Bible verses or their notion of morality. Same-sex sexual behavior is also viewed as wrong because it is seen as annulling God's sexual design. Same-sex unions, they say, do not fulfill the procreative purpose of sexual intercourse and are an attack on families as the basic unit of society. This is the case even though many lesbian and gay people have children from earlier heterosexual marriages, insemination, or other means. In addition, sexuality is viewed as good only within marriage, so those representing the rejecting-punitive view require lesbian and gay people to be celibate (Hodge, 2005). To impose this on an entire group is unjust, as all humans have a right to sexuality (Nugent & Gramick, 1989).

If one grew up in a rejecting-punitive church, one no doubt received the negative messages about same-sex sexual identity cited above and many other messages of the same type. They came through religious teachings (for example, reading of the scriptures or other sacred texts, sermons, or discussions). They also observe prohibition of openly lesbian and gay clergy or religious leaders and isolation or avoidance of identified lesbian and gay people. Often sermons include admonitions against same-sex thoughts or deeds and say they are mortal sins. Church members internalize the prohibition "thou shall not be gay" (Lease et al., 2005).

Rejecting-punitive views are prevalent in many Christian churches, Jewish synagogues, and Islamic mosques and create conflict for lesbian and gay members (Yakushko, 2005). The most notable rejecting-punitive views in the United States, however, exist among the Christian churches. These are the churches we hear from the most in America in terms of their negative views of lesbian and gay people. In a study by Melton (1991) of Christian religious organizations, 72 percent were found to condemn lesbian and gay people and to call their same-sex attractions an abomination. The word "abomination," however, specifies a violation of ritual purity rather than referring to a moral or ethical violation (Schested, 1999).

Since the 1950s, scientists have learned a great deal about the wide variety of human sexual orientations and behaviors. Some religious denominations have been able to gain new understandings in response to these discoveries. But others have not been able to find a way to reconcile this information with their traditional belief systems. The congregations who allow the science of human sexuality to influence their understandings of scriptural principles often construct new theologies and do away with their institutions' oppression of sexual minorities. Their congregations vote to be inclusive. As noted earlier, religious groups that interpret scripture with a greater emphasis on historical context and allow for greater variations in interpretation also report less prejudice and discrimination against lesbian and gay people (Nelson, 1982; Nungesser, 1983).

Conservative interpretations of the Bible passages cited above are also countered by liberal interpretations (Brammer, 2004). During the past 30 years, a growing number of biblical scholars, theologians, and clergy have commented on how difficult it is to draw conclusions about lesbian and gay issues from the Bible. At the time it was written, there were no words for "gay," "lesbian," or "homosexual." These words did not exist in classic Greek or Hebrew. They did not appear in the Bible until 1946 (Mancini & Rzeznik, 1993). These words would not have had meaning before that time. In addition, the ancient world most likely did know of hostility to "homosexuality" (Burr, 2009). The fact that the word "homosexual" was not coined until the middle part of the 19th century presents challenges when attempting to discern what, if anything, the Bible says about it (Tolbert, 2002). Again, conservative Christians seem to pay no attention to these facts.

Churches with the rejecting-punitive view have the most organized political opposition against lesbian and gay people. Evangelical Protestants are the most organized in their opposition to lesbian and gay people, although Catholics and other Christian sects have also strongly opposed them (Miceli, 2005). This includes the Lubavitch sect of Judaism, which preaches abhorrence of same-sex sexual behaviors (Enron, 1993). Lesbian and gay people have no "religious citizenship" in most denominations (Yip, 2007).

Summary

Heterosexism is always in the background, if not the foreground, of the lives of lesbian and gay people. It also influences conservative religious views of them. Most religious denominations in the United States have highly negative views of lesbian and gay people. Many insist that to avoid burning in hell one must convert to heterosexuality. The rejection-punitive religious view is the most severe and troublesome to lesbian and gay people.

Two

Views of Some Major Denominations

O f the wide range of religious faiths active in the United States, not all
denominations (or all churches within them) take a rejecting-punitive
view toward gay and lesbian people or same-sex attractions. The positions
reviewed in this chapter represent a broad sample of religious positions. While
most, if not all, of these denominations have long had lesbian and gay members,
few developed official policies on the subject before the late 1960s (Clark, Brown,
& Hochstein, 1990).

Protestantism has hundreds of different denominations. Each has its own hier-
archy and tenets. Churches range from fundamentalist and evangelical to moderate
(Methodists, Congregationalists, Episcopalians) to Universalist/Unitarians. Protestantism emerged as a reaction to centuries of religious domination by the Roman
Catholic Church. This change was part of the European Renaissance. It included
the Lutheran Church (Martin Luther in Germany), Methodist Church (John Wesley
in England), Presbyterian Church (John Calvin in Scotland), and other mainstream
Protestant denominations such as Episcopalians and Baptists. Some Protestant
denominations have internal divisions; for example, the Missouri Synod is the more
conservative branch of the Lutheran Church, and the Southern Baptist Convention holds more fundamentalist views than the Northern Baptist Convention.

Some churches appeared in America after the Protestant Reformation, including Seventh-Day Adventists, the Church of Jesus Christ of Latter-Day Saints, Jehovah's Witnesses, and Christian Science (Cummings & Cummings, 2009).

Jehovah's Witnesses

The Jehovah's Witness organization began in the late 1800s in Pennsylvania as a small Bible study group. During the early 1900s it became an international organization called the Watch Tower Bible and Tract Society of Pennsylvania. Jehovah's Witnesses teach that "homosexuality" is "detestable," "an abomination," "abhorrent," and caused by demon possession. "Homosexuals" are expected to remain celibate. One must suppress desire, longing, feelings of attractiveness, love, and sexual fantasies about others of the same sex. People who do not conform completely to the sect's doctrines and practices, including a strict prohibition against being gay, are "disfellowshipped"—a severe form of ostracism in which fellow members avoid all contact with them. Some also consider celibate lesbian and gay people to be unsuitable for membership (Judge, 2006).

Church of Christ

The only creed of this church is the Bible, which is considered the infallible guide to heaven. In the past, church doctrine on "homosexuality" was taken from Bible verses such as Leviticus 18:22 (instruction to men: "Do not lie with a man as one lies with a woman; that is detestable.") The official current Web page of the church stated: "'Homosexuality' is a choice made by those who desire the unnatural. God remains consistent in His condemnation of 'homosexuality.' By the written Word of God, the church does not condone or embrace 'homosexuality,' but a 'homosexual' can repent and be forgiven by God" (Church of Christ, 2008).

United Church of Christ

This church has begun to reach out to lesbian and gay people. Television ads communicate that everyone is welcome in their churches. A newer statement from the church says that it has "addressed the concerns of lesbian, gay, bisexual, and transgender people in church and society, calling for welcome, inclusion, and justice." This church also supports gay marriage and stands for ending discrimination and violence against lesbian and gay people (United Church of Christ National Bodies, n.d.). Many of its pro-lesbian and -gay stances can be found on the Human Resource Campaign 2010 Web site: http://www.hrc.org/issues/5055.htm.

Southern Baptist Convention

The Southern Baptist Convention (SBC) is the largest Protestant denomination in the United States. It is the most public in denouncing lesbian and gay people. It goes further than most Christian denominations in condemning not only lesbian and gay sex but anyone with a lesbian or gay sexual orientation. In 1996, it declared that even the desire to engage in a same-sex relationship is sinful. The SBC also expresses antipathy for heterosexuals and institutions that accept or support lesbian and gay people (Bennett, 1998).

The SBC has passed numerous resolutions on lesbian and gay issues. It asserts that it will preach, teach, and politically organize against these people and their supporters, and has gone on record as supporting discrimination against lesbian and gay people. Although the SBC traditionally permitted congregations to make their own decisions on morality questions, it issued a rare amendment to its constitution in 1992 stating that it would bar any congregation that acted to approve or endorse "homosexual" behavior. This would include congregations that bless lesbian and gay unions or ordain lesbian or gay clergy (Bennett, 1998).

Southern Baptists consider the Bible to be a literal rendering of God's word. They dismiss scientific, cultural, and linguistic views that other people of faith support. For example, the SBC dismisses as irrelevant the idea that, with the many translations of the Bible in existence, the original words are subject to misinterpretation (Bennett, 1998).

In recent years, the SBC has become aggressively more negative toward lesbian and gay people. Recently a Baptist preacher said that gay people were out to rape children in order to recruit them and that the only way to stop this was to kill them (Right Wing Watch, 2009). The SBC opposes civil rights for lesbian and gay people. It forbids them to become members of the church; members who disclose their sexual identity are often excommunicated. The SBC holds, however, that with repentance, forgiveness and transformation through Jesus Christ can happen (see http://www.hrc.org/issues/5051.htm for more views of the SBC on lesbian and gay people).

Mormon Church

The Mormon church, whose formal name is the Church of Jesus Christ of Latter-Day Saints, is also fiercely antagonistic toward lesbian and gay people. Like other conservative religious groups, its antigay rhetoric has intensified as social acceptance of same-sex marriage, civil unions, and domestic partnerships has become more widespread.

It argues that those who say they are attracted to someone of the same sex are misguided or willfully sinful. "Homosexuality" is seen as Satan's work, the devil trying to thwart God's plan for humankind. The Mormon Church excommunicates those who persist in saying they are lesbian or gay. The church stated: "We cannot stand idle if they indulge in immoral activity" (Hinckley, 1998, as cited in Church of Jesus Christ of Latter-Day Saints, n.d.). This church pronounced that "homosexuality" was antithetical to God's will and destructive to the family. It is increasingly vocal in opposition to same-sex relationships, because in its view sex is to be used for procreation and to enhance marital intimacy.

For years, the church counseled lesbian and gay members to marry and live a heterosexual life. In 1988, the church softened its position somewhat. While it still holds that sex is only permissible within the context of a heterosexual marriage, it acknowledges that marriage is not a cure-all for "homosexuality" and encourages gays instead to remain celibate (Dove, 2000). The Mormon Church also encourages gay and lesbian people to adopt heterosexuality, but it does not have any official ties to organizations that work to change sexual orientation (Vance, 2008).

Because of its opposition to same-sex marriage, the Mormon Church supported Proposition 8, for a constitutional amendment that would change the state constitution to define marriage as being between a man and a woman, in California in 2008. In a letter dated June 29 of that year, the church leadership called for members to work hard to pass Proposition 8; the church spent nearly $190,000 to help pass it (McClatchy, 2009; see http://mormonsfor8.com/).

Surprisingly, in November 2009, the Mormon Church supported a local ordinance in Salt Lake City that banned discrimination against lesbian and gay people in housing and employment. It was an unexpected progressive move by the church (Becker & Knox, 2009/2010).

Judaism

Orthodox Judaism follows the Torah according to the letter of the law. It holds that sexual relations between people of the same sex are sinful, based on two passages from the Bible: Leviticus 18:22 and 20:13. These passages are viewed as evidence of God's stand on the matter. Jewish law elaborates by stating, in more specific terms, that Leviticus forbids anal penetration between two men. Although the Torah does not address sexual relations between women, Jewish law instructs them to also not be involved in same-sex sexual relations (Bennett, 1998).

The four major movements within Judaism take different positions on same-sex attraction. Members of the Orthodox Jewish community, which with 900,000 members is the most traditional branch of Judaism, welcome all Jews as members but view gay sexual behavior as an "abomination." Conservative Judaism regards gay relationships as against Jewish law. This movement, with 1.4 million members, forbids its clergy to officiate at weddings for same-sex couples or to ordain openly gay or lesbian rabbis. Reform Judaism, the largest Jewish movement in the United States, with 1.7 million members, welcomes LGBT people as members and clergy. Reconstructionist Judaism, the smallest of the four major movements, with 130,000 members, fully supports LGBT people, welcoming them as members and as clergy. It also forbids employment discrimination based on sexual orientation. Reconstructionist rabbis have been given permission to perform same-sex wedding ceremonies following traditional Jewish rituals since 1993 (Human Rights Campaign, n.d.).

To a great extent, the differences among the positions are determined by attitudes toward changing social conditions. The movements that most strongly believe in the need for religion to change with the times are also the most accepting of gay and lesbian people (Bennett, 1998), and the more liberal and progressive Jewish groups support lesbian and gay civil rights (Sands, 2007).

Roman Catholic Church

The Roman Catholic Church considers a lesbian or gay sexual orientation sinful and rejects all lesbian and gay sexual expression (Nugent & Gramick, 1989). It considers lesbian and gay orientations as unnatural and disordered. The construct of original sin developed in the fourth century A.D., when Saint Augustine used the story of Adam and Eve to explain how the human race often chooses evil instead of good. This led many Christians to believe that sin is primarily disobedience (Brown-Taylor, 2000).

Bishops, Catholic organizations, and individual Catholics have called upon church leaders to stand up for the rights of lesbian and gay people, but they have not made much progress. The Vatican is the ultimate authority for the Catholic Church. A declaration by Pope John Paul II repeated an official condemnation of same-sex sexual orientation and banished lesbian and gay support groups from access to church property and church funds. The organization Dignity serves lesbian and gay Catholics. It often holds clandestine services in spaces leased from other denominations. Catholic priests are not allowed to serve as celebrants in these services. In an effort to avoid discovery and sanctions by church officials, Catholic priests often travel outside their diocese to lead Dignity's services (Barret & Barzan, 1996; Dworkin, 1997).

The same papal declaration also suggested that antigay violence may be understandable (Bennett, 1998). A document by Pope Benedict XVI stated that "homosexual" behavior is not a "morally acceptable option. Even the inclination toward "homosexual" behavior shows a tendency toward moral evil (Ratzinger, 1986). A leading Roman Catholic cardinal said in 2009 that "'transsexuals' and 'homosexuals' will never enter the kingdom of heaven" and that "homosexuality" constitutes "acting against nature and the dignity of the human body [and] is an insult to God" and a sin. Still, this cardinal opposes discrimination against lesbian and gay people (*Raw Story*, 2009).

Other Conservative Churches

Many evangelical, Pentecostal, and smaller independent Bible churches are adamantly opposed to same-sex relations. They oppose any support or recognition of what they think is immoral or evil and a serious threat to family values (Nugent & Gramick, 1989). But not all churches in this category take an antigay stance. One Denver pastor, at Highland's Church, tells his congregation that there is no hate in his church and lesbian and gay people can embrace their sexual orientation as God-given and seek fulfillment in committed same-sex relationships. This evangelical church is out of the evangelical mainstream, and some members have left because of the gay-friendly approach of the church (Gorski, 2009).

United Methodist Church

Several other denominations have mixed views about lesbian and gay persons. For example, the United Methodist Church teaches that lesbian and gay people have the same sacred worth as heterosexuals. It welcomes them as members and it commits itself to ministry to all people, regardless of sexual orientation. Yet it also considers lesbian and gay sexual activity sinful. According to the Book of Discipline (United Methodist Church, 2004), which spells out the official beliefs agreed upon by the General Conference of the United Methodist Church, the church does not condone the practice of "homosexuality" and considers it incompatible with Christian teaching. Lesbian and gay people cannot serve as lay persons in services or as ministers. No church funds can support or promote the acceptance of "homosexuality" (United Methodist Church, 2004). Still, this denomination is considered moderate when compared to more conservative churches because it supports civil rights for lesbian and gay people. However, it is more conservative than other denominations such as the United Church of Christ (Bennett, 1998).

> **To sum up the United Methodist Church position:**
> A gay or lesbian person is considered equal to a heterosexual person.
> Gay or lesbian sex is regarded as a sin.
> Gay and lesbian people are welcome as church members.
> Ministers are forbidden from blessing gay and lesbian unions.
> "Self-avowed practicing" (noncelibate) gay and lesbian individuals may not be ordained.
> The church supports basic human rights and civil liberties for all gay and lesbian people. (Bennett, 1998, p. 15)

Episcopal Church

The Episcopal Church is the U.S. branch of the larger Anglican Communion. Neither the Anglican Communion nor the Episcopal Church have doctrinal statements of faith like other denominations, but they have different views about "homosexuality." In 2009, the Episcopal Church voted to lift a moratorium on ordaining lesbian and gay bishops and to allow local clergy to bless same-sex unions, especially in states where same-sex marriage is legal (R. P. Jones & Cox, 2009). A split between the Anglican Communion and the Episcopal Church has been talked about but has not occurred, though conflict continues. Like many other denominations, the Episcopals' practices differ from church to church and are heavily influenced by lay members (Conan, 2007). Because of these differences in practices and because the church does not have an official doctrine, it is difficult to compare Episcopal beliefs about "homosexuality" to those of other denominations. However, its views on "homosexuality" are typically considered moderate to liberal (Donnelly, 2001).

Evangelical Lutheran Church in America

The Evangelical Lutheran Church in America (ELCA) formed in 1982 when the American Lutheran Church, the Association of Evangelical Lutheran Churches, and the Lutheran Church in America joined together (Evangelical Lutheran Church in America, n.d.).

The ELCA does not have a statement of its own on human sexuality. The topic of "homosexuality" is being deliberated and there is not an official stance or statement at this time. However, the ELCA does officially state that they welcome lesbian and gay people to their congregations. Additionally, the ELCA rejects discrimination, assaults, and harassment involving lesbian and gay people. Although the ELCA does not officially sanction same-sex unions, they leave the decision up to individual pastors to provide pastoral care in this matter (Evangelical Lutheran Church in America, n.d.).

In August, 2009, the ELCA did claim a policy by voting to lift a ban that prohibited sexually active lesbian and gay people from serving as ministers. Individual congregations will be allowed to hire them as clergy as long as they are in committed relationships. Before that, they had to be celibate to serve as clergy. Not all church members are happy with this change, and some have suggested that congregations and members may split off from the denomination ("Leaders to Allow," 2009).

Unitarian Universalism

The Universalist Church of America began in 1793 and the American Unitarian Association in 1825. In 1961 these two groups joined to form the Unitarian Universalist Association of Congregations. Unitarian Universalism is a "liberal religion that encompasses many faith traditions. It includes people who identify as Christians, Jews, Buddhists, Hindus, Pagans, Atheists, Agnostics, Humanists, and others" (Unitarian Universalist Association of Congregations, 2008b). Unitarian Universalism promotes acceptance, affirmation, and advocacy, as evidenced in their online statements about lesbian, gay, bisexual, and transgender people (Unitarian Universalist Association of Congregations, 2008a, 2008c). The Unitarian Universalist Association in 1996 became the first mainline denomination in the United States to adopt a position supporting legally recognized marriage between members of the same sex. It also allows for nonheterosexual people to be ordained as ministers (see http://www.uua.org/visitors/worship/ministers/6961.shtml).

Metropolitan Community Church

The Metropolitan Community Church serves a largely lesbian and gay membership (Lukenbill, 1998). It began with a gathering of 12 people led by the Rev. Troy Perry in Huntington Park, California, on October 6, 1968. Today it has grown to over 43,000 members with 300 congregations in 22 countries. Its core values are love, community, spiritual transformation, and social action. It celebrates lesbian, gay, and queer people. It is a movement that faithfully proclaims God's inclusive love for everyone (see http://www.mccchurch.org/).

Other Liberal Churches

Moravian, Friends, and some other churches also have made strong statements of official support for lesbian and gay people and have endorsed same-sex relations as fully compatible with Christian morality (Nugent & Gramick, 1989).

Differences and Some Progress

There are differences of opinion within Christianity and Judaism, even turmoil, about gay and lesbian sexual identity. There are also contradictions in stances within some churches, such as the United Methodist Church. The voices of Christianity are multiple, varied, and sometimes confusing. The influence of progressive and liberal religious groups is not nearly as strong as that of churches with a rejecting-punitive viewpoint, and they are also not as well-organized at the grassroots level (S. Diamond, 1998; White, 1994).

Some churches remain closed to accepting lesbian and gay people. But things are better today than they were during uncritical fundamentalist condemnation of "homosexuality" and rejection of lesbian and gay people. Many churches support continuing dialogue on these issues (Nugent & Gramick, 1989).

Council on Religion and the "Homosexual"

A movement for advocacy and support for lesbian and gay people within the church began in 1964 with the founding of the Council on Religion and the "Homosexual" (Tigert, 1996). The goals of the Council were to (1) educate clergy, church leaders, and congregations about lesbian and gay life and to listen to lesbian and gay people, (2) reach new understandings about religion and same-sex attractions, (3) communicate accurate information about lesbian and gay people through the church press, and (4) train clergy to work effectively as counselors for lesbian and gay people. Council members have taken two primary directions in relation to the institutional church. Some remain and work for justice within the church by forming advocacy and support groups. Others have left to create churches and ministries that are focused on the needs of lesbian and gay people.

Several denominations, such as Unitarian Universalists and the Quakers/ Friends, have led the way in supporting and accepting lesbian and gay people in their congregations. Other church congregations voted to become part of the Welcoming Church movement and say that God has called the church to be an inclusive community that affirms the diversity of human sexual orientation. This is the case even if church law or tradition does not support this view (Tigert, 1996).

Summary

Churches and denominations range, in their approach to gay and lesbian people, from rejecting-punitive to accepting. A number of churches accept lesbian and gay people, although some of them still hold the view that same-sex relationships are sinful. Welcoming or gay-positive churches are totally accepting and affirming of lesbian and gay people and do not think they are sinful. The Council on Religion and the "Homosexual" helped some churches and ministers to be more affirming.

Three

Effects of Religious Condemnation of Same-Sex Attraction

Churches with a rejecting-punitive approach cause the most conflict for lesbian and gay members. Conflict results when people are motivated to become romantically involved with someone of the same sex but their religion warns that they will burn for an eternity in hell for doing this. Religious lesbian and gay people may believe that this will really happen.

People who think they might be lesbian or gay learn at an early age that conservative religions believe that same-sex attractions are sinful (Barret & Barzan, 1996). Many people realize during adolescence or young adulthood that they are not heterosexual. Conflict between sexual and religious identities can begin in adolescence. Negative messages in church may delay lesbian or gay identity development or acceptance of it. People may learn at an early age to be ashamed of their same-sex attractions and hide them from others. Being open about their attractions may cause strain with family members who hear the same negative messages in church (McGrady & McDonnell, 2006). Lease and Shulman (2003) surveyed families with a lesbian or gay member. More than two-thirds of them (69 percent) were attending religious institutions that preached that lesbian and gay relationships are unacceptable, sinful, and immoral.

Having a strong religious belief and a strong sense of being lesbian or gay can create excruciating conflict and intense pressure (Barret & Barzan, 1996; Yip, 1998). Most lesbian and gay people who follow a conservative religion feel forced to choose between it and their sexual identity. Some deny or suppress their sexuality so as to accept their religion or suffer with the knowledge that their church considers them sinful (Ritter & O'Neill, 1995). Some hope that if they pray or behave well God will take away the conflict. Some may leave the church, but the church often makes this decision for them. Lesbian and gay people are often told that they are no longer welcome in their church (Barret & Barzan, 1996). One minister told a gay person that if he acted on his sexual impulses the church would shun him until he repented of his sin. And the minister said he was only acting out of love. Most likely other gay members were told the same thing (Burr, 2009). Conservative branches of other religions, such as Islam and Judaism, also do not accept same-sex attractions and create similar psychologically damaging environments for lesbian and gay people (Bhurga, 1997).

Schuck and Liddle (2001) studied 32 gay men, 26 lesbians, seven bisexual women, and one bisexual man, ages 18 to 65. Nearly two-thirds reported having experienced conflict between their religion and same-sex attractions. The most common sources of conflict were religious teachings in church. They were taught that sex between members of the same sex was sinful. Perhaps the most damaging teaching was that God rejected them and they would go to hell. Biblical passages were used to condemn same-sex relations. They were instructed to pray for forgiveness and overcome their same-sex attraction. Some felt there was no place for them in their church.

Wolkomir (2001) examined cases of men whose gay sexuality created conflict with a fundamentalist Christian belief system. Some of the men converted to conservative Christianity as adults, while most were born into conservative or fundamentalist Christian families. Being Christian meant being heterosexual, getting married, and having children. They were taught that these acts paralleled the marriage of Jesus to the church and the rebirth of believers. Celibacy, however, was accepted as it was seen as a marriage to God. Those who chose not to meet one of these requirements were viewed as not fully participating in their faith.

The men's sexuality did not work well with beliefs that damned them as sinners and discredited them as Christians. Conservative Christians labeled the gay men in Wolkomir's (2001) study as abominations, sinners who defiled God's plan for the universe, were unworthy of heaven, and would go to hell. The men feared that this would happen to them because they felt they were unworthy of God's love and salvation. They also worried that friends and family would reject them. Most of these men, therefore, kept their same-sex desires a secret and presented themselves as heterosexual Christians. But this created another problem: not being sincere or authentic. They felt guilty about the secret. This could result in severe compartmentalization (Gross, 2008). Some participated outwardly in their religious organizations but inwardly were involved in a powerful struggle between their religious beliefs and their sexual identity (Barret & Barzan, 1996).

Most of the 33 young male respondents studied by Kubicek et al. (2009) were raised as either Protestants or Catholics. Those who described their religious upbringing as Christian, Pentecostal, or evangelical typically reported hearing severe heterosexist messages, including "gay is bad; gays go to hell" or "you'll burn." Sermons seemed to often bring up "homosexuality," making the young men feel uncomfortable or fearful. Catholic respondents noted that the church preached that sex in general was sinful rather than focusing only on "homosexuality."

About half of the men studied by Kubicek et al. (2009) felt they had little choice about attending religious services while growing up. Some went four or five times a week. The young men described having considerable anxiety and believing that they would eventually be sent to hell. It was not just that being gay was a sin. They were told they had a demon inside, which others in the church said needed to be cast out.

Respondents also reported hearing heterosexist messages from family members, particularly from those who were religious. Quite a few had close family members who were ministers or pastors. This was particularly common among African American respondents. Family members would pray for them to be "normal" and said that gays would burn in hell. Many were not "out" to their family members due to not wanting to hear these messages or believing that they would be forced from their home or rejected by family members. Several respondents reported being forced from their homes because they disclosed their sexual identity. A brother told his gay brother that he was no earthly good, was a sinner, and had no purpose (Kubicek et al., 2009).

Hearing and internalizing the negative messages often had a detrimental effect on respondents, especially if they had a strong religious commitment. Some questioned their goodness and experienced self-hatred. Some reported being depressed and contemplating suicide. Some fasted or overate to alleviate their feelings of despair and hopelessness. Some described feelings of fear and guilt for having sexual attraction to other men. They asked for God's forgiveness or for those feelings to be turned off. For several respondents, hiding a part of their identity represented a lie that was another burden or sin. In the more extreme cases, self-hatred at times resulted in respondents taking out their frustration on lesbian and gay people. The negative messages were less harmful for those without a strong religious or spiritual commitment. When in church they usually did not listen to the negative messages or did not absorb much of them (Kubicek et al., 2009).

Latino, African American, and Asian American lesbian and gay people may struggle more with who they are. Already stigmatized due to their racial and ethnic identities, they experience multiple oppressions (Greene, 2007). They also struggle with who they think others in their culture and religion want them to be. Most feel strongly tied to their communities. They may experience conflicting norms and values and competing demands from family members or peers to choose one identity over another. The pressure will likely be to reject their lesbian or gay identity. Religious beliefs can also be a tool to raise the tensions and discord (Greene, 2007). Another pressure is that their communities provide the means of survival for the culture so they need to not disrupt their community with their nonheterosexual sexual identity. Family expectations often take precedence over personal wishes (Chan, 1992; Wooden, Kawasaki, & Mayeda, 1983).

In addition to hearing negative comments about lesbian and gay people, those with disabilities face another major obstacle. Family members may refuse to provide transportation for them to meet other lesbian and gay people. Lesbian and gay organizations may also not make themselves accessible (Greene, 2007).

Social class can also be an obstacle. It can make a big difference as to whether people can attend costly venues where lesbian and gay people often meet. Being poor heightens the stress of identifying as lesbian or gay if one wants to go to these venues (Greene, 2007). But there are less expensive or free places to also meet others.

Mental Health Issues

Some lesbian and gay people may have mental health issues due to negative attitudes about same-sex attractions (Meyer and Dean, 1998; Otis and Skinner, 1996; Ross and Rosser, 1996; Wagner, Brandolo, & Rabkhi, 1996). Participation in an organized religion can be detrimental to psychological health because of the negative messages they receive about their sexual identity (Gage Davidson, 2000; Mahaffy, 1996).

Many of the mental health issues result from the stress created by the conflict between religious beliefs and sexual identity (Almazan, 2007). At the least, people face cognitive distress when trying to reconcile the two. Furthermore, the lack of religious affirmation and acceptance causes tension, misery, distress, and adjustment difficulty (Gonsiorek, 1995). Being called immoral or bad strikes at the core of one's sense of self-worth and personal value. It also engenders a deep sense of shame and self-hatred that is difficult to reverse (Ritter & O'Neill, 1995). People who experience this may start to regard themselves as evil (Gonsiorek, 1995). This can also result in low self-esteem, depression, alienation, fear, anxiety, guilt, and suicidal ideation (Allen & Oleson, 1999; Lease et al. 2005; Schuck & Liddle, 2001; Wolkomir, 2001; Yip, 1998).

A study by Yakushko (2005) identified several significant factors that can raise or lower self-esteem in lesbian and gay people who adhere to conservative religious beliefs and practices. Having a sense of social support appears to relate to higher levels of self-esteem in those who are religiously committed. A sense of existential well-being in life may also contribute to higher levels of self-esteem. As in other studies (for example, Vincke, De Rycke, & Bolton, 1999), self-esteem for lesbian and gay people was associated with the amount of distress they experienced in acknowledging and embracing their sexual orientation. The more distress, the lower their self esteem became.

The causes of the inner conflict experienced by many lesbian and gay people are both intrinsic and extrinsic. Intrinsic causes generally include internalized moral ideals or fear of divine retribution (Ritter & O'Neill, 1989). Extrinsic causes include acceptance of antigay religious doctrine (Yip, 1997b), negative outlooks on lesbian and gay people and their experiences (Rodriguez & Ouellette, 2000a; Shallenberger, 1996, 1998), and the religious beliefs of family members and friends (Mahaffy, 1996; Rodriguez, 1997). The rejecting-punitive religious context seems responsible for both intrinsic and extrinsic causes of the conflict experienced by lesbian and gay people who self-identify as religious. It is also the case that many adherents of rejecting-punitive religions believe that one cannot be both lesbian or gay and Christian, or that being lesbian or gay means that one does not believe in God.

Conservative religion can clearly be a damaging influence in the lives of religiously affiliated lesbian and gay people (Gage Davidson, 2000; Hancock, 2000; Patterson, 1995; Ritter & O'Neill, 1989; Ritter & Terndrup, 2002; Wood, 2000). Conservative religion may have damaging consequences for lesbian and gay people who either have been brought up in a conservative church or have attended one at some time in their lives.

Barriers of Heterosexism and Religious Conflict in the Coming-Out Process

One of the most important events in the lives of lesbian and gay people is the process of coming out or establishing their sexual identity. The process necessitates being resocialized. Developing a lesbian or gay identity requires separation from the norms, values, and traditions of heterosexual culture and resocialization into lesbian and gay culture. Much of this resocialization takes place during the process of coming out. One unlearns being heterosexual or separates oneself from a heterosexual identity and rejects the stereotypes associated with being lesbian or gay and the ideology that heterosexuality is the only acceptable and normal sexual identity (Herdt & Boxer, 1993).

When coming out, reaching the goal of acceptance is often not easy because of heterosexism. If religious conflict is also involved, the coming-out process is made more difficult. Conflict between sexual identity and religion usually shows up early in the coming-out process and may continue throughout the process or as far as one goes in the process.

When the process of coming out begins, conflict between religion and same-sex attractions will likely intensify. This can lead some people to integrate or reconcile the two. For others, the distress of living with this conflict can be exacerbated. The latter situation may prevent some people from accepting their sexual identity or present an extreme challenge to reaching this goal.

The first approach to coming out is addressed in the most established and comprehensive coming-out model, developed by Cass (1996), which has some empirical support (Brady & Busse, 1994; Cass, 1984). In this model, changing perceptions make up an interpersonal matrix that accompanies the different stages. Perceptions include those of oneself (for example, "I am lesbian or gay"), one's behavior (for example, "My behavior represents a same-sex sexual identity"), and the responses of others (for example, "Others think I am lesbian or gay"). The model has six stages:

1. *Identity confusion:* "Who am I?"

2. *Identity comparison:* "I am different."

3. *Identity tolerance:* "I am probably lesbian or gay."

4. *Identity acceptance:* "I am lesbian or gay."

5. *Identity pride:* "I am lesbian or gay!"

6. *Identity synthesis:* "My sexual identity is a part of me."

At each stage, conflict occurs within or between perceptions. For example, at stage 1 (confusion), the experience of same-sex thoughts, feelings, or behaviors conflicts with perceptions of having a heterosexual identity. Resolution of the conflict at each stage results in advancement to a new stage, resulting in increased congruency between perceptions of one's behavior, self-identity, and others' beliefs about oneself (Cass, 1996). The goal is to integrate one's identity into one's overall perception of oneself. Integration provides consistency between one's perceptions of one's behavior and one's self, and between one's private and public identities (Rust, 2003).

For those with a religious identity from a rejecting-punitive church, integration would also include reconciliation between one's sexual and religious identities. When this or heterosexism keeps one from advancing through the stages, one is said to be in a state of identity foreclosure (Cass, 1996). This happens when one experiences cognitive conflict about one's sexual identity and cannot accommodate new information related to being lesbian or gay. When in foreclosure, one's identity development is stalled (Marszalek, Cashwell, Dunn, & Jones, 2004). The stages are discussed in more detail below.

Stage 1: Identity Confusion

Before the coming-out process begins, one views oneself as heterosexual and does not think of oneself as lesbian or gay. Once questioning of one's sexual identity begins, the first stage, identity confusion, begins. This is the first moment of incongruence as perceptions of oneself as lesbian or gay are at odds with one's heterosexual thoughts, feelings, or behaviors (Langdridge, 2008). However, one wonders whether information about same-sex sexual identity is relevant to oneself. This is one of the most difficult stages. One feels different from others who may be talking about getting married and experiencing other normative events (Burr, 2009). Considerable distress or inner turmoil can be experienced.

Such turmoil is typical because what one is questioning is not a normative developmental event (Cass, 1996). One has not anticipated or prepared for this kind of experience and often faces it alone (Reid, 1995). The confusion stage can last for years with a vague sense that something about oneself is different and one experiences inner turmoil or a sense of alienation that is not communicated to others (Burr, 2009).

Cass (1996) identified several possible pathways in the early stages. One of three pathways is taken at the confusion stage. One may find a lesbian or gay identity relevant and desirable, accept its relevance but not its desirability, or find it both irrelevant and undesirable. In the latter case, one stops behaviors that could be viewed as lesbian or gay, blocks access to information about being lesbian or gay, and avoids provocative situations. One may use irrational or magical thinking to deny that one is lesbian or gay ("I must be going through a phase; I'm not really attracted to same-sex people"). Or one does not attach thoughts and emotions to being lesbian or gay. One does not think about this or have any feelings about it (Marszalek & Cashwell, 1998).

People at the confusion stage often have negative thoughts about themselves due to heterosexism. This is what for many lesbian and gay people causes emotional turmoil. Those who experience additional religious conflict may experience guilt, shame, depression, and fear of rejection from family, friends, and their church. This can slow the coming-out process or even shut it down completely, resulting in foreclosure. Both heterosexism and religious conflict can bring a person to this place. People who experience religious conflict and foreclosure and drop out of the coming-out process may experience conflict all of their lives between their sexual feelings for others of the same sex and the antigay values of their church.

Lesbian and gay people who are in a rejecting-punitive religion are more likely to feel negatively about their sexual orientation (Tozer & Hayes, 2004). Either they do not reach acceptance of their nonheterosexual orientation or they may deny their same-sex attractions altogether because of their feelings of guilt and unworthiness (Lease et al., 2005). They may have existential questions such as these: Why me? What does my life mean? How am I to live? Where do I belong? Can I really be lesbian or gay and still be an upstanding person (Wilcox, 2002)?

Another issue that may arise for people at this early stage is the effect of a change in sexual identity on all of one's other identities. In addition, changes in self-concept often happen. Clients often have negative thoughts about themselves as potentially lesbian or gay (E. F. Levy, 1995).

Stage 2: Identity Comparison

Both the second and third pathways in the confusion stage are examples of identity foreclosure. If one does not foreclose because one cannot suppress one's lesbian or gay identity, or because one accepts it, one enters stage 2, identity comparison, moving from a belief that one is heterosexual to a belief that one might be lesbian or gay. This involves a change from an immediate concern with personal identity to a concern with social alienation. The continuity of one's past, present, and future has been broken, so one must also find new meaning in life. Many expectations that one had before, such as a heterosexual marriage, become irrelevant (Langdridge, 2008).

People at this stage tentatively accept the possibility of being lesbian or gay but are not yet able to define their same-sex feelings and thoughts and are still experiencing confusion. Cass (1996) thought that the confusion could result in a sense of alienation from one's family of origin, support networks, and society generally. One may also still think that being lesbian or gay is a temporary phase or that one is attracted to only one person and will not have other same-sex attractions (Burr, 2009).

One of four pathways is taken at stage 2, based on how one sees oneself and the consequences one anticipates:

1. One may develop a positive self-evaluation and anticipate high rewards.

2. One may develop a positive self-evaluation but anticipate low rewards and reject the lesbian or gay identity (foreclosure); if this fails, however, one is likely to conclude that one is probably lesbian or gay.

Heterosexism and Religion

3. One may develop a negative self-evaluation but perceive high rewards; this can lead to the desire for a heterosexual identity.

4. One may develop a negative self-evaluation and perceive low rewards. This can also lead one to reject a lesbian or gay identity and strive for a heterosexual identity.

People who do not foreclose will probably acknowledge a lesbian or gay identity. But a negative self-evaluation can result in self-hatred and possibly self-destructive behaviors such as self-mutilation or suicide attempts. If religious conflict is a factor and one has heard in church that being lesbian or gay is immoral or evil, self-hated and self-destructive behaviors may intensify. Or, according to Chew (1999) one may hold on more strongly to religious beliefs as a defense against accepting a lesbian or gay identity.

Stage 3: Identity Tolerance

In this stage, one comes closer to committing to a new identity or acknowledging that one is "probably" lesbian or gay. One might begin to associate with other lesbian or gay people, engage in sex with a person of the same sex, and develop new lesbian or gay support networks (Cass, 1996). These developments help to counteract feelings of isolation and alienation (Burr, 2009). According to Marszalek et. al (2004), people at this stage use causal, if-then logic to reason that if they have same-sex attractions and feelings, thoughts, or actions then they are probably lesbian or gay. This acknowledgement, however, does not necessarily lead to viewing themselves positively. They may feel that they are inferior to those with heterosexual attractions.

One of six pathways is taken at this stage:

1. One may develop a positive view of self as probably lesbian or gay and experience positive contacts with other lesbian and gay people.

2. One may develop a positive view of self but experience negative contacts with other lesbian and gay people, devalue them, and reduce contact with them (identity foreclosure), and then reevaluate one's conception of oneself as lesbian or gay as less positive.

3. One may develop a negative view of self but experience positive contacts with lesbian and gay people. These positive contacts can eventually lessen one's negative self-evaluation.

4. One may develop a negative self-evaluation and experience negative contacts with lesbian and gay people. This can lead to avoidance of contacts (identity foreclosure), but a negative self-evaluation is modifiable if future contacts are positive.

5. One may develop a positive self-evaluation as partly lesbian or gay and experience negative contacts with lesbian and gay people. This can lead to a devaluation of lesbian and gay people (identity foreclosure).

6. One may develop a positive self-evaluation and experience positive contacts with lesbian and gay people. This can lead to greater commitment to being lesbian or gay (Cass, 1996).

If one has moved this far in the coming-out process, one can still be stopped by foreclosure with continued negative views of oneself whether or not one experiences positive contact with other lesbian and gay people. Religious conflict can keep one from evaluating oneself as positive if one's church reinforces a negative view of lesbian and gay people and those who associate with them. Most likely a person in intense religious conflict about being lesbian or gay will not reach the later stages of Cass's model.

Stage 4: Identity Acceptance

In the identity acceptance stage, one begins to feel that being lesbian or gay is valid and may prefer being around others who are lesbian and gay. One has answered the questions "Who am I?" and "Where do I belong?" and discloses the new identity to more people, decreasing the incongruence between one's self-perceptions and the perceptions of others or between one's positive evaluation of self and the negative evaluations of others. One may still use coping strategies such as "passing" as heterosexual. Continued "passing" at this stage is seen as identity foreclosure (Cass, 1996).

Stage 5: Identity Pride

In this stage, one often devalues all that is heterosexual and values all that is lesbian or gay. One is likely to disclose one's lesbian or gay identity in many areas of one's life. This is risky, due to widespread prejudice and discrimination (Matthews, 2007), and negative reactions tend to reinforce one's negative perceptions of heterosexuals. One may attempt to resolve the incongruence between self-acceptance and devaluation by others by disregarding negative opinions (Cass, 1996). The Internet offers virtual groups that can help a person to come out and also to make disclosures anonymously (McKenna & Bargh, 1998).

People may experience anger when they realize that heterosexism that was internalized from a heterosexist society prevented an earlier coming out. They may feel pride about being part of a community of lesbian and gay people, and may become activists on behalf of the community (Cass, 1996; Marszalek et al.,

2004). Those in antigay churches are less likely to make widespread disclosures, feel pride about being lesbian or gay or about other lesbian and gay people, or become activists in the lesbian and gay community—especially if they cannot devalue their religion or disregard their church's negative opinions of lesbian and gay people. Some may move against the church because of their anger (Chew, 1999). One study found that self-disclosure was highest if there was little attachment to a church (Savin-Williams, 1990).

Many lesbian and gay people feel alienated from or hostile toward their church as one of the strongest sources of their oppression. But many remain committed to their church (Yakushko, 2005). Religious identity is embedded in the psyche. Religion also offers comfort for someone in torment and soothes anxieties. Religious affiliation can serve as a central organizing aspect of identity to such a degree that a person cannot relinquish it even at the price of conflict with his or her sexual identity (Haldeman, 2004).

Overcoming internalized heterosexism is a key challenge during the coming-out process (Garnets, Herek, & Levy, 1990; Gonsiorek, 1993; Herek, 1992; Malyon, 1982). Most lesbian and gay people manage to develop a positive identity. But they may not disclose their sexual identity to others for some time, if ever (Herek, 1995), especially if they are in religious conflict. No matter how they feel about themselves, people who disclose themselves as lesbian or gay invariably deal with stereotypes, prejudices, and hostility (Kitzinger, 1991). Those in a rejecting-punitive church may be thrown out of their church. There are also fears of harassment and violence.

Stage 6: Identity Synthesis

In the sixth stage, Identity Synthesis, people gradually modify the "us against them" stance of the previous stage. They experience less anger about heterosexism and realize that not all heterosexuals are heterosexist. They increase contact with supportive heterosexuals and may bring some of them into their support networks. At this stage one experiences congruence between perceptions of one's self and one's behavior and between one's private and public identities. More psychological integration is experienced, and being lesbian or gay is consolidated with the rest of one's identity (Cass, 1996). Cass pointed out that identity synthesis may not emerge until the 30s or later.

In this last stage, one may contemplate existential issues such as what it means to be lesbian or gay or how one's sexual identity affects one's relationships with others (Marszalek et al., 2004). If one has been in religious conflict and reaches this stage, then one has come to terms with oneself and rejected the church's view of lesbian and gay people. Few people in religious conflict, however, reach this stage. Instead, they opt out of the process long before. According to Chew (1999), some may gravitate back toward religion by seeking out a Welcoming church. Some tolerate the inconsistency between their original religious institutions and their sexual orientation.

Moving through the Stages

The early stages of identity development, confusion and comparison, may result in shame and other negative feelings (Lewin, 1993). In the two middle stages, identity tolerance and identity acceptance, one is tested with the outcomes of disclosures. One may experience hostility, rejection, and perhaps isolation. One also has to accept that one is lesbian or gay. For people in religious conflict, these stages could be too difficult to negotiate in a positive way; they could experience increased rates of depression, suicidal ideation, and suicidal attempts. Heterosexism affects most lesbian and gay people when coming out. They usually experience negative feelings about themselves when they first recognize their same-sex attractions (Goffman, 1963; Gonsiorek, 1993; Hetrick & Martin, 1984; Meyer, 1995; Neisen, 1990; Smith, 1988; Stein & Cohen, 1984).

People at later stages of sexual identity development, identity pride and identity synthesis, show greater psychological well-being, happiness, kindness, sexual satisfaction, and mental and physical health, as well as comparatively lower levels of loneliness, anxiety, and suicidal ideation (Minton & McDonald, 1985; Shannon & Woods, 1991; Woodman & Lenna, 1980). On the other hand, coming out raises questions about their social acceptability. And there is awareness that a drastic change has happened. Their place in the social order has changed. According to Goffman (1993), they are stigmatized or have a spoiled identity. Because stigma is always attached to a lesbian or gay identity, they have to continually cope with it and manage it (Herdt & Boxer, 1993). Bohan (1996) identified stigma management and overcoming internalized heterosexism as key elements for positive psychological adjustment. This begins during the final stages of the coming-out process. One declares a nonheterosexual identity in defiance of heterosexism and reconstructs stigmatized parts of oneself. (Chapter 4 discusses ways to cope with stigmatization.)

Other Perspectives on Coming Out

Many criticisms exist of all coming-out models, including the Cass model. Queer theory, for example, is a radical challenge to coming-out models that describe, and implicitly prescribe, a fixed identity and happy acceptance of the social world as the final (ideal) state of identity development. If the end point of successful identity development is contentment, this is looked at as politically conservative (Langdridge, 2008).

Missing pieces also characterize coming-out models such as interactions with one's environment or social context; the fact that one takes an active role in constructing one's sexual identity (Horowitz & Newcomb, 2001); historical effects such as generational differences (Parks, 1999); and race, ethnicity, and membership in other groups (Gove, Bimbi, Nani'n, & Parsons, 2006). As noted earlier, developing multiple identities can be difficult (Wallace, Carter, Nani'n, Keller, & Alleyne, 2002). Sexual identity often remains secondary or tertiary to other identities and roles (Phellas, 1999). People may prioritize the development of a racial or ethnic identity over a sexual identity in response to many psychosocial and environmental barriers associated with race, ethnicity, and socioeconomic status (Wallace et al., 2002).

Another Coming-Out Model Focused on One's Church and Religious Experiences

Chew (1999) presented three stages of coming out—personal, private, and public—in which religion can play an important role. Those in the personal stage do not identify as lesbian or gay and have nothing to disclose. Even if they did, they would not be comfortable with disclosure of their sexual orientation. They may never have distanced themselves from their church or may be embracing the church more strongly to defend against a lesbian or gay identity. They may be in stage two or three of the Cass model.

Those in the private stage are fairly comfortable with their sexual identity and somewhat comfortable with disclosures to others. They have disclosed to a few friends and relatives but have not publicly identified themselves as lesbian or gay. They may be moving away from the church because of their anger at heterosexual institutions. They are likely to be in stage four or five of the Cass model.

Those in the public stage experience a high degree of comfort with their sexual identity, are comfortable with disclosure, and have disclosed at home, at work, and in social situations. They also publicly identify as lesbian or gay. This stage corresponds to the sixth stage of the Cass model.

Most people studied by Chew (1999) endorsed beliefs in God or a higher power and in an afterlife. About one-fourth reported that they attended church regularly. Less than 10 percent were atheists or agnostics. Those in the personal stage were more likely to believe in God, experience closeness to God, and believe in an afterlife. They tended to use personal prayer more than those in the private stage of the coming-out process. Those from Welcoming congregations tended to participate more in church activities and also tended to integrate their religious beliefs into many aspects of their lives.

A relationship between religion and the personal stage of the coming-out process was found for both women and men, particularly if they attended inclusive Welcoming churches. Women from non-Welcoming churches who were in the public stage tended to be low in religious commitment compared with males or other females. Men from non-Welcoming churches who were in the private stage tended also to be low in religious commitment

Three moves happened more often for men: (1) a move toward believing in a supreme being during the personal stage as a way to assuage guilt or prevent suspicion about their sexual orientation, (2) a move away from the church during the private stage due to anger at heterosexist institutions, and (3) a gradual return to religion as they integrated their sexual orientation. Women appeared to continue to move away from a belief in a supreme being as they moved through the coming-out stages, particularly if they were not attending a Welcoming church. It may be that the traditional view of God as a father figure is seen as patriarchal and thus more likely to be rejected by women.

More men than women reported attending Welcoming churches. Men from Welcoming churches who were in the private and public stages tended to use prayer more often than men from non-Welcoming churches. Men were more likely than women to report church attendance, personal prayer, and belief that their ideas about religion influence their philosophy or way of life. Women from Welcoming churches did not show the same trend toward becoming less religious as they moved through the coming-out stages as women from non-Welcoming churches (Chew, 1999).

Success Factors in Coming Out

Bringaze (1998) did a national study on factors contributing to success in the coming-out process. The sample consisted of leaders in the lesbian community. Nineteen items were identified as success factors. Two factors were helpful for the majority of participants (66 percent): having gay friends and reading. Meditation and self-study was the next most helpful factor (43.3 percent), followed by gay social organizations (40 percent), counseling (35 percent), and gay bars and role models (30 percent). Between 13.3 and 20 percent reported that noncounseling support groups, prayer, or religious or spiritual communities were helpful. Two significant statistical correlations were being out to at least one family member and experiencing a closer relationship with one's family after coming out. These were key success factors.

In the Cass model of coming out, the most important success factors were associating with or seeking out other lesbian and gay people. Cass emphasized the importance of these relationships in reducing feelings of alienation and differentness. Other success factors were investigation of the incongruence between one's earlier perceived self and the emerging self. In Cass's model, a developmental stage involves questioning one's sexuality and comparing oneself to others. Self-help resources such as readings provide information on issues of sexual orientation and can provide validation. This can be especially helpful as success factors to women in more rural and conservative areas with no access to a lesbian and gay community.

In the Bringaze (1998) study prayer was useful to few women (16.6 percent); 25 percent rated it as not helpful, and nearly half (46.7 percent) said it did not apply to their situation. Perhaps because of the intolerant views of many churches, these respondents sought alternatives to organized religion and prayer. Only 13.3 percent identified a religious or spiritual community as helpful. They felt alienated from organized religion. Thirty-five percent rated individual counseling as helpful.

Over 90 percent felt satisfied and had a positive view of their life as lesbians. Still, a significant number reported contemplating suicide (21.8 percent), turning to drugs and alcohol (25 percent), isolation (48.4 percent), and depression (30 percent). Harassment was experienced by 53.3 percent, and 16.6 percent experienced physical violence because of their sexual orientation (Bringaze, 1998).

Summary

Rejecting-punitive religion can have many negative effects on religious lesbian and gay people. It can delay coming out, cause them to hide their sexual orientation, and cause excruciating conflict due to being told, for example, that they are sinners and are going to hell. They may also have mental health issues such as low self-esteem, depression, anxiety, guilt, or suicidal ideation. Almost all lesbian and gay people go through a coming-out process, but it can be stalled because of heterosexism and conflict between sexual and religious identities. A number of models of coming out have been developed. The Cass model involves six stages, during which conflicts with religion can delay or stall the process; some people never come to accept their lesbian or gay sexual identity. The Chew model involves three stages—personal, private, and public—each of which can be influenced by religion. Coming-out models have limitations. Factors that have been identified in successful coming out include having friends and connections in the gay and lesbian community and having access to educational and self-help materials.

Part II

Dealing with Conflict Between Religious and Sexual Identities

Four

Strategies for Reconciling Religion and Sexuality

*L*esbian and gay people who experience intense conflict over their sexual and religious identities have a difficult choice to make. Choosing religion over sexuality risks denying a crucial part of themselves. But choosing sexuality over religion puts them in conflict with religious beliefs most have held since childhood. This conflict often drives people to seek ways to resolve the distress they are experiencing. Means to do this are discussed below and in chapter 5. This chapter focuses on what lesbian and gay people figure out to do for themselves to resolve the conflict and remain lesbian or gay, although some try to get rid of their same-sex desires. In the next chapter, sexual reorientation is discussed. The sole purpose of this intervention is for outsiders to resolve the conflict by changing lesbian and gay people to heterosexual.

Resolving Cognitive Dissonance

Research among lesbian and gay people indicates that conservative religion can contribute to cognitive dissonance when it conflicts with one's sexual desires (Leong, 2006; Schuck & Liddle, 2001; Thumma, 1991; Yip, 1997a, 2005). Conflict or psychological tension results from the condemnation of same-sex attractions by one's religion and awareness that one is a target of this condemnation because of one's sexual attractions (Festinger, 1957; Rosario, Yali, Hunter, & Gwadz, 2006). When one feels tension between two psychologically inconsistent thoughts, beliefs, value systems, or practices, one is in a state of cognitive dissonance. This produces a negative mental state and is emotionally uncomfortable (Festinger, 1957).

One usually cannot remain in a state of cognitive dissonance without it negatively influencing mental and physical health (Rosario et al., 2006). When the psychological tension is intolerable, one is motivated to reduce the tension (Thumma, 1991). One can reduce tension by eliminating or changing one of the two conflicting thoughts, beliefs, value systems, or practices. A successful outcome is a state of cognitive consonance in which anxiety and conflict are reduced (Cooper & Fazio, 1984; Festinger, 1957).

Some participants studied by Leong (2006) decided to live with the dissonance. Participants studied by Beckwith (2007) used a variety of coping strategies to reduce or get rid of their same-sex attractions. These strategies included (1) intrapsychic defense mechanisms; (2) sexual and relational solutions; (3) emotional coping; (4) hiding; (5) religious solutions; and (6) escape, release, and suicide. Attempting suicide was seen as the only solution for eight participants. None of the other strategies eradicated participants' attractions. Some lesbian and gay people studied by Rosario et al. (2006) also attempted to reject their sexual identity through (1) defense mechanisms such as suppression or repression, (2) self-directed behaviors such as avoidance of lesbian and gay people, or (3) immersion in heterosexual activity. Some people studied by Beckwith (2007) committed to sexual abstinence or heterosexual marriage or struggled in other ways against same-sex desires. Some might seek sexual reorientation therapy or an ex-gay ministry with the goal of becoming heterosexual through spiritual intervention (Yip, 2007). Chapter 5 presents a detailed critique of this intervention.

Some people want to keep their same-sex attractions and block their religion's rejection of it. Some may transfer their religion's emphasis on a moral and righteous life to their intimate relationships and commitments with others (Beckwith, 2007). Others alter their religious beliefs. This may involve (1) reframing God as embracing all people (Leong, 2006), (2) reinterpreting Bible verses that condemn lesbian and gay people, (3) focusing on Bible verses that express love and acceptance of all people, (4) believing that lesbian and gay people are God's creations and that all forms of sexuality are created by God (Wilcox, 2002), or (5) believing that God loves them as they are (Rosario et al., 2006).

Mahaffy (1996) found that an evangelical religious identity predicts greater internal and external dissonance for lesbians between their religious and sexual identities. Efforts at resolution included changing one's religious beliefs, disaffiliation from the religion, or living with the dissonance. Thumma's (1991) study of a gay evangelical group found that it was difficult for participants to reconcile gay and evangelical identities. They eventually reconciled the dissonance they experienced by changing to a congregation that accepted them as both Christian and gay.

When gay Mormons experience conflict with their religious and sexual identities, they may attempt to deny their sexual orientation, change it, remain celibate, experience suicidal ideation and attempts, and in some cases find resolution (R. Phillips, 2005). Some Mormons report self-inflicted punishments for same-sex behavior and fantasies or masturbation as well. Other means include acceptance of the church's teachings on and proscription of "homosexuality," acceptance of these teachings but participation in covert same-sex sexual activity, rejection of these teachings but abstinence from same-sex activity, active resistance to church teachings on "homosexuality," and participation in same-sex sexual behavior while attempting to change church policy regarding it (R. Phillips, 2005). Not many leave the church. For those reared in religious traditions such as Mormonism with their unique beliefs, practices, traditions, and history, changing one's religious affiliation is difficult. It often involves a profound shift in religious identity more likely through an internal conversion than externally switching to another religion (Vance, 2008).

Dissonance-reducing strategies used by lesbian and gay Adventists include denial of "homosexuality," seeking professional help to change their sexual orientation, suicide attempts, prayer, further immersion in religion, using religious rituals to deter same-sex sexual activity, and heterosexual marriage (Drumm, 2001). For Adventists and Mormons counseled not to act on their sexual orientation and to change it or remain celibate, suicidal ideation or attempts and suicide itself are not uncommon (Drumm, 2001; R. Phillips, 2005).

Lesbian and gay Adventists and Mormons are instructed that if they are unable to change their sexual orientation they should remain celibate. Both groups have reported that they have been unable to maintain celibacy. Most abandon it as an unviable strategy and report that when they attempt to refrain from all same-sex behavior, they experience significant unhappiness, loneliness, and isolation (Drumm, 2001).

Some religious lesbian and gay people try to alter their church by challenging it, saying that as a gathering of humans, it can be wrong, as human nature is fallible. Another strategy involves leaving the social environment that reinforces the dissonance and creates the tension—the church (Gross, 2008). But some people are unable to leave their faith (Yip, 2000). One can also believe without belonging to a church; some stop attending church in order to remain true both to their faith and to themselves. Those who retain their faith but leave the church are using a strategy of avoidance or defection (Davie, 1994).

Some who leave or distance themselves from religious communities do so because they fear stigmatization. But the vast majority want to reject an institution that has rejected their sexuality (Yip, 2007). This may lead to an alternative spiritual or religious connection. Some have found more gay friendly religious groups in mainstream churches, gay churches, or gay-positive religious groups. They want an inclusive church that accepts their sexual identity (Beckwith, 2007). Thumma (1991), who studied a group of eight religious gay people, found that both their religious beliefs and their sexual identity were important to their self concept. In a church more friendly to their sexual identity, they were able to renegotiate their religious and sexual identities and change from having a negative view of themselves to a positive view.

Some lesbian and gay people have created their own spiritual ceremonies and rituals (Rosario et al., 2006). Others stay in their traditional churches; their loyalty is a barrier to looking for alternative churches, and they cannot easily abandon their cultural heritage (Schuck & Liddle, 2001). In a study by Gross (2008), only 20 out of 395 participants turned to more inclusive churches. Others who continue in a traditional church and are openly lesbian or gay are perceived as unrepentant. They may hope to incite change within the church. Some studied by Davie (1994) remained affiliated with their church because they thought the church would change. Increasingly, lesbian and gay Christians are seeking social justice within their churches. Many, however, say they are growing weary of the slow progress (Yip, 2007). Only 16 percent of those studied by Schuck and Liddle (2001) reported staying in their original church in order to change attitudes there. Some, however, were willing to experience the dissonance and attend services and participate actively in the church.

It is an extreme action when lesbian and gay people discard their religious faith altogether. But it is also an extreme action when they leave their lesbian or gay lives. This is the aim of groups and organizations collectively known as the ex-gay ministry. Most likely responding to pressure from church authorities, lesbian and gay church members attempt to refrain from practicing a lesbian or gay life or seek to change their sexual orientation through spiritual intervention. In less extreme cases, believers maintain their religious faith outside of the church and disengage from their religious communities (Yip, 2007). Of those studied by Yip, 60 percent were affiliated with a religion but only 38 percent practiced their faith publicly or participated in church activities.

A study by D. I. Garcia, Gray-Stanley, and Ramirez-Valles (2008) of Latino gay Catholics found that many used the strategies described above to cope with the dissonance between their sexual and religious identities. Their current levels of commitment to and participation in Catholicism varied. They used different paths to reconcile their sexual identities and Catholic values or leave the church.

Many participants studied by D. I. Garcia et al. (2008) abandoned Catholicism. They joined other traditional religions or denominations that they perceived as friendly to lesbian and gay people. For other participants in this study, religion and spirituality remained a significant force in their lives. The majority of these participants reported having a religious and spiritual life that they relied on for support and strength. This group included activists; many were active in their churches or congregations. Religion shaped their activism, and it is possible that their activism affected their levels of religious and spiritual investment. Their activism or civic involvement, with few exceptions, did not take place through their participation in church, but through community organizations working on HIV/AIDS and lesbian and gay issues.

Those who remained in the Catholic Church resolved the differences between religious teachings and their same-sex attractions in several different ways. Some hid their same-sex attractions (B. M. Berger, 1981; Fellows, 1996). They attended religious services regularly but were not openly gay in their churches and did not discuss their sexual lives. Others criticized religious teachings on same-sex attractions and decreased their participation in and commitment to Catholicism, attending church only on special occasions like weddings and funerals. Some participants made a distinction between institutionalized religion and personal spirituality. They also noted that their same-sex attractions were strictly between them and God (B. M. Berger, 1981; Thumma, 1991).

Rosario et al. (2006) cautioned that managing cognitive dissonance associated with religious and sexual identities takes time. It involves investigation and experimentation with different responses to the cognitive dissonance. Most eventually reach a stable solution when they either reject their religion or integrate their religious and sexual identities. Rejecting religion without finding an adequate substitute for the support it provided can result in increased stress and lead to substance abuse, high-risk sexual activity, or other behaviors that put their health at risk.

Compartmentalization

Another strategy used by lesbian and gay churchgoers studied by Beckwith (2007) and Rodriguez (1997) was compartmentalization—keeping one's religious and lesbian or gay identity separate. Some compartmentalize the church into one section consisting of the doctrines of the church and another consisting of priests who are more accepting of lesbian and gay people. But, according to Rosario et al. (2006), those who compartmentalize their religious and lesbian and gay identities may not realize the difficulty of maintaining this state over time. Compartmentalization is usually a transitional phase rather than a long-term solution.

Revisionist Ideological Work

Strategies mentioned above to overcome cognitive dissonance involve altering one's religious beliefs, reinterpreting Bible verses that are usually seen to condemn lesbian and gay people, and moving toward more inclusion in the church. B. M. Berger (1981) indicated that these strategies require remedial or revisionist ideological work. In an ethnographic study, Wolkomir (2001) assessed a group of gay Christian men called Accept. This was a group in the Metropolitan Community Church in the southeastern United States. The men in Accept wanted to sidestep the power of their church and revise traditional Christian ideology. In order to accommodate their sexuality, they had to go through a process of ideological maneuvering through which they could construct moral identities and mitigate psychological distress.

Before joining Accept, the men were in a dilemma due to conflict between their Christian and gay identities. They had committed themselves to Christianity, often in childhood. Later they experienced a sexual attraction to another male that created conflict with their long-standing religious beliefs. When they felt that the attraction was an enduring one, they began to feel inauthentic as Christians. This resulted in anxiety, shame, fear of rejection by their families, feeling unworthy of Christian fellowship, and fear of not attaining eternal salvation. The men desired resolution and used revisionist ideological work to alter the meaning of their Christian identity. In this way they hoped to accommodate their sexual desires and behaviors (Snow, Rochford, Worden, & Benford, 1986).

Religious identities are ideologically anchored in the unchanging sacred and divine realm (P. Berger, 1967). To challenge religious ideology risks tampering with the divine and divine authority. Members of Accept chose not to challenge divine authority but instead created new meanings in the secular realm (Wolkomir, 2001).

The men had strong beliefs in God and in the Bible as God's word and therefore could not challenge biblical truth. Instead, they challenged traditional interpretation of the Bible. To them, conservative interpretation reflected human biases. They also located Bible passages that contradicted antigay interpretations. To make being gay and Christian compatible, they rejected any interpretation of the Bible that condemned gay relationships. They claimed that conservative Christians historically used the Bible to oppress and exclude certain groups of people from being considered good Christians and from entering the Kingdom of Heaven. The conservative Christian attack on gay people added up to intolerance. In Bible study meetings, the men deconstructed the Bible verses commonly used to denounce same-sex attractions, studied the verses as they appeared in the original language, and arrived at a new interpretation (Wolkomir, 2001).

As noted in chapter 1, the Bible has been published in various English translations of the original Greek and Hebrew texts (Walton, 2006). It has been translated, in whole or in part, into more than 2,000 languages and dialects. Translation inevitably involves interpretation. Also, "normal" and "right" are socially constructed categories and thus unstable, unfixed, and mutable (Kahn, 2006).

Affirming Views

To transform restrictions against being gay, Accept members applied secularized notions of social justice to their situation. They elevated the principle of inclusiveness—the importance of including all people in God's love and recognizing that because God loves everyone equally, humans should do the same. Good Christians include all others in their love, whereas excluders fail the test of moral character. In this way, they came to view their same-sex attractions and themselves in a positive light (Sherkat & Ellison, 1997).

For the men to think of these new views as legitimate, the new meanings had to be known as truth or shifted into the divine realm. They linked the views either to specific scriptural passages or to widely accepted religious principles (Wolkomir, 2001).

Inclusiveness versus Exclusion

Accept members also linked their new ideology to the divine realm by redefining the biblical basis for good and evil. They interpreted the Bible as aligning goodness with inclusiveness and evil with exclusion, and thus considered their revised ideology to be a biblically mandated truth not of their own making. The link between good (inclusiveness) and bad (exclusion) provided evidence that their revised ideology reflected biblical truth and reflected what good Christian behavior was (Wolkomir, 2001).

Downside of Revision

A difficult problem for marginalized groups when they attempt ideological revision is their belief in the dominant ideology of their religion. A subordinate group is rarely able to completely reject the dominant world view. Too many understandings of one's self and the world depend on this view to totally discard it. These gay men were not ready to renounce Christianity as the basis for their moral identities. So, despite ideological revision, they remained marginalized within their heterosexist Christian church (Wolkomir, 2001).

The ideological maneuvering of stigmatized groups, when it becomes public, will likely also provoke a backlash. When gay Christians advocate reconciling "homosexuality" and Christianity, other groups emerge to reassert the impossibility of such a move. Existing studies of identity reconstruction in marginalized groups show that creating new identities requires subverting the dominant ideologies that impose stigma on them (Francis, 1997; Karp, 1992; Ponticelli, 1999; Schwalbe & Mason-Schrock, 1996; Thumma, 1991).

Positive Outcomes

The study by Wolkomir (2001) showed how a group of men resisted stigmatization by maneuvering around and within dominant ideologies. The goal was to reconcile their sexuality with religious beliefs when they were unwilling to relinquish either one. The gay men in this study accomplished this revision through step-by-step ideological maneuvering. However, the revision was selective. The larger, legitimating structure of Christian ideology remained intact. Much of the oppressive ideology was still in place.

On the other hand, they created a moral identity that generated feelings of worth, acceptability, and authenticity. Members of oppressed groups can reduce psychological distress and empower themselves to work for social change. For the gay and Christian men in this study, ideological revision positively affected their mental health. Depression declined, and in some instances suicidal desires were reduced. Their desire to engage in anonymous sex or other risky sexual behaviors diminished as well. Ideological revision, therefore, dramatically altered individual lives in this group of gay men (Warner, 1995).

Oppositional Identity Work

McQueeney (2009) studied lesbian, gay, and heterosexual-but-affirming members of churches in the South. The participants challenged the Christian belief that same-sex relations were sinful. The researcher obtained data from 200 hours of participant observation and 25 in-depth interviews in two Protestant churches. One church was predominantly black, working class, lesbian, and evangelical. The other church was mostly white, middle class, heterosexual, liberal, and gay-affirming. The sample was predominantly black and working class. This study viewed the ways in which participants modified their sexual identities in order to make them compatible with their religious identities. The respondents engaged in oppositional identity work to challenge lesbian and gay stigma and present good Christian identities. Discredited identities had to become credible ones (Schwalbe & Mason-Schrock, 1996).

The strategies used included the following:

- ❧ Some black lesbians deemphasized same-sex attractions so they would be secondary to their Christian identity. A few black lesbians suggested that sexuality is irrelevant to one's character. By minimizing same-sex attractions, they felt they would be seen as good Christians, but the concept of same-sex relations as sinful was unchallenged.

- ❧ Most lesbian and gay people (black and white) attempted to normalize their sexuality through monogamy, manhood, or motherhood. They felt that they could then claim that they were normal regardless of their sexual orientation. Some working class black gay people normalized their same-sex attractions in portraying Christian manhood. White lesbians also used a normalizing strategy that focused on their similarity to heterosexual Christians. They supported monogamous relationships and valued being good mothers. But these normalizing strategies relied on conventionally gendered models and practices grounded in white middle class respectability. Black lesbians used a masculine leader-provider model and a feminine nurturer-helper model for their relationships. But this reinforced two gender systems that devalued the feminine role.

- ❧ Some lesbian and gay respondents defined themselves as more generous and moral than "condemning" Christians who excluded lesbian and gay people. They claimed that their sexual attractions gave them a special calling as Christians. Their mission was to save lesbian and gay souls and to make Christianity more inclusive. Some white heterosexual-but-affirming church respondents developed a sense of having a special moral identity because of their mission to include the excluded.

For some black lesbians, the cost of being ostracized from the black community was too high to challenge institutional structures such as heterosexual marriage and cultural ideologies such as the sinfulness of same-sex attractions. But they did find comfort in the black lesbian community at another church. Some worshipped at a traditional black Baptist or Pentecostal church where they were not out. They could stay connected to the black community but be true to their identity by also attending the gay-affirmative Faith Church in the afternoon. At this location, they experienced cultural solidarity and the freedom to be open with friends and lovers.

Critical Rethinking of Religious Ideas

Gay respondents studied by Kubicek et al. (2009) dealt in a variety of ways with heterosexist messages. But most of their strategies involved critically rethinking what they had been taught in church about same-sex attractions.

One strategy was to critically evaluate the source of heterosexist religious messages, including the origins of the religious text. Respondents believed that interpretations of religious texts vary dramatically and that the Bible can be translated in different ways. Several respondents asserted that religious scripture was written or recorded by people driven by their own particular perspectives and motives (Kubicek et al., 2009).

Some respondents also mentioned people and groups who appeared to be hypocrites, saying that observing such hypocrisy enabled them to feel confident that the people who judged them for being gay were not expressing God's actual attitude toward gay people. Several commented that their churches taught that it is wrong to judge others but that church leaders and other members of the congregation were judgmental of them. Respondents also observed that pious people making antigay remarks demonstrated their hypocrisy, especially when those people engaged in what respondents identified as sinful, dishonest, or morally questionable behavior. This included adultery or, in one case, throwing a party with paid strippers (Kubicek et al., 2009).

The young men in the study frequently identified logical contradictions in antigay religious doctrines. They thought about the contradictions, discussed these issues with friends, read relevant texts, kept a journal, or engaged in an internal dialogue with themselves. The most frequently cited contradiction was that gay people will be punished by God versus the concept that God is a loving, omniscient, perfect creator. Respondents reported a period of confusion, wondering why God would make them gay. The idea of being created gay led the majority (30 out of 36) to feel that their same-sex attractions were not a mistake. To reach this perspective, respondents relied on the idea that a loving God would not create people in a way that is wrong or that dooms them to hell (Kubicek et al., 2009).

A number of respondents referred to the concept that "God creates everything for a reason." Sexual desire was therefore seen as something acceptable and a valued part of a person's life: The question was why God would give you something that he did not want you to use (Kubicek et al., 2009).

As part of the effort to find a religion or faith that would provide them with tranquility and acceptance, several respondents reported having visited or wanting to visit a gay church. The idea of such a church was appealing, with several looking forward to an environment that would be accepting.

Most of the young men who initially adhered to the assertion that the Bible says "homosexuality" is an abomination were able ultimately to accept their sexuality. Although many respondents had gone through periods of self-judgment, nearly all of them had adopted a more accepting attitude by the time they were interviewed. Their gay-affirming outlooks provided relief from intense shame and guilt (Kubicek et al., 2009).

It seems crucial for lesbian and gay people to critically evaluate beliefs and scripture as discussed above. According to Fowler's (1981, 1996) theory of faith development, an important religious development is the ability to consider the utility and veracity of specific religious beliefs for oneself rather than relying on outside authorities. Fowler considered this development an indication of religious maturity. Definitions of religious maturity, however, vary by religious groups (Decker, 1993). For this reason, the name for critical evaluation of beliefs was changed by Fowler to "postconventional religious reasoning."

People who use more postconventional religious reasoning have less traditional religious beliefs (Haan, Smith, & Block, 1968), broader principles in moral reasoning (Emsberger and Monaster, 1981), and a preference for less literal interpretations of the Bible (Harris, Schoneman, & Carrera, 2002). They may also exhibit less internalized heterosexism than those who use less postconventional religious reasoning. These behaviors may help those in conflict with their sexual attractions and religion to reduce the conflict.

Stigma Management Strategies

The centrality of stigma related to one's lesbian and gay identity was studied by Crocker (1995). Lesbian and gay people's characters can be stigmatized by rejecting-punitive Christian religious doctrine and its adherents as bad, immoral, and otherwise negative. The more importance is placed on a stigma by oneself or by others, the more it affects one's identity (Goffman, 1963).

Crocker and Major (1989) identified three major strategies used to manage stigma or protect oneself from being stigmatized: (1) attributing negative characterizations to prejudice or discrimination; (2) devaluing domains in which stigma makes it unlikely they will excel; and (3) comparing themselves and their outcomes with others who share their stigma rather than with nonstigmatized people.

In a study by Yip (1997a) of 60 gay Christians in England, four stigma management strategies were identified: (1) attacking the stigma, (2) attacking the stigmatizer, (3) positive personal experience, and (4) the ontogeneric argument. These strategies were used interchangeably and collectively to dismiss the credibility of the institutionalized church and the validity of its position on being lesbian or gay. Attacking the stigma included challenging the correctness and accuracy of Biblical passages used to condemn same-sex attractions (see chapter

1). This can be achieved through invalidating the conventional interpretation of these passages, shifting focus from these passages to broader Christian principles of love and respect for all, or challenging the relevance of these passages to today's society. Attacking the stigmatizer is a strategy in which lesbian and gay people dismiss the credibility of the church as their moral guardian and undermine or ignore negative church doctrine. Use of positive experience entails adherence to basic Christian moral values by living in a monogamous relationship. The ontogeneric strategy involves the belief that all sexual identities were created by God and thus blessed by God.

Essentialism

Essentialism is the belief that one was born (genetically determined) with a lesbian or gay sexual orientation (Fuss, 1989). Some participants in Kubicek et al.'s (2009) study of gay men said that they knew when they were young that they were attracted to others of the same sex, or that their behavior was different from that of other boys. For some respondents, such memories confirmed that their sexual orientation had been fundamental to them since birth.

Many say God made them this way. This removes blame and guilt and can be empowering and politically expedient (Fuss, 1989). This belief is also one way to cope with religious and identity conflict. Most antigay religious groups believe that sexual orientation is freely chosen and can be changed. The belief of most lesbian and gay people, however, is that change is not an option (Wilcox, 2002).

Separating Religion from Spirituality

More than half of the respondents studied by Schuck and Liddle (2001) said they were spiritual rather than religious. Spirituality is another way that some resolve the conflict between sexual and religious identity (Mahaffy, 1996; Rodriguez, 1997; Shallenberger, 1998). Religion is equated with traditional churches and with official church doctrine. Spirituality refers to the personal, subjective, and unsystematic expression of faith. So a shift is made from the institutional to the personal (Yip, 2002). Spirituality relies on an internal authority, meaning that the expert is the person him- or herself; truth comes from personal experience. Value is also placed on personal insight (Barret & Barzan, 1996). In addition, people can see their own life events as a source of authority. Spirituality is multidimensional, with numerous pathways, and has no clear-cut boundaries; it is amorphous (Bosivert, 2007; Shallenberger, 1998). For some people, spirituality does not include affiliation with any religious doctrine.

Newer forms of spirituality borrow teachings, beliefs, and rituals from Buddhist, aboriginal, New Age, and other religious traditions. Spirituality can also consist of beliefs about the importance of nature or the connectedness of life. One might describe one's spirituality simply as a search for inner peace or a commitment to being a good person (Hodge & McGrew, 2006). Or it can focus on a search for meaning, purpose, and values (Frame, 2003).

Many gay respondents studied by Kubicek et al. (2009) desired acceptance and tranquility. This led some to explore beliefs such as Kabbalah and Wicca or paganism. Respondents described seeing friends develop greater clarity or change in other ways and attributed the changes to these beliefs. Spiritual practices, including meditation or connecting to a natural or spiritual being, provided some of the support and tranquility that their religious upbringing failed to provide. Some developed their personal spirituality as a way to continue to connect to a higher power and experience its support.

Kubicek et al. (2009) asked respondents to explain how they differentiated religion and spirituality. While some had difficulty saying how the two concepts differed, most seemed to agree that spirituality was connected to nature and that it is generally internalized, emphasizing an individual connection to a higher power (Koenig, McCullough, & Larson, 2001). Being a spiritual person meant that one did good things and believed in good things such as love, happiness, good fortune, and relating to another person. Spirituality was often described as related to a belief in karma (the idea that all the good and all the bad you do adds up in the end) (Kubicek et al., 2009).

Religion was most often described in terms of rules that included having to go to church on Sunday, adhere to the teachings of the minister or priest, read the Bible each day, or say a prayer at night. Respondents often described religion as being structured and practiced externally by attending services and prayer groups. Some respondents felt that people who said they were religious were not necessarily the closest to God or a higher power.

For many who decided to develop a personal spiritual system, the primary motivation was the rejection they felt from the religion in which they were raised. This led some young men, who had heard that they could not be both Christian and gay, to develop a sense of spirituality (Kubicek et al., 2009).

A sense of spirituality was important for a number of reasons. For some, it provided a sense of purpose in life, or the idea that there "is something more." For others, it ensured that they had someone to help them with their problems. Others said they received strength to overcome challenges such as family and relationship problems. Their personal relationship with the spiritual world contributed to their having the inner strength to overcome hardships (Kubicek et al., 2009).

Some respondents believed that the religion one was raised in had a strong influence on any belief system developed later in life. In other words, if one was raised as a Christian, discarding all of the beliefs from that religion would be difficult. Those who had developed an individual spirituality retained the idea of a single benevolent God and belief in the general tenets of Christianity, such as the possibility of redemption and the importance of kindness. A few respondents felt that one could not be totally spiritual without some religion (Kubicek et al., 2009).

Spirituality provided the respondents a sense of support and acceptance that for many was not available in organized religion. The young men acknowledged that they often had a great deal of help in their spiritual exploration. Support came from friends, family members, members of religious communities, and the gay community (Kubicek et al., 2009).

Spirituality was also a source of strength for gay students attending a religiously affiliated liberal arts college. The coming-out process can motivate some lesbian and gay people to search for a spiritual identity, due to the conflict between religious teaching and their developing awareness of their sexual identity (Love, 1997). Some students equated religion with spirituality but later rejected both. Later, the students often came back to spirituality, leaving religion behind (Love, Bock, Jannarone, & Richardson, 2005).

A spiritual identity may buffer the impact of negative religious experiences (Gage Davidson, 2000). Lesbian and gay people with a strong spiritual identity seem to experience better psychological health than those who depended solely on an affiliation with an organized faith group (Lease et al., 2005; Zinnbauer et al., 1997). Lesbian and gay respondents who had high existential well-being, or spiritual lives, had positive outcomes. They experienced higher self-esteem, lower internalized heterosexism, and a lower sense of alienation than those who expressed a sense of religious well-being. This seemed to result from having to seek more comprehensive answers to the meaning of existence and faith than when in organized religions (Tan, 2005).

Distinguishing spirituality from religion helps family members accept their children's sexual orientation. Spirituality facilitates understanding and acceptance (Lease & Shulman, 2003).

Queer spirituality also exists. In the Christian, Jewish, and Muslim traditions, same-sex relations are viewed as non-normative because they do not produce life. Queer spirituality opposes this view. It also opposes dominant religious world views that favor a heterosexual perspective. As an example, the biblical story of Adam and Eve and procreation does not reflect queer experience, nor would they want it to. Also rejected are heterosexual privilege, patriarchy, and male hegemony.

Queer spirituality chooses marginality as central to the meaning of the queer experience in the world. Marginality is seen as power—such as the collective power of lesbian and gay people when they celebrate the Stonewall events of 1969, or the way that lesbian and gay people's disclosure of their sexual identity empowers others to do the same. Queer spirituality also deals with fears of the erotic or the sexualized body (erotophobia). Fear of the erotic stems from teachings of Christianity that frown on nonprocreative erotic activity. Queer spirituality affirms the value and worth of a variety of sexual experiences (Boisvert, 2007; M. Jordan, 2007).

Some lesbian and gay people abandon all spiritual activities because of the residual pain from earlier religious struggles; neither religion nor spirituality hold their interest. This is partly because they fear trusting anything that is even remotely similar to teachings that have created intense suffering in their lives (Barret & Barzan, 1996). Some experience grief and loss as they abandon religious institutions, but anger at all religious organizations modifies their experience of loss (Ritter & O'Neill, 1995).

Summary

Responses that lesbian and gay people use to cope with conflict between their sexual and religious identities include resolving cognitive dissonance, compartmentalization, revisionist ideological work, oppositional identity work, critical rethinking of religious ideas and postconventional religious reasoning, and stigma management. Although these methods are helpful, many of them leave some problems with the church unresolved. Essentialism, or the belief that one was born lesbian or gay or created that way by God, can be empowering and help to resolve conflict. Many people find spirituality to be a source of strength that is easier to access than continued participation in organized religion.

Five

Unworkable and Unethical Cures for Same-Sex Attraction

When lesbian and gay people cannot resolve the conflict between their sexual identity and a conservative religious identity, they may seek therapy to change their sexual orientation to heterosexual (Beckstead & Israel, 2007).

Treatments offered to change same-sex attractions have been biological, behavioral, cognitive, psychoanalytic, or religious. Most of these treatments are still attempted today, although the biological treatments are rarely used. They included cauterization of the spinal cord, clitoridectomy, castration, ovary removal, lobotomy, convulsive treatments such as electric shock or drugs, radiation, and hormonal treatments such as steroids (Nugent & Gramick, 1989).

Today, some behavioral treatments are still used, such as electric shock or nausea-inducing drugs paired with same-sex erotic material. These treatments focus on changing same-sex attractions by pairing them with negative consequences. Cognitive therapy offers to eliminate cognitive blocks to heterosexuality. Psychoanalytic treatment offers to repair uncompleted gender identity through gender lessons and support groups that encourage participants to adopt traditional gender roles (S. L. Morrow & Beckstead, 2004). When such treatments are not successful, some people seek sexual reorientation therapy (SRT). Other terms for this so-called therapy include "reparative therapy," "reorientation therapy," "conversion," and "transformational ministry." The term "reparative therapy" implies that lesbian and gay people are in need of repair; the term "reorientation therapy" implies that they were once heterosexual and need to be reoriented to this identity again (Bieschke, Paul, & Blasko, 2007). Transformational ministry is a term used by religious groups that try to change sexual orientation.

The term SRT is used in this book to refer to all treatments that attempt to change individuals' sexual orientation or at a minimum reduce their same-sex thoughts, feelings, and behaviors. Both professionals and nonprofessionals practice SRT around the world. Most human services organizations are strongly opposed to SRT because its assumption of pathology and promotion of intolerance violate their ethical principles (Johnston & Jenkins, 2006). This includes the National Association of Social Workers (2003), the American Psychological Association (1998), and the American Psychiatric Association (2000).

As noted earlier, rejecting-punitive churches instill the belief in lesbian and gay members that God does not love same-sex-attracted people who cannot or will not change. The SRT route has a steep price (giving up one's sexual identity), but some lesbian and gay people are willing to pay this price (Tozer & Hayes, 2004). One reason for hope for a "cure" may have come from their belief in miracles ("with God, nothing is impossible") (Beckwith, 2001).

Reasons some lesbian and gay people seek SRT may include the following:

- ❦ to be relieved of the conflict between sexual and religious identities,

- ❦ to live in conformity with the ideal of heterosexuality and avoid the social stigma of same-sex attractions,

- ❦ to reduce religious guilt,

- ❦ to avoid rejection by one's church community, and

- ❦ to overcome fear of eternal damnation. (Tozer & Hayes, 2004)

The therapeutic benefits sought by the 20 participants in a study by Beckwith and Israel (2007) were developing secure opposite-sex emotional relationships, increasing gender identity congruence, and decreasing same-sex sexual behaviors and thoughts. They said they believed that these outcomes would resolve their previously distressing emotions related to being "lost and alone" or feeling like a "sissy or tomboy" or a "fag, dyke, or pervert."

In a study of 68 self-identified lesbians and 107 self-identified gay men ranging in age from 16 to 73, mostly urban and educated, Tozer and Hayes (2004) found that those who saw religion as a central organizing principle in their lives tended to seek SRT. They also tended to internalize heterosexism. Those who had not internalized heterosexism were not likely to seek SRT. One's religious orientation did not matter as much as internalized heterosexism as to who sought SRT and who did not.

Those with what Tozer and Hayes (2004) called a "quest identity" to religion were more flexible and adaptable and were also not likely to seek SRT. They were open to doubt and uncertainty in general, perhaps specifically regarding religious doctrine about sexual identity. They may have an easier time accepting a nonheterosexual identity. Tozer and Hayes also reported that those in the later phases of identity development were less likely to seek conversion therapy. These people were further along in managing their identity and may have developed coping mechanisms such as a social support group and increased self-esteem so that their sexual identity was fulfilling and meaningful. For gay people, identification with the gay community was found to increase understanding of, coping with, and acceptance of a gay identity. Increased contact for both lesbians and gay men in a community was a way to redefine their identities in a positive direction (Tozer & Hayes, 2004).

SRT represents collusion with the part of clients that they feel is their problem (Greene, 2007). Those who seek SRT were found to attend more religious services per week, rely on God to provide direction for behavioral change, have a personal relationship with Jesus, and report that the idea of Christian conversion prompted them to consider changing their same-sex attractions. They felt they had no choice but to consider changing their sexual identity as they were not going to abandon their religion of origin (Schaeffer, Hyde, Kroencke, McCormick, & Nottebaum, 2000). Some would rather attempt to change their sexual orientation in order to retain the religious and social rewards associated with heterosexuality, while others may feign a heterosexual conversion in order to remain part of their church community (Beckstead & Morrow, 2004). Schaeffer et al. credited high religious motivation for achieving greater success in abstaining from same-sex sexual behavior. But participating in SRT was not found to help decrease same-sex sexual behavior.

A number of others have reported SRT as unhelpful at best and harmful at worst. Haldeman (2001) reported harmful results such as low self-esteem, depression, social withdrawal, and sexual dysfunction. These findings were seen in clinical practice among gay people following unsuccessful SRT. In a qualitative study of 202 SRT consumers, Shidlo and Schroeder (2002) found that fewer than 5 percent experienced a shift in their sexual identity. Many others in their study reported harmful effects including depression, suicidal thoughts, low self-esteem, relationship impairment, and spiritual harm.

Some of the practices of SRT are demonstrated in a case reported by Markowitz (1998). Typically in SRT with gay men, the practitioner attempts to evoke attraction to women and heterosexual sexual fantasies. Participants are shown heterosexual pornographic magazines and movies. In one case, homework was assigned including taking the magazines home between sessions and masturbating while looking at the pictures of women. When the client reported that none of this interested him, the practitioner became cold, aloof, and disapproving. The client, who felt ashamed and humiliated, was told to invest more effort in the assignment. On one occasion, the client reported that his favorite fantasy was kissing his best male friend. The practitioner told him to never be alone with this friend again and to imagine that feces and vomit covered this person. The practitioner told the client that he would end up alone, unloved, and persecuted. The client left therapy after he fabricated stories about experiencing heterosexual fantasies. He also reported that he took a girl to his senior prom. His parents felt relieved that he was now living a normal life. Four months later, however, he attempted suicide and checked himself into a psychiatric hospital. There, an affirmative practitioner helped him come to positive terms with his sexual identity (Markowitz, 1998).

Ethical Issues with SRT

Attempts to "cure" same-sex attractions are not ethical, because there is nothing wrong with being lesbian or gay. The American Psychiatric Association no longer views lesbian and gay people as mentally ill. Nearly all major medical and professional service organizations repudiate SRT. But SRT proponents interpret this as evidence that modern psychiatry, medicine, psychology, and other helping professions have a liberal bias (Morris, 2002). Conservative religious authorities view themselves as the only ones worthy of trust about what to do about same-sex sexual attractions (Ream & Savin-Williams, 2005).

Many therapists who practice SRT are also unethical in another way: A majority of the participants in SRT surveys report that they were given prejudicial and misleading information about same-sex sexual attractions. Lesbian and gay life was distorted. For example, participants were told that all lesbian and gay people have unhappy lives. At the least, this is psychologically harmful. Unfortunately, most practitioners of SRT operate outside the ethical mandates of any professional organization (Haldeman, 2004).

SRT has shown no empirical evidence of success. Methodologies of studies purporting to demonstrate change in sexual orientation through SRT have been severely lacking and theoretically unsupported (S. L. Morrow & Beckstead, 2004). As SRT has no empirical validation and reinforces damaging messages about same-sex attractions, practitioners must challenge the underlying beliefs that clients have about changing their sexual orientation. And they should encourage them to find support from lesbian and gay communities. As noted earlier, increased contact with other lesbian and gay people is one way to redefine one's sexual identity in a positive direction. People further along in coming out can also be positive role models and promote self-acceptance (Tozer & Hayes, 2004).

It is unlikely that people would seek to change their sexual orientation unless they were being punished in some way, or feared punishment, for their same-sex identity or behavior. The motivation to seek SRT cannot be separated from the potential for rejection, ridicule, and violence. Self-hate and self-loathing can also develop. Many people seeking SRT have internalized condemnation of their sexual orientation. If they feel they are morally wrong, they may excuse the rejecting behavior of many of the loved ones in their lives. They often have had no exposure to those who are faithful to a religion or spirituality but have not internalized heterosexist values or have unlearned negative attitudes (Greene, 2007).

Practitioners who treat clients seeking to change their sexual orientation should critique, not reinforce, distorted views of lesbian and gay people. They should not collude with clients' negative assumptions about themselves just because they believe the assumptions are true or are based on religious faith. When beliefs are psychologically harmful to a client, the practitioner should seek to explore them and critique their harmful effects as well as their origins. Divergent opinions about lesbian and gay sexual orientations exist across religious and cultural groups. There are many ways to interpret or understand a cultural or religious proscription (Greene, 2007).

Persistence of SRT

As noted earlier, "homosexuality" has been removed from the *Diagnostic and Statistical Manual of Mental Disorders (DSM)*, and the evidence of positive mental health among lesbian and gay people is overwhelming (American Psychiatric Association, 1973, 1980, 1987, 1994, 2000). Yet many people still hold negative views about any form of sexual variation from heterosexuality. This includes many human services professionals (Rothblum, 1989). Some physicians, psychiatrists, psychologists, nurses, counselors, and social workers refuse to surrender the illness-oriented perspective on same-sex sexual identity. Some of these practitioners attempt to "cure" lesbian and gay people and reorient them to heterosexuality (Kelly, 1994). In a study of the treatments used by 139 psychologists with lesbian and gay clients, K. M. Jordan and Deluty (1995) reported that 6 percent approved the use of aversion techniques to try to change sexual orientation, though none of them claimed to use such techniques themselves. Some 11 percent, however, reported use of alternative methods such as psychoanalytic techniques for the same purpose. Viewing same-sex sexual orientation as unacceptable predicted both the support of aversion techniques and the use of alternative SRT techniques.

Conservative psychoanalytic psychiatrists such as Socarides (1992, 1995) have called for "homosexuality" to be reinstated in the *DSM* as a mental illness.

Psychotherapists such as Nicolosi (1991) and Socarides continue to publish books in which they present "homosexuality" as pathological and recommend treatments for conversion to heterosexuality. These practitioners, however, cannot present any evidence that their techniques are effective (for example, Fernandez, 1990; Haldeman, 1991).

This is not to say that spontaneously occurring shifts in sexual practices or identity do not occur over a person's lifetime (Haldeman, 1995). In the best survey to date in terms of both sample size and methodological rigor (Laumann, Gagnon, Michael, & Michaels, 1994), most young people who reported adopting same-sex sexual practices at some point also reported giving them up later. Some women experience fluidity in sexual identity. Yet spontaneous shifts are quite different from attempts by practitioners to force change (Hadelman, 1995).

No matter what the research says or how strongly professional organizations oppose attempts to change sexual orientation, the SRT movement continues to flourish. The goals of the National Association for Research and Therapy for "Homosexuality" (NARTH) include preserving the pathology myth of "homo-sexuality" and encouraging "homosexuals" to believe they can change their sexual orientation (Hadelman, 1995). SRT practitioners believe there is no such thing as a "homosexual" person, but that everyone is intrinsically heterosexual and "homosexuality" is a condition, not an intrinsic part of a person (Fellows of Research Institute, 2005).

Conservative religious groups that condemn "homosexuality" and actively support antigay legislation support this organization, headed by Joseph Nicolosi and Charles Socarides. The group welcomes former and potential "ex-gay and lesbian" people. Members must accept NARTH's dogma that "homosexuality" is an illness. Members will be dropped from the organization if they do not accept the organization's dogma (Drescher, 1998).

Religious SRT Practitioners

Rejecting-punitive religious groups also advocate the use of SRT, but they want to "cure homosexuality" not because they consider it sick but because they con-sider it immoral and believe that "homosexuals" must convert to heterosexual-ity to be saved from their immorality and sin (Haldeman, 1994). They want clients to rely on the power of prayer and doctrinal prohibitions. They also want their clients to strengthen willpower, reduce desire, and limit same-sex behavior (Besen, 2003; Ritter & O'Neill, 1989). Church-affiliated practitioners attempt to coerce lesbian and gay people not to act on their same-sex sexual attractions through programs that combine religious exhortation, prayer, Bible study, group pressure, brainwashing, and corrective sexual experiences. These "interventions" are often intermixed with elements of 12-step self-help programs (Haldeman, 1994; Rosenberg, 1994).

The religious groups include the Exodus Movement, with over 135 chapters in the United States, Asia, and Europe; Courage, a Roman Catholic group with about 15 U.S. centers; Evergreen International, in Canada and Australia; Homosexuals Anonymous, with chapters throughout the United States, and Jews Offering New Alternatives to Homosexuality (JONAH) (S. L. Morrow & Beckstead, 2004). Parents and Friends of Ex-Gays (P-FOX) supports the families and friends of ex-gay people (Markowitz, 1998). Some of these groups provide residential programs in which one can spend up to a year trying to change (Rosenberg, 1994).

Ex-gay groups say they will convert lesbian and gay people who want to be heterosexual through a process of gender socialization, prayer, and group and individual counseling. Many of their procedures come from aversion therapies that have been rejected by mainstream psychology and psychiatry. Ex-gay groups' activities range from exorcisms at urban churches to rural retreats where gay and lesbian people can live while they try to gradually adopt a changed sexual orientation (Fetner, 2005).

SRT practitioners usually claim that their clients successfully choose to replace an immoral "homosexual" life with a moral heterosexual life. They never report any scientific data, however, of actual cures from same-sex sexual attractions (Gonsiorek, 1996; Haldeman, 1995). In one program reviewed by Rosenberg (1994), the men who "converted" took varied roads afterward. Some reported that they "became heterosexual," married, and had children. Many became celibate and dedicated their lives to God. Most acknowledged, though, that they still experienced same-sex sexual fantasies (Gonsiorek, 1996; Haldeman, 1994). Heterosexual marriage was only a facsimile of heterosexuality because same-sex dreams, fantasies, and attractions continued (Pattison & Pattison, 1980).

Despite the many treatment failures and the dubious successes, SRT practitioners never seem to abandon their goals. Early in 1998, full-page ads ran in *USA Today,* the *New York Times,* the *Washington Post,* and other newspapers that portrayed testimonials from people who claimed that they were once lesbian or gay but became heterosexual. The ads were financed by conservative Christian groups. They claimed that lesbian and gay people seeking help through organizations such as Exodus, Love in Action, and Homosexuals Anonymous could become heterosexual and be saved from sin, shame, and emotional emptiness. Other messages conveyed in the ads were that the only morally acceptable sex happens within heterosexual marriages and that one cannot be both Christian and lesbian or gay (Fetner, 2005; Painter, 1998).

Discredited Approach

A review of the empirical literature indicates that it is not possible for one to change sexual orientation. Few people have reported that they believe they have made a shift in sexual orientation. But it is difficult to validate these self-reports. And there have been neither accurate measurement of sexual orientation before and after intervention nor long-term follow-up studies (Bieschke et. al, 2007).

Not only is SRT scientifically unproven, but serious ethical questions arise about using any form of therapy that causes harm to clients (Gonsiorek, 1996; Haldeman, 1994; Isay, 1990). It is ethically wrong for a practitioner to support or participate in ineffective, detrimental treatments (Brown, 1995, 1996). In December 1998, the American Psychiatric Association's board voted unanimously to repudiate any therapy with the sole goal of turning lesbian and gay people into heterosexuals. The board agreed that these therapies can cause depression, anxiety, and self-destructive behavior (their position statement can be found here: http://www.psych.org/Departments/EDU/Library/APAOfficialDocumentsandRelated/PositionStatements/200001.aspx). As noted earlier, attempts to change sexual orientation are also ethically irresponsible because a lesbian or gay identity is not a psychiatric disorder (Gonsiorek, 1982a, 1982b).

Given the fear of damnation that some people experience, it may seem difficult to oppose the right of practitioners to attempt SRT. This therapy, however, is as blatantly prejudicial as were schools of therapy based upon racism or sexism (Hadelman, 1995). No ethical practitioner engages in any of these practices today (Haldeman, 1991; Stein, 1988). A client's request for SRT does not justify providing it. Gay-affirmative theorists and practitioners indicate that people who desire to change their sexual identity are in a stage in the coming-out process prior to reaching a positive lesbian or gay identity (Atkinson & Hackett, 1998).

Those who criticize SRT argue not only that changing one's sexual orientation is impossible but also that attempting such a change can be harmful (Haldeman, 1991, 1994; LeVay, 1996; Martin, 1984; T. F. Murphy, 1992, 1997; Stein, 1996). Haldeman (1991), after describing what he called the "inadequate and questionable science" (p. 150) of conversion treatments, said that mental health providers who use such interventions "commit consumer fraud, as this damaging practice simply does not work" (p. 160).

In line with the latter reasoning, on August 14, 1997, the American Psychological Association passed a resolution, based on its ethics code, that affirmed basic principles concerning treatments to alter sexual orientation. The resolution supported the "dissemination of accurate information about sexual orientation and mental health, and appropriate interventions in order to counteract bias that is based in ignorance or unfounded beliefs about sexual orientation" (American

Psychological Association, 1998, p. 934). In essence, the resolution requires a full discussion by the therapist of the client's potential for happiness as a gay, lesbian, or bisexual person and communication that no scientific evidence exists that conversion treatments work. The American Psychological Association elaborated on its earlier stance that having same-sex attractions is not a mental illness and recommended that practitioners refrain from using sexual reorientation interventions until these treatment modalities are placed under empirical scrutiny to assess risks, benefits, and long-term outcomes.

Other mental-health provider associations such as the American Medical Association, American Academy of Pediatrics, American Counseling Association, and National Association of Social Workers (NASW) have made similarly strong policy statements against sexual reorientation therapy (Beckstead, 2002). In 1993, NASW stated the following:

> Social stigmatization of lesbian, gay, and bisexual people is widespread and is a primary motivating factor in leading some people to seek sexual orientation changes. Sexual orientation conversion therapies assume that "homosexual" orientation is both pathological and freely chosen. No data demonstrate that reparative or conversion therapies are effective, and in fact they may be harmful. NASW believes social workers have the responsibility to clients to explain the prevailing knowledge concerning sexual orientation and the lack of data reporting positive outcomes with reparative therapy. NASW discourages social workers from providing treatments designed to change sexual orientation or from referring to practitioners or programs that claim to do so. (Svensson, 2003)

Alternatives to SRT

If a client remains steadfast in his or her desire to reorient to heterosexuality, no action is better than the wrong action. The practitioner should have available a bibliography of resources that factually refute the prevailing myths and misconceptions about SRT and that offer positive images of lesbian, gay, and bisexual people. Practitioners cannot collude, even peripherally, with a practice that is discriminatory, oppressive, and ultimately ineffective in achieving its stated ends (Tozer & McClanahan, 1999).

Practitioners should inform such clients of their profession's stand regarding the use of therapies that operate from an assumption that same-sex orientations are pathological. An affirmative practitioner can also encourage clients who are troubled about sexual identity to focus less on the label of lesbian or gay than on their own unique experiences. This can help them take the time to consider their needs and feelings rather than rushing to acquire the "right" identity (Tozer & McClanahan, 1999).

A practitioner in this situation can reiterate that he or she is not attempting to recruit the client to a lesbian or gay orientation, but at the same time is not willing to support the notion that such an orientation is bad, immoral, invalid, or unhealthy. It can be powerful for someone with the social authority of a practitioner to say these things (Tozer & McClanahan, 1999).

Some respondents studied by Kubicek et al. (2009) were engaged in a personal struggle to alter their sexual desires. Respondents who had been raised in religious settings were more likely to have believed at some point that their sexual orientation could be changed, a view that also was expressed often by religious leaders and family members. Several respondents with a religious upbringing had been told that prayer could make them heterosexual, and such assertions were often reinforced with stories of gay people who had become heterosexual through prayer. Relatively few of the respondents reported trying to change their sexual orientation, although many reported feeling pressure from their families and religious communities. The journeys these individuals described were difficult and painful, but in every case led to the conclusion that their sexual orientation could not be altered.

Summary

Some lesbian and gay people seek therapy to change their sexual orientation to heterosexual. But such therapies are not ethical, because there is no empirical proof that they work and because they seek to change something that is not pathological. Many SRT practitioners tell their clients that as lesbian or gay people they will have miserable lives, which is a falsehood. Most human service organizations have come out against SRT for these reasons.

※ **Part III** ※

Helping Lesbian and Gay Clients Work through Conflict

Six

Working with Religious Lesbian and Gay Clients

Some lesbian and gay people experience little or no conflict with their religious identity. But others feel distress over conflict between their religious beliefs and their sexual attractions (Beckstead & Morrow, 2004; Haldeman, 2004; Yarhouse & Tan, 2004). Some of the people in the latter group seek assistance from practitioners. Schuck and Liddle (2001) found that, after friends, the two greatest sources of help reported by their lesbian and gay participants were therapists and clergy. Thus it is important for practitioners to know how to help effectively.

The first issue for practitioners to address is the need to counter the negative societal messages experienced by lesbian and gay clients. Practitioners can work with clients' internalized heterosexism and can help them reframe issues in a more positive light. They can highlight the inherent human worth of each person regardless of sexual identity (Gage Davidson, 2000; Pachankis & Goldfried, 2004). Practitioners can emphasize that all aspects of self and identity are worthy of respect, and that bodies and sexuality are inherently good (Heyward, 1984). This replaces a model emphasizing redemption from sin with one that accepts and affirms everyone (Struzzo, 1989). Practitioners can also help clients separate nonaffirming doctrine from faith practices and principles that support lesbian and gay people. They can provide information about affirming faith groups, practitioners, or faith leaders to help challenge the notion that being lesbian or gay is incompatible with having a religious identity.

Practitioner Preparation

In order to work with religious lesbian and gay people, practitioners have to be affirmative. They have to prepare themselves by acquiring accurate information, exploring their attitudes toward lesbian and gay people, and developing skills to work with the difficult and complex issues these clients are dealing with.

Acquiring information about lesbian and gay people is the easy part of preparation: There are many books, Web sites, and continuing education courses available. Examining biases toward sexual minorities and exploring one's own religious upbringing for negative messages regarding same-sex attractions is more difficult (Barret & Barzan, 1996; Fassinger & Richie, 1997; Frame, 2003; Israel & Selvidge, 2003; Kocarek & Pelling, 2003). This exploration is essential, however, if one's work with gay and lesbian clients is to succeed.

We all grow up in a society that blatantly expresses a negative attitude toward lesbian and gay people. Like others in this society, most practitioners see themselves as nice people who want to do no harm. But everyone has internal biases and prejudices (Rudolph, 1992). McHenry and Johnson (1993) argued that a non-gay practitioner treating a lesbian or gay client can unconsciously collude with the client's self-hate. An example is the practitioner whose gay client tells of moving in with his lover and who, at a moment when congratulations and celebration are appropriate, says nothing. This portrays rejection of the client. Acknowledging happy events such as a new dating relationship, successful disclosures at work, or becoming a parent help lesbian and gay clients feel understood (Barret & Barzan, 1996).

Because a practitioner has power to which clients could be susceptible, the practitioner must focus on correcting or managing any such negative messages (Beckstead & Israel, 2007). Practitioners must recognize how their biases, agendas, and emotional reactions will contribute to or reinforce clients' fears and beliefs. For example, a practitioner's internalized heterosexism may be expressed through negative representations of same-sex relationships. The client has to be able to reflect fully on his or her feelings, needs, perspectives, and on ways to resolve sexual orientation conflicts (Lasser & Gottlieb, 2004). A practitioner's biases or lack of affirmative knowledge should not interfere with this process.

Biased practitioners can push negative views of same-sex relations. They may insist that clients overcome their lesbian or gay sexual identity because of their heterosexism or, in some cases, religious beliefs. Practitioners need to explore and modify their heterosexist and religious biases, because they can affect every step in the therapeutic process (Beckstead & Israel, 2007).

Practitioners have to understand that heterosexism permeates most social institutions and will influence their attitudes, and that it is important to be vigilant about this and to avoid projecting heterosexism onto clients. Throughout this process, practitioners must also be aware of the difference between heterosexist and affirmative therapy. Practitioners have to help clients explore and embrace complex and conflicting perspectives, confront misinformation and the ways in which the clients' religious culture is oppressive in its views of lesbian and gay people. They should encourage clients to get new perspectives and accurate information (Beckstead & Israel, 2007). Is the practitioner willing to illuminate the pernicious role of heterosexism in this culture? Can the practitioner balance the professional demands of neutrality with an appreciation for the myriad ways in which lesbian and gay sexual identities are actively discouraged by the larger society (Tozer & McClanahan, 1999)?

In the past, lesbian and gay people reported significant distress over the level of bias they experienced from practitioners (Rudolph, 1992). Simply being aware of heterosexist biases is not sufficient. Working through these attitudes with an affirmative peer or supervisor, combined with a strong commitment to see all clients as worthy people, will reduce the likelihood of projecting negative attitudes toward lesbians and gay people (House & Holloway, 1992).

The pervasiveness of heterosexism results in a socially devalued status for lesbian and gay people, and it affects their relationships with family members, partners, friends, and coworkers. Heterosexism informs every aspect of their lives (Garnets, Hancock, Cochran, Goodchilds, & Peplau, 1991). Practitioners must be able to recognize the impact that their sexual orientation has on the entirety of lesbian and gay clients' lives. Not the least of the challenges for them is the development of a healthy self-esteem in an environment full of hostility, stigma, and violence.

The practitioner should also have the skills to confront client misinformation and the ways in which the clients' cultures are oppressive and ensure that the practice environment does not support such biases. Clients should receive validation, achieve enhanced self-understanding, and discover a variety of resolutions. Clients can also be informed of research about what can be changed in attitudes, identity, and life choices and what cannot—for example, one's basic sexual orientation (Beckstead & Morrow, 2004; L. M. Diamond, 2003; Shidlo & Schroeder, 2002).

Most important are the ethical aspects of working with clients in conflict between their religion and their sexual identity. Of primary concern is respecting the values and life experience of the clients and upholding their right to self-determination. Clients must be encouraged to make decisions for themselves. Regardless of his or her personal values, the practitioner should not judge clients' experiences of religion or sexuality. When a client is experiencing distress about pressure from family or religious institutions, a practitioner must not demean the client's history as something to overcome. Conservative religious beliefs should not be marginalized (Haldeman, 2002, 2004). The practitioner should not attempt to talk clients into valuing or devaluing their religion or sexual attractions. Clients have to make their own valuations. Practitioners can help clients to understand the effects of their social environment on them. But it is not their task to provide advice or direction but to help clients to explore the many challenging questions associated with identity conflicts and to suggest alternative courses of action for consideration (Haldeman, 2004).

Work has to be done with the whole of a client's complex situation. A practitioner can help a client to explore and eventually live more comfortably within a sexual identity that is consistent with his or her personal values and beliefs (Throckmorton & Yarhouse, 2006). The practitioner should make clear that it is the client's right to choose among options.

Practitioners must also keep in mind that the ramifications of clients' decisions can be considerable. If one's lesbian or gay identity is expressed to members of a conservative religion, the potential losses of family and religious community are not easily replaced. And the loss of a religious institution can mean loss of meaning and comfort. Similarly one faces difficult challenges if one chooses religious expression instead of same-sex expression (Haldeman, 2004).

As clients gain new perspectives and more accurate information, they can make informed decisions (Haldeman, 2004; Lasser & Gottlieb, 2004). A practitioner and client may agree that, at the outset, it is unnecessary to decide what the final outcome will be and they only need to agree on the process by which the client will make his or her decisions about sexual identity (Beckstead & Israel, 2007).

When lesbian and gay people decide that their religious and family affiliations are more important than their sexual orientation, they will not come out as lesbian or gay. They think they would lose everything important to them. They want to stay with their community of faith and may want to become celibate. They may request enrollment in an ex-gay ministry, but as stated in chapter 5, this is not an ethical treatment, and although a practitioner cannot prevent a client from seeking it, it is not ethical to recommend it.

Many clients who seek help to resolve conflicts between their sexual and religious identities have already lost friends or family members. Many have been told they would be condemned for eternity unless they changed their sexual orientation. It is important that the practitioner acknowledge these losses and threats. A practitioner can assist a client to develop knowledge about more lesbian- and gay-affirmative forms of religious practice and spirituality. Finding faith-based alternatives can be empowering (D. R. Morrow & Tyson, 2006).

Practitioners should usually avoid disputing religious beliefs and values (W. B. Johnson, 2004). In unusual cases in which practitioners believe they should dispute religious beliefs, they can follow guidelines for raising considerations that "create dissonance between discordant beliefs" (W. B. Johnson, 2004, p. 261; see also W. B. Johnson, 2001). This may involve logical, empirical, and functional disputations. (These are discussed in more detail in chapter 7.)

Some of the most challenging situations for practitioners involve conservative parents who reject their child's lesbian or gay identity. In these cases, it is important to remember that parents are critical stakeholders in their children's lives. Their support is essential especially to an adolescent. The practitioner's focus on the ways in which the parents' religion promotes love and acceptance of their adolescent can be a better way for communication and problem solving than an approach that underscores their religion's behavioral proscriptions. The practitioner may, however, bring to the foreground existing religious beliefs that may have receded to the background. This can happen during parents' initial emotional reactions to learning that their adolescent has experienced same-sex attraction or has identified as lesbian or gay. A concern can arise if family members bring up passages from the Bible or other sacred texts that support the teaching that same-sex behavior is immoral. It is useful to try to understand the conflict from each family member's perspective, to point out possible tensions among beliefs or values, to explore a variety of approaches to the topic, and to offer to navigate both the religious and sexual identity concerns (Yarhouse & Tan, 2004).

Contacting local lesbian and gay organizations to learn more about local resources is necessary. Many larger cities have lesbian and gay hotlines or newspapers that provide information about religious and spiritual organizations that welcome lesbian and gay people. They may also identify clergy who are affirming of lesbian and gay people and open to discussing religion and spirituality and conflicts with sexual identity. *Stranger at the Gate* (White, 1994) is a book that addresses lesbian and gay spiritual experiences. These resources can be shared with clients and their families.

Four general stages are recommended for the practitioner and client to go through for those in conflict with their sexual and religious identities: assessment, identification of goals, interventions, and resolution. Assessment and goal identification are discussed in this chapter and interventions and resolution in the next two chapters. Chapter 7 focuses on clients experiencing intense or moderate conflict between their sexual and religious identities, and chapter 8 on those who are comfortable with their sexual identity. While going through these stages, practitioners should leave assumptions behind in an effort to be open to understanding a client's experience (Shapiro, 1996).

Assessment

The client's motivation for seeking sexual identity therapy should be assessed early in the first meeting. Some clients may be internally motivated because of their judgments about their same-sexual identity or behavior. Others may be externally motivated, for example by receiving an ultimatum from their parents or heterosexual partner. Often clients will mention conflict between religious beliefs and their sexual orientation. The question to ask is: What is it about your same-sex attraction that brings you in to see a practitioner? (T. R. Johnson, 1995; Koenig, 1993).

Assessment lays the groundwork for eventual goal development and for deciding how open the client is to a lesbian or gay identity. The client's psychosocial history is carefully reviewed for meanings associated with religious and sexual expression. In order to understand a client's religious and sexual conflicts, the practitioner can explore answers to these questions: How do you define religion and spirituality? What role does religion and spirituality play in your life? What are your attitudes toward deity and religious community? What are your religious leaders' views and the doctrines of your church on sexuality, gender roles, and same-sex relations? What do you believe is your deity's judgment of same-sex attractions and of you? What does your religious affiliation mean to you? This information helps the practitioner understand what it means for the client to live by the normative teachings of his or her religion, to have same-sex attractions, and to act or not act on these attractions (Buchanan, Dzelme, Harris, & Hecker, 2001; Yarhouse & Burkett, 2002).

Additional questions include the following: Are you strongly attached to family and church? Are you attached to your community of faith through tradition, fear, a combination, or some other reason (Haldeman, 2004)? Would you risk losing these connections if you disclosed your sexual identity? If so, what would replace them? If you chose to not disclose, would you have anonymous sexual encounters? How would you manage your guilt over this (Beckstead & Israel, 2007)? It is also useful to know what steps the client has already taken to deal with the conflict (see chapters 4 and 5).

Several questionnaires are available for assessing participation in religious activities and level of commitment to religious beliefs. The Religious Commitment Inventory-10 (Worthington et al., 2003) and the Santa Clara Strength of Religious Faith Questionnaire (Plante & Boccaccini, 1997) both have some degree of validation. One can also create a semistructured interview so that the client can elaborate on responses (E. Garcia, 2007).

More information about religious identity and conflict with one's sexual identity can be attained through other additional questions that follow. Questions with scales have different ranges of numbers or phrases to respond to. In addition, those who have affirmed a sexual identity of lesbian or gay or have not can have conflicts with their religion. So all of the questions are relevant to assessment for both groups of clients. Practitioners can order the questions differently than done here. Some questions are asked again in a different way to allow the client to rethink them and perhaps answer differently.

Religious affiliation: What is your religious affiliation? Christian? Catholic? Jewish? Buddhist? Hindu? other (Yarhouse & Tan, 2004)?

Religious conversion: How did your conversion experience come about? Who was the most influential person(s) in your conversion experience? Did it change your life? How did it affect you emotionally? How has it affected your relationships? How did it affect your understanding of your religious and sexual identities (E. Garcia, 2007)?

Religious practices: What religious activities do you participate in? How often do you participate? How important is this participation to you? How does it make you feel (E. Garcia, 2007)?

Religious beliefs: What do your religious beliefs say about who you are? Do you struggle with your religious beliefs? In what ways do your beliefs influence your actions? Do they help you cope with stress? What do they tell you about your sexuality? How does your religious identity interact with your sexual identity? Have you experienced conflicts between these two identities (E. Garcia, 2007)? How religious are you on a scale from 1 (not religious) to 10 (very religious)? On the same scale, how spiritual are you (Yarhouse & Tan, 2004)?

Relationship with God: Do you feel you are close to God? How close? When do you feel closest? Most distant? What makes it difficult to feel close to God? What would you have to do to be fully accepted by God (E. Garcia, 2007)?

Influence of religion: How much does religion influence your life? Rate it on a scale from 1 (not at all) to 5 (totally) (Yarhouse & Tan, 2004).

Parents' influence: What influence does your mother have on your relationship to God? How about your father (E. Garcia, 2007)?

Sexual history: When was the first time you had sex? What was it like? How old were you? Who was your partner? How did you feel about it? What does it mean to you now (E. Garcia, 2007)?

Sexuality: How do you feel about your sexuality (E. Garcia, 2007)? Have you ever tried to resist your same-sex attractions (Yarhouse & Tan, 2004)? How important is sexuality in defining who you are? What would you like your sexuality to involve? Is there anything you would like to change about your sexuality (E. Garcia, 2007)? Are you erotically attracted to men, women, or both? Rate your experiences of sex with men or women on a scale from 1 (highly appealing) to 4 (not at all appealing) (Savin-Williams, 2009). How did your religious or spiritual views help you deal with identifying as lesbian or gay? How did they hinder this?

Sexual fantasies: What people are in your sexual fantasies? What is their gender? How do you feel about this? What emotions do you have (E. Garcia, 2007)?

Sexual desires: What are your sexual desires? How often do you think of these desires? What would have to happen to make them come about (E. Garcia, 2007)?

Current sexual behavior: What current sexual behaviors do you engage in? Who else is involved (E. Garcia, 2007)?

General view of sex: What general views do you have about sex and sexuality (Beckstead & Israel, 2007)?

Dating history: When did you have your first boyfriend or girlfriend? What was this experience like (E. Garcia, 2007)?

Emotions about same-sex relationships: What emotions, needs, difficulties, and joys have you experienced in past and present same-sex relationships (Beckstead & Israel, 2007)?

First kiss: What feelings did you have after your first kiss? What was your partner like? How did you feel physically? Emotionally?

Current relationship: How would you describe your current relationship? Do you feel close to your partner? What is your sexual relationship with your partner like (E. Garcia, 2007)?

Dreams for future relationships: What do you want in your future relationships? What will influence your engaging or not engaging in same-sex behavior in the future (Buchanan et al., 2001; Yarhouse & Burkett, 2002)?

Feelings about sexual orientation: What feelings have you had about your awareness of your changed sexual orientation? Have you felt confused, scared, angry, sad, happy, or other feelings (Yarhouse & Tan, 2004)?

Happy people and integrated people: Do you know any lesbian or gay people who are happy, or who have integrated their sexual and religious identities or resolved conflicts between the two (Beckstead & Israel, 2007)?

Chances for happiness: Do you think you will be happy if you identify as a lesbian or gay person? Which fits better for you—being lesbian or gay or being heterosexual (Tozer & McClanahan, 1999)? How happy are you—very, somewhat, or not so happy (Yarhouse & Tan, 2004)?

Imagining daily life: Can you imagine what your daily life would be like if you lived with a same-sex partner (Tozer & McClanahan, 1999)?

If married: What were your reasons for marrying? Do you feel commitment to your partner? What has intimacy been like with your partner (Beckstead & Israel, 2007)?

Accepting lesbian or gay identity: What feelings did you have when you accepted your lesbian or gay identity—relief, joy, peace, fear, or other feelings (Yarhouse & Tan, 2004)?

Sexual identity assessment: Do you think of yourself as heterosexual, bisexual, lesbian, gay, or something else (Savin-Williams, 2009)? Are you comfortable with your gender? Your sexual identity? If not comfortable, how do you feel about your sexual identity? Can you alleviate the feeling if it is negative? How likely is it that you will overcome the negative feeling? How often do you think about this conflict? What are your thoughts about the conflict? Have you shared this struggle with anyone? What was their response? Was it helpful? What do you want to happen (E. Garcia, 2007)? Rate the following on a 0 to 10 scale: your level of same-sex attractions, your level of distress as a result of your same-sex attractions, your level of distress when managing your religious beliefs and same-sex attractions (E. Garcia, 2007).

Masculinity/femininity: How masculine do you feel? How feminine? How strongly do your identify with men? With women? (E. Garcia, 2007)?

Religious trauma: How have you been affected by religious doctrine that is critical of the way you live or feel? What specific experiences have you had? Has this influenced your self-esteem or contributed to guilt, shame, or internalized heterosexism? Low self-esteem and internalized heterosexism are considered risk factors for depression, suicidal feelings, and substance abuse—have you experienced any of these (D. R. Morrow & Tyson, 2006)?

Losses: What losses have you experienced because of your same-sex attractions? How have they affected you (D. R. Morrow, 2003; D. R. Morrow & Tyson, 2006)?

Coping mechanisms: What is your main way of coping with distress? With feelings (Lazarus & Folkman, 1984)? What coping methods did you use when the situation could not be changed through behavior? What did you feel? Did you try to solve problems in your situation? (Lazarus, 1991)? Are you usually able to find solutions for problems (E. Garcia, 2007)?

Religious coping: What is your main religious coping mechanism? Is it positive? Do you think of religion in terms of spiritual support (God will take care of you), collaboration (you and God are united in getting through the conflict, you get support from your congregation), or benevolent religious reframing such as belief in God's divine will? Has religion been harmful for you? Do you feel discontent with your congregation or with God? Do you see your situation as God's punishment (E. Garcia, 2007)?

Morals: How has religion affected your morals (for example, perceptions of what is good and what is bad)? How much do you rely on authorities for answers and how to run your life (Beckstead & Israel, 2007)?

Ex-gay ministry groups: Have you worked with or met people from ex-gay ministry groups? If so, what kind of experience did you have?

Openness to lesbian or gay identity: How open do you feel, if at all, to considering a lesbian or gay identity for yourself? Would you consider exploring the lesbian and gay community? Have you read books about being lesbian or gay, been in support groups, or attended a reconciling church where lesbian and gay people are welcome (Beckstead & Israel, 2007)?

Other identities: How connected are you to lesbian and gay culture? What other social resources are available to you (Beckstead & Israel, 2007)? Do you have struggles in terms of race, ethnicity, culture, national origin, social class, or individual differences in gender, age, and ability status? Do any of these characteristics impact your sexual identity or restrict the your viewpoint and choices?

The lesbian and gay community: What concerns do you have about being or not being validated within the lesbian and gay community (Bing, 2004)?

Rejection and acceptance: Who in your surroundings would reject you, and who would accept you, as lesbian or gay (Tozer & McClanahan, 1999)?

Family: Are you and your family able to openly discuss issues related to culture and sexuality and to support an identity that defies or contradicts traditional cultural standards?

Choices: Do you feel you have to choose between your religion and culture and the lesbian and gay community (Folayan, 1992; Glock, 1992; McCarn & Fassinger, 1996)?

The trauma of religious oppression on the psychological health and well-being of lesbian and gay people can cause mood and personality disorders (Shafranske, 1996). A practitioner may want to assess how clients have coped with their attractions, conflicts, differentness, and painful emotions. Mood and personality disorders may have developed as a result of inadequate external support and internal resources. Some behaviors are maladaptive, such as denial, passivity, substance abuse, suicide attempts, disconnection from emotions, and avoidance or hatred of lesbian and gay people. Others are adaptive, such as attaining self-worth and identity from sources other than heterosexist communities (Beckstead & Morrow, 2004).

Practitioners may need to help clients distinguish between problems arising from dealing with same-sex attractions and behavior (for example, sexual compulsiveness, objectification of others, lack of assertiveness, and intimacy problems) and those experienced regardless of sexual orientation (Beckstead & Israel, 2007). Psychological issues can contribute to conflicts about sexual orientation. For example, a client with obsessive-compulsive disorder may ruminate on fears of being lesbian or gay that have no relation to same-sex attractions (Beckstead & Israel, 2007).

As suggested above and in chapter 2, the struggle between sexuality and religion can have mental health consequences. Attempts at reconciling these identities are associated with depression, guilt, shame, suicidal ideation, and difficulty accepting one's sexual identity (Schuck & Liddle, 2001). The most severe consequence is suicide. In a tragedy reported in the national news media, Stuart Matis and Clay Whitmer committed suicide after trying to reconcile being both gay and Mormon (Miller, 2000).

Other Assessment Activities

McGrady and McDonnell (2006) suggested using an exercise called the Circle of Self to assess clients' relationships with others. Clients are given a drawing of a large circle that represents the self and asked to note in the circle factors that influence how they see themselves, how they interact with others, and what contributes to their worldview. Factors could include age, education, ethnicity, family, gender, race, religion, spirituality, sexual orientation, socioeconomic status, and whatever else the clients consider relevant. Different colors and shapes can be used. When this task is finished, clients can be asked to describe the circle with reference to sexual orientation and religion and spirituality. Questions can be asked such as: How did you decide which factors to include in the circle? What is the significance of the colors and shapes you used? Why did you place certain factors in relation to each other? What factors were not included? Why?

McGrady and McDonnell (2006) also developed a writing activity to be done at home and brought to the next session with the practitioner. Clients are asked to reflect on influential factors in their lives and write about them so as to attain clarity about their impact. Also to be included are times when they heard messages about sexual orientation from the church or church members. When they bring their writing to another session, the practitioner can ask them about their reactions to the assignment: What were your emotional reactions? What effect has religion or spirituality had on you as a lesbian or gay person? What influence has religion or spirituality had on your life, past and present? What traditions, practices, or beliefs do you want to keep? Have you discovered any form of spirituality apart from the church and organized religion? Who are you as a spiritual or religious person? Has this influenced how you see yourself as a lesbian or gay person? What do you see as your next steps?

Goal Identification

Following assessment, the client and practitioner together identify goals and interventions. Practitioners have to be prepared for clients to want to be in charge of their lives and where they are going. Lesbian and gay people frequently experience taking charge of their lives. Because they often feel different from other family members, they may separate early from the family. If they acknowledge their sexual orientation, this may lead to rejection by their families. They have learned, therefore, to trust their own experiences rather than the dictates of their family (Barzan, 1995; D'Augelli, 1992).

Clients may choose various paths such as investigating a lesbian or gay identity, returning to their original community of faith, or other options. Whatever a client's goals are, the practitioner should provide support. Practitioners should show neither skepticism nor enthusiasm and neither agree with nor discourage decisions the client makes (Haldeman, 2004).

Another goal may be to overcome myths and stereotypes. Practitioners can challenge myths and stereotypes by providing accurate information. They can provide affirming literature and facilitate involvement with lesbian and gay community groups. It may be particularly helpful for a client to meet others with similar values, interests, and cultural backgrounds. Haldeman (2004) pointed out, however, that a practitioner may need to help a client understand how self-loathing can be projected onto the lesbian and gay community. One can recognize how negativity toward this community may be a reflection of internalized heterosexism. Haldeman suggested discussing any fears a client may have of exposure or other consequences that might result from exploring lesbian and gay venues. Such a discussion can help the client dispel inaccurate perceptions of being lesbian or gay, become less anxious about self-disclosure, find helpful resources, feel more normal, resolve feelings of being alone, and find a place to belong and fit in (Beckstead & Israel, 2007). The community can also help the practitioner to get to know lesbian and gay people and the diversity within the community (Matthews, 2007).

Although some clients may come to see a same-sex relationship as essential and fulfilling, others clients may not. A client who is primarily attracted to the same sex with little or no heterosexual attraction may still want to live as a heterosexual. But, seeking to create a significant heterosexual attraction may prove futile and disappointing. Nevertheless, the client may decide to adopt a heterosexual or bisexual identity and enter into or remain in a heterosexual relationship. This could happen with a person of the opposite sex who does not emphasize the sexual components of the relationship but focuses on emotional intimacy and is comfortable with a partner who is same-sex attracted. A client who pursues this route will need to take into account the short- and long-term consequences of self-disclosing to those he or she dates or wants to marry. Practitioners can help clients in this situation achieve integrity with themselves and others when deciding on the best relationship outcome for themselves with current or potential partners (Beckstead & Israel, 2007).

The most important task for practitioners may be to facilitate positive self-identifications. This includes reframing issues in a more positive light. Highlighting inherent human worth emphasizes the value of each person regardless of sexual identity (Gage Davidson, 2000; Pachankis & Goldfried, 2004). Everyone is accepted and affirmed (Struzzo, 1989). According to Beckstead and Morrow (2004), those who stopped trying to reject their attractions and reframed them in a positive light found the most peace in their lives, regardless of behavioral or identity outcome. Acceptance and affirmation seem to give people permission to be who they are and not hate or fear their sexual feelings. It also helps them to evaluate any negative messages they internalized about same-sex attractions, eliminate negative views of these attractions, and hear alternate perspectives about such attractions. There are a variety of ways to view an attraction—as a sin, burden, emotional need, normal feeling, impulse, test, joy, or gift, and as unimportant or essential. A client can decide which framework best fits with his or her values and developing perspectives.

Finally, practitioners can help lesbian and gay clients find safe places to explore spirituality and religion. They can help clients distinguish between non-affirming faiths and faith practices and principles that support lesbian and gay people (Horne & Noffsinger-Frazier, 2003). Practitioners can also challenge the myth of incompatibility between religious and sexual identities by providing information on affirming faith groups (Heerman, Wiggins, & Rutter, 2007).

Informed Consent

Clients often enter work with a practitioner confused about the course of action they wish to pursue. Some clients may be leaning toward a certain course, while others may have clearly determined the direction they would like to pursue. Developing out of a consumer model of service delivery and valuing of client autonomy and self-determination, informed consent has emerged as a critical part of establishing treatment goals (Corey, Corey, & Callanan, 1998). What is most important in this process is to help each client make a truly informed decision about the kinds of goals they have for treatment and how those goals match the services that are available (Throckmorton & Yarhouse, 2006).

Summary

Practitioners who intend to work with lesbian and gay people in conflict with their religion should first assess themselves for heterosexist biases, acquire accurate knowledge about the lesbian and gay community, and develop the skills to work with people experiencing religious conflict. The choice of direction is up to the client. But whatever decisions a client makes will have significant ramifications for his or her life, especially in terms of losses. Practitioners also have to understand heterosexism, how it can be internalized, and how it impacts the lives of lesbian and gay people.

The first steps in working with a client on these issues are assessment and goal identification. Many questions and exercises can be used during these steps. Informed consent can be useful because it contains the goals clients have for treatment and how they match the services available.

Seven

Clients with Little or No Openness to a Lesbian or Gay Identity

*T*his chapter addresses two kinds of religious lesbian and gay clients: those who, although they have same-sex attractions, are not open to a lesbian or gay identity or integration of this identity with their religion, and those who are somewhat open to a lesbian or gay identity.

Acceptance of being lesbian or gay is not for everyone with same-sex attractions. Lesbian and gay people with strong religious beliefs cannot always reconcile them with their lesbian or gay identity. For some, familial rejection and religious condemnation are too powerful to overcome. Deeply held religious beliefs can be a more important part of the self than sexual identity. Many people's religious beliefs and experiences add solidity, structure, and comfort to their lives. A religious community can serve as a surrogate family (Haldeman, 2001). When religion and sexuality are in conflict, the potential losses are a tremendous obstacle to giving up religion (Schuck & Liddle, 2001). Abandoning religion would cause grief and would mean leaving traditions that have been part of the family for generations (Ritter & O'Neil, 1995). For some people, religion is too central to their identity. Adopting a lesbian or gay identity would go against their moral convictions and cause too big a shift in their core identity and sense of purpose. They may also believe it would cause damnation in the afterlife. Faced with the costs mentioned, it can seem easier to give up same-sex desires. Some such clients may have even read self-help books on being lesbian or gay or attended a gay-positive church, but none of this felt right to them, so they went back to their conservative church (Haldeman, 2004).

Some people who have same-sex attractions experience excruciating conflict that most likely cannot be resolved through the development of a lesbian or gay identity (Haldeman, 2002). To reject and give up what is an integral part of themselves may be damaging (Wagner, Serafini, Rabkin, Remien, & Williams, 1994). They suffer harm when they feel compelled to sever religious attachments because of their sexual orientation (Thumma, 1991). Most lesbian and gay people studied by Schuck & Liddle (2001) said it was difficult to accept a lesbian or gay identity. The mean difficulty rating for all respondents was 4.0 on a scale of 1 to 7, 4.4 for those experiencing religious conflict, and 3.3 for those without religious conflict.

These clients may describe their concern as "I think I'm gay, but I really don't want to be. Can you help?" Some lesbian and gay people have struggled with same-sex attractions during much of their lives but never outwardly identified as lesbian or gay. The practitioner must respect their right to self-determination in terms of their values and desires (Beckstead & Israel, 2007).

The conflict these clients experience often results in cognitive distress (Rodriguez & Ouellette, 2000), which can be overwhelming (Barret & Barzan, 1996; Ritter & O'Neill, 1995). As discussed earlier, the majority of conservative faiths place lesbian and gay people in a bind: they must live in denial of their sexuality in order to accept their religion or suffer with the message that they are sinners.

Lesbian and gay people in this situation believe their sexual attractions are a burden to be overcome. They may be depressed and despondent. Practitioners can use a variety of interventions to help them reach clarity about what kind of life they want (Haldeman, 2004).

The same interventions also will help those who are undecided about whether they want to adopt a lesbian and gay identity but are partially open to that option. When practitioners help clients to identify, sort out, examine, and prioritize the multiple dimensions of their lives, they may become clearer about who they are and what they want (and do not want). The rest of this chapter discusses interventions that may assist these clients to determine more clearly what their goals are (Beckstead & Israel, 2007). Practitioners can select from these interventions what might best fit with their clients.

The interventions are extensive in order to help clients fully explore their situation and make the best decisions for themselves. Together, clients and practitioners review the interventions and the clients agree to them before they begin.

Even when clients are not open to a lesbian or gay identity, certain steps seem to help them accept themselves and consolidate a positive identity. A practitioner can help correct the harmful effects of antigay socialization on their self-concepts (Haldeman, 1996, 2002). Techniques from diverse theoretical orientations (see Fassinger, 2000) may be used to help clients identify, evaluate, and replace internalized negative beliefs with feelings of worth, acceptance, self-understanding, and belonging (Bing, 2004; Tozer & McClanahan, 1999).

In general, the practitioner's task is to provide a safe environment in which the client is free to explore the many challenging questions associated with identity conflicts. The practitioner is also responsible for providing accurate information and suggesting alternative courses of action. Difficult challenges face a person who chooses religious expression instead of same-sex attraction. The repression of same-sex feelings and the attempt to live in a heterosexual or celibate manner can exact a great psychic toll. The practitioner faces unique challenges with clients in this situation. Many therapists may have difficulty talking about any course of action that subverts one part of identity for another. Some believe that it is easier to find a new religious affiliation than to change or repress one's sexual orientation, so they attempt to overtly or subtly guide the client in this direction. But this may be an inappropriate choice for some clients. Similarly, some religious counselors may be at risk of ignoring their client's realities because of a scripturally induced rigidity about the way in which clients should live their lives. Again, clients have the right to live lives that are consonant with their personal values, not someone else's values (Haldeman, 2004).

Interventions

The following interventions have the purpose of helping clients in conflict to think through their dilemma carefully. Hopefully they will feel better about themselves and reach full clarity about what they want to do about their sexual identity.

Group Therapy

Practitioners may want to develop a therapy group for clients in conflict. Clients may feel safer in a group for people who are exploring their ambivalence and conflicts about sexual identity than in a group that is identified as being for lesbian or gay people. Recruiting members for such a group may be difficult, because clients may not want to admit to having attractions to others of the same sex. But for some such clients, a group could be a place where they could be known and feel accepted (Beckstead & Israel, 2007).

Group therapy can help in developing self-acceptance and a positive self-identity. A heterogeneous group with female and male members from diverse cultural backgrounds can be helpful. This kind of group has differing perspectives and goals. It can increase exploration of a variety of solutions, provide feedback about misinformation, and enhance respect for diversity. Members are interested in questioning, dialoguing with, and relating to each other. They may learn to validate their own choices, values, and relationships. Above all, a group setting can desensitize anxiety and provide opportunities to develop authentic relationships and emotional closeness (Beckstead & Israel, 2007).

Support Networks

Lesbian and gay clients can also benefit from support networks, that have been developing since the 1970s. Virtual networks also exist on the Internet. The immediacy of the Internet provides unmediated communication among people all over the world (Henrickson, 2009). These networks are particularly important for those with little access to other support networks because of their geographical location or fear of disclosure.

The Gay Christian Movement began in 1976. It was renamed in 1987 to the Lesbian and Gay Christian Movement. It has contributed to the confidence and social visibility of its members. This organization has two basic functions. One is to provide a safe platform for identity reinforcement and community building. If desired, participants can explore integration of their sexuality and religious faith. The second function is to mobilize members for social action to challenge discrimination. This is a strategy to challenge religious orthodoxy and heterosexism within religious communities. Participating in this kind of action may not be the right or comfortable choice for everyone in these networks (Yip, 2007).

Affirming Theological Literature

Another form of help is lesbian- and gay-affirming theological literature. This literature focuses on undermining traditional Christian views on sexuality. It also undermines the moral authority of religious authority structures and conservative Christians who subscribe to it. Authority structures and believers are locked into traditions that uphold moral absolutism. Believers rationalize this as preserving a moral order sanctioned by religious tradition and divine authority. This literature argues that these interpretations are socioculturally inaccurate. They do not take into account today's reality and current understanding of human sexuality (Yip, 2007).

Socratic Questioning

In order to help clients think through their situation in more depth, Socratic questioning can help. For example, what about the person would result in rejection by church members or family? What assumptions does a person have about coming out or making disclosures? Such questions can begin an internal dialogue and bring to the surface cognitive distortions (Heerman et al., 2007).

Addressing Cognitive Distortions

Cognitive distortions need to be addressed, such as the fortune-teller error (predicting that things will turn out badly for oneself), all-or-nothing thinking (one failure leads to the perception of one's whole self as a failure), and catastrophizing (exaggerating the importance of setbacks) (Beck & Alford, 2008).

The triple column exercise helps to overcome cognitive distortions. Clients can be encouraged to list their thoughts in three columns: automatic thoughts, irrational thoughts or cognitive distortions, and rational responses (Heermann et al., 2007). An example: automatic thought (no one will like me if I am gay); irrational thought (some might not like you, but not all people in your life will feel this way); rational response (a few people might not like me if I am gay, but I have good friends who are not likely to change their opinion of me).

Rational–Emotive Behavioral Therapy

For clients who think that they are morally bad, unworthy, or sinful because of their religion, rational–emotive behavioral therapy can be useful. The practitioner works to help clients identify irrational beliefs underlying their emotional distress, clarify the link between irrational beliefs and their current distress, and move from irrational, absolute, evaluative beliefs toward rational thinking. Beliefs are irrational when they are logically inconsistent, do not fit with empirical reality, are absolute and dogmatic, cause emotional upset, or obstruct clients' progress toward their goals. The primary intervention is disputation or challenging the irrational beliefs. At the same time, the practitioner suggests rational alternatives that are likely to lead to less disturbed emotional and behavioral outcomes (W. B. Johnson, 2004).

Clients with conflicts between their religious and sexual identities often experience clinical depression. This results from accepting religious doctrines even if they cause destructive outcomes for oneself (W. B. Johnson, 2004).

As emphasized before, it is important to remain neutral while clients decide whether to accept or reject a lesbian or gay identity. But practitioners can help change thoughts related to depression. If a client's depression is driven by strong demanding and judgmental beliefs about same-sex attraction, it is important to help change these thoughts. This involves a profound philosophical change or attitudinal shift in how clients think about a problem. If clients are thinking the worst, such as "if I am gay that would be awful, even catastrophic, or prove that I am worthless and evil," they need a fundamental shift in their attitudes and thinking (W. B. Johnson, 2004). This kind of shift results from disputes.

Logical disputations can help clients recognize unreasonable and arbitrary irrational beliefs. Questions can be asked such as: How is being gay a catastrophe? To not disappoint your parents, do you think that you absolutely must not do certain things? Where is it written that feeling attracted to someone of the same sex is one of life's greatest calamities?

Functional disputations can help clients determine how their irrational beliefs create and sustain self-defeating emotions and behaviors and how they will suffer less if they adopt more rational beliefs. Harsh judgmental thoughts bring about depression. Questions can be asked such as: Do you feel less depressed if you say to yourself that your sexuality is awful or you think you are worthless?

More specialized disputations are needed when clients persist in seeing themselves as damned and worthless. This might include encouraging them to challenge judgmental religious doctrines. Generally, religious beliefs should not be disputed unless they cause pain and emotional and behavioral dysfunction. Strong dogmatic beliefs that cause depression have to be addressed. Jesus said nothing about being non-heterosexual. Instead he emphasized kindness, mercy, and love. You say God created you. Was God wrong in the way you were created (W. B. Johnson, 2004)?

Narrative Perspective

The narrative perspective focuses on stories that clients bring to practitioners. It offers an approach for helping clients to understand problems and their impact on them. Drawing from Foucault's (1965, 1980) idea that constructed ideas shape people's lives, White and Epston (1990) focused on the effects of "dominant stories." They explained that at times, a person's story is problem-saturated and can negatively impact his or her happiness. The narrative approach aims to release clients from problem-saturated stories by helping them to understand, deconstruct, and rebuild or re-story them (Winslade & Monk, 1999), demonstrating that hope and change for the better are possible (McLean & Marini, 2008).

Lesbian and gay clients often come with a dominant story of internalized social, political, cultural, and religious oppression. Foucault (1980) called these stories "restraining narratives." Clients can be helped to understand how some problems causing distress come from expectations imposed on them by the dominant culture. This culture prescribes that the preferred sexual orientation is heterosexual and all other forms of sexuality are deviant (McLean & Marini, 2008). Clients are encouraged to break away from these stories and consider alternatives offering greater promise (Goldenberg & Goldenberg, 2004).

Deconstruction helps clients examine falsehoods in the majority group's dominant narratives. Clients are asked not to blindly accept or internalize these dominant narratives (Andrutsopoulou, 2001a, 2001b). Deconstruction also opens up space to explore preferred ways of being and helps clients to resist the influence of the problem (White, 1995), reclaim power, and have more say in who they are and how they want to be (Buchanan et al., 2001).

Separating one's identity from the problem is called *externalizing* the problem. This begins the process of developing alternative stories (Goldenberg & Goldenberg, 2004). Clients start thinking about what their story could be. Externalizing conversations are a way to help clients objectify their problems and separate them from themselves. This is accomplished with the idea that the problem is a thing outside of themselves but has an influence on them. This releases the problem as internal or inside oneself (Roth & Epston, 1996). Once the problem is seen as external or outside the self, clients can act in relation to it (White, 1993).

For clients with conflict between their religious and sexual identities, the problem-saturated story would be one of conflict between their religion and sexual orientation. Often they have never questioned their religious identities. In this approach, their beliefs are explored so as to understand underlying influences and effects. This allows them to become separated from the story that is predominantly influencing them and "re-story" it in a way that fits better with their preferred way of being (White, 1993).

Another narrative strategy is the use of questions. Questions are a means of deconstructing religious identities and exploring preferred ways of being. Questions could include the following (adapted from Freedman & Combs, 1995, and White, 1995):

- In what ways do your religious beliefs and practices impact your sexual identity? In what ways do they guide your life?

- How does your family's religious background affect your sexual identity?

- How do your church and your religion affect your sexual identity?

- Are you aware of ways that religious beliefs or practices influence you?

- How do your religious practices facilitate your sexual identity?

- How do they diminish or limit your quality of life?
- Have you found support to help you live the new story and maintain the story?

Specific deconstruction questions include the following:

Externalizing the problem: What does your church (or synagogue, mosque, or other faith community) say to you? What do you think about your relationship with your church?

Challenges in lesbian and gay spirituality: What do you think about your relationship with God (or the supreme being, nature, Buddha, or other higher power)?

Opening space for alternatives questions: Has spirituality been a support to you? Are you able to consider different ideas?

Preference questions: Do you feel comfortable with your religious or spiritual beliefs? Do you want them to guide you? How do your religious or spiritual beliefs direct you to live? Would you consider changing your religious or spiritual beliefs?

Story development questions: Can you look at your sexual identity differently now than you did before?

Meaning questions: If you look at your sexual identity in a different way, what kind of person does this say you are?

Questions to extend the story into the future: How do you see your sexual identity and religion developing in the next year? What impact will your sexual identity have on your religion, and vice versa, during the next year?

These are a sample of the multitude of questions that may be asked of clients who are in conflict with their sexual and religious identities. They provide an opening to explore preferred ways of being within one's spiritual and religious beliefs. When deconstructing religious beliefs, the emphasis is on not being blind to the influences of the beliefs on one's life. Religious identity becomes a thing outside of the person that exerts an influence on the person. When the problem that was internal becomes external, this allows one to act in relation to the problem (White, 1995).

This is an abstract process but can help remove the power of the punitive elements of a religious identity, which have often remained unquestioned (Buchanan et al., 2001).

Independent Thinking

Encouraging clients to independently explore their own and alternative religious beliefs can also be helpful. Practitioners can help their clients to use their own experience as a primary point of reference, rather than that of outside authorities. This may assist in the resolution of internalized religious proscriptions regarding lesbian and gay behaviors. In order to do this, practitioners, including religious counselors, may want to present themselves as other than an authority, so that the client's independence or postconventional functioning (see chapter 4) can be used to search out new approaches to the conflict between their religious and sexual selves. This approach also shows respect for clients' ability to act as the ultimate authority on their religious experience. At the same time, it allows the practitioner to respect clients' experience of their feelings about same-sex attraction (Harris, 2001).

The goal of this type of intervention is to allow clients to move from knowing based on authority to knowing based on their own experience, intuition, and reasoning. For clients who have known only one source of religious authority, the first step in the process of developing a postconventional approach to religious reasoning is to foster an awareness that there is diversity among religious authorities. However, it may be most effective to ask the client to critically explore these alternatives and evaluate the utility of the beliefs expressed by multiple sources.

The idea of emphasizing the client's right to base judgments upon his or her individual experience may be particularly powerful on yet another level. For many lesbian and gay people, socialization has taught them to disregard their experience (Anderson, 1994; Brown, 1986). These interventions dignify the right of lesbian and gay clients to make judgments based on their experiences of religious involvement. This can be a powerful mode of combating the cultural invalidation of their experience (Harris, 2001).

Countering Misinformation

Clients' choices are often restricted because they believe erroneous heterosexist stereotypes about lesbian and gay people (Greene, 2003; Shidlo & Schroeder, 2002). Conservative religious people may adopt a variety of labels growing up. They may consider themselves different and unacceptable, lost and alone; perverts, sissies or tomboys, abominations, evil, damned, worthless, inferior, and not good enough. These self-concepts cause considerable distress and can motivate people to try to be heterosexual. They may see this as the only way to change negative self-identities (Beckstead & Morrow, 2004).

The practitioner can help clients to understand that their negative self-labels are a result of social influence, and provide insight about the emotional impact of being subjected to and believing these labels. Hopefully, most clients will decide to reject such labels and consider more affirming and accurate self-concepts. Some clients, however, will hold on to the labels (Beckstead & Israel, 2007). The social devaluation of lesbian and gay people can contaminate them to such a degree that they cannot shake loose from it (Greene, 2003; Malyon, 1982).

Clients who are conflicted may believe that being lesbian or gay means a life of promiscuity, disease, loneliness, and misery (Krajeski, Myers, Valgemae,

Pattison, & Mansell, 1981; Rosik, 2003). Practitioners can provide accurate information to counter these beliefs. They should acknowledge that lesbian and gay people face numerous challenges that may have an adverse effect on their emotional wellbeing, but should also make clear that gay and lesbian people can experience happiness, productivity, and family relationships. This enables clients to envision a fulfilling life as lesbian or gay people. Practitioners can also help clients to find affirming faiths and faith practices and principles that support lesbian and gay people (Horne & Noffsinger-Frazier, 2003).

Bibliotherapy

Fear, guilt, and shame can also be neutralized through readings that accurately depict the lives of lesbian and gay people. Schuck and Liddle (2001) asked participants in their study what book topics they wanted. Of more than 30 books they considered helpful, several dealt with religion and same-sex attraction. Books mentioned by more than one participant all dealt specifically with religion and spirituality. Many other books addressed same-sex orientation in general. Bibliotherapy can include books such as Helminiak's (1994) *What the Bible Really Says about "Homosexuality,"* McNaught's (1988) *On Being Gay,* and Boswell's (1980) *Christianity, Social Tolerance, and "Homosexuality."* These and other books can help clients see new positive images of spiritual leaders and life paths (Frame, 2003). Another helpful book is *The Feeling Good Handbook* (Burns, 1990), which challenges cognitive distortions and irrational thoughts. Clients who feel that they will never be able to form lasting commitments because of their belief that lesbian and gay relationships do not work can read Berzon's (1988) *Permanent Partners: Building Gay and Lesbian Relationships That Last.* Lesbian and gay people who are members of racial or ethnic minorities may especially benefit from reading Loiacano's (1989) "Gay Identity Issues Among Black Americans: Racism, Homophobia, and the Need for Validation" or Chan's (1989) "Issues of Identity Development Among Asian-American Lesbians and Gay Men."

Limits to Behavioral Science

Interventions such as those discussed here help some people feel better about themselves, but behavioral science cannot fully resolve religious issues. There is a need for other corrective experiences. This includes developing a network of support, including friends and a connection to the lesbian and gay community—for example, membership in a gay-affirmative group or community such as Evangelicals Concerned, which is dedicated to the reconciliation of same-sex orientation and conservative religious faith. There are also many reconciling congregations in the United States that have pastoral staff who are not affected by a negative view of same-sex attraction. They can help clients talk their conflicts through and refer them to other affirmative ministers and congregation members. If the client chooses even temporarily to investigate the lesbian and gay community or explore living as a lesbian or gay person, these community resources may serve as helpful aids (Haldeman, 2004). Practitioners cannot condemn a client's religion even if it tells its members that lesbian and gay people will burn in hell. But they can propose ways to explore alternative theological perspectives (Scasta, 1998).

Practitioners can encourage clients to seek out other lesbian and gay people who are integrating their spirituality in their daily lives. Living models are powerful inspirations to struggling people, especially those who may be isolated in rural areas with few opportunities for support. Practitioners can also develop a list of religious and spiritual resources to share with clients. This could include affirming local places of worship, religious and spiritual groups, and clergy as well as readings on affirming theology and spirituality (Haldeman, 2004).

Each person has to determine the course he or she will embrace. The choice may be to stay in or return to the original community of faith. Clients might make an informed choice to seek spiritual support for living as a celibate person or suppressing or managing their same-sex attractions. Others may choose a different religious community once their experience validates this choice. Others may start a coming-out process (Haldeman, 2004).

Some people will eventually find a home in a welcoming and affirming religious tradition. But, as noted before, not all religious lesbian and gay people are able to relinquish their conservative traditions. Some leave their churches while coming out but eventually return to them. Some manage to resolve conflicts without abandoning either religion or sexual orientation (Schuck & Liddle, 2001). Others maintain their religion either by reconciling their sexual identity with their religion or by concealing their sexuality (Barret & Barzan, 1996; Fellows, 1996). Some may attend religious services but never discuss their sexual identity.

Some people who resolve conflicts between sexual identity and religious beliefs may experience transformation. In his transformational learning theory, Mezirow (1997) indicated that the process of transformation is often precipitated by a disorienting dilemma. The conflict between religious and sexual identities is one such dilemma (Merriam, Caffarella, & Baumgartner, 2007; Taylor, 2000). Baumgartner (2001) explained that a disorienting dilemma may be a process or a series of experiences rather than a single, isolated event. Resolving the schism between religious beliefs and sexual identity can be mentally and emotionally difficult, and internalized heterosexism can be painful. This can last for years, or even for a lifetime (Yip, 1997a), until a transformation or a dramatic change in one's views and beliefs take place.

Clients who are not open to being lesbian or gay may come in and out of treatment until they reach a resolution. These are not short-term cases, and practitioners must be patient and respectful of their clients' decisions regarding religious issues (Meara, Schmidt, & Day, 1996).

Summary

Clients with a conflict between their religious and sexual identities may not be open at all to a lesbian or gay identity and may choose to give up their same-sex sexual attractions in order to stay in their community of faith. Other clients may be somewhat open to considering a lesbian or gay identity. The practitioner can provide interventions that allow both kinds of clients to make informed choices about their lives. Clients can accomplish this by participating in therapy groups, reading affirmative theological literature, overcoming cognitive distortions, creating and thinking about narratives, independent thinking, receiving accurate information about being lesbian or gay, using bibliotherapy, talking with others in the lesbian and gay community, and perhaps attending more welcoming churches or having conversations with affirmative ministers and congregations. Practitioners cannot influence clients' decisions or condemn their religious community or theology. Clients have the right to self-determination and to decide what is right for them.

Eight

Clients Who Are Open to a Lesbian or Gay Identity

Some lesbian and gay people who have accepted their sexual orientation have been affected to some degree by their conservative religion, but they are willing to question it. Others may never have encountered negative rhetoric against lesbian and gay people or never internalized it. In a study by Rodriguez and Ouellete (2000a), some participants did not seem to have encountered antigay religious rhetoric. Twelve out of 40 respondents, or 30 percent of the sample, reported never having experienced conflict between their sexual identity and their religious beliefs. Nine of the 12 reported having fully integrated these two identities.

Affirmative Practice

Traditional gay-affirmative practice can be used with such clients. According to W. B. Johnson (2004), an affirmative approach rests on several assumptions:

- Lesbian or gay sexual orientation is largely genetic and biological.

- It is enduring or lifelong.

- Attractions are basically unchangeable.

- Attempts to change or convert sexual orientation are ethically questionable and often harmful.

- Ethical and appropriate practice involves affirmation of lesbian and gay identities, reduction of internalized heterosexism, and eventual integration into a lesbian or gay life and community.

- Each person has unconditional value and worth regardless of sexual orientation.

S. L. Morrow and Beckstead (2004) added two other assumptions of affirmative practice: that lesbian and gay and heterosexual identities are equally valid, and that specific practitioner knowledge, awareness (particularly self-awareness), and skills are central to competent practice with same-sex-attracted people. Affirmative therapy challenges oppressive stereotypes and systems of thought, including religious thought. It celebrates and advocates the validity of lesbian and gay people and their relationships (Tozer & McClanahan, 1999). It also attempts to challenge negative messages that most clients have received all of their lives about same-sex attractions. Practitioners can assist the client in coming out, identity development, and addressing other issues, such as relationships with partners and parents and work and career choices.

A major part of affirmative therapy is to focus on the effects of heterosexism in clients' lives. The following questions serve as a way for therapists to help clients consider the effects of heterosexism in their lives.

- Do you think you will have happiness being lesbian or gay? Is there anything you would have to give up or anything you would want in your life that you do not have now? What are the costs?

- When you say you are not accepted by society, are there specific others who do not accept you? Imagine their faces. Would any of those people embrace or celebrate you as you are?

- Do you know any happy lesbian or gay people? Have you spoken to them about their reactions to discovering their sexual identity? Do you assume that they were proud and satisfied? Why do you think they are happy?

- If you have religious concerns, what messages did you receive from your religious community about same-sex orientation? Do you know any lesbian or gay people in your faith? Was questioning allowed in your faith? How were you encouraged to view life, only from a biblical perspective or from multiple perspectives (Tozer & McClanahan, 1999)?

It can be a moving experience for both client and practitioner to deal with these kinds of questions within a supportive environment. It is powerful to witness someone recognizing the layers of myth, stereotype, and oppression that can alienate people from themselves. In many instances, clients who initially present with pronounced levels of internalized heterosexism, once given permission and initial assistance in questioning that heterosexism, progress rapidly (Tozer & McClanahan, 1999).

Negative Views of Religion

The oppressive force of organized religion in the lives of most lesbian and gay people has no institutional parallel. For this reason, many lesbian and gay people see organized religion in a negative manner (Haldeman, 2001). Many lesbian and gay Christians are critical of institutionalized religion. They tend to reject the heterosexist beliefs of the church. Instead, they focus on their own Christian beliefs and faith (D. L. Levy, 2008). Many lesbian and gay people from judgmental religious backgrounds may attempt to discover the origins of Christian beliefs about same-sex attractions. They talk to people in their churches, read books, or investigate online for answers (Webster, 1998). Those with negative views of their churches may reject their old beliefs that same-sex attractions are a sin and may come to devalue church teachings and to believe that their church and the Bible are not 100 percent correct (Yip, 2003). They are likely to develop new beliefs about themselves, their church, their God, and their world (D. L. Levy, 2008). They choose ideologies and behaviors that fit them, and may integrate these ideologies and behaviors into one unified identity (Beckstead & Israel, 2007).

Taking Action

Most people in this group take some kind of action. For lesbian and gay people from a Christian background, that action can be rejecting Christianity totally or finding and following a more accepting religion or spiritual practice. Others may continue to follow the Christianity of their church but in a modified way. Other conservative religious people construct affirming self-concepts—such as altering religious and cultural beliefs so as to feel welcome within society and their deity's plan, redefining sin and the meaning of being lesbian or gay, believing that their deity continues to love them because of or despite their sexual attractions, and feeling spiritual outside of the context of religion. They may join an affirmative religion or remain faithful within their religion but self-identify as being lesbian or gay (Perlstein, 1996). Eventually, they may leave their church.

Another action may be educating heterosexual Christians about sexuality. This might include disclosing to others in their church community. Disclosure may create discourse and change within the community. In addition, lesbian and gay Christians may create a formal or informal support network with others in their area (Shallenberger, 1996). Finally, if there is little encouragement and continued discrimination, some may be inclined to move out of their faith communities into more supportive environments (D. L. Levy, 2008). By far the most common response for those studied by Schuck and Liddle (2001) was to stop attending the offending religious institution.

Finding Alternatives to Traditional Religion

Some lesbian and gay people remain in their denomination but find individual congregations within it that are more gay-affirmative (Schuck & Liddle, 2001). At present, there are a number of gay-friendly congregations, as well as numerous mainstream denominational "reconciling congregations" that welcome lesbian and gay people and affirm their spiritual needs (Haldeman, 2001).

Others renounce their religion altogether and join non-Christian religions. This is most likely to happen in larger cities that have a culture conducive to exploring alternative religions and spirituality such as meditation, spiritual groups, and Eastern religions (Barret & Barzan, 1996; D. I. Garcia et al., 2008; Schuck & Liddle, 2001).

Spirituality

Some may abandon all religious groups and teachings and consider themselves spiritual, while others maintain no religious or spiritual ties at all. In a study by Schuck and Liddle (2001), more than half of the respondents considered themselves spiritual rather than religious. They maintained a spiritual life or maintained their faith privately. Forty percent reinterpreted religious teachings.

When one holds religious authority in low esteem, one's views about one's sexual identity become more positive in contradiction to the official church views (Buisson-Fenet, 1999). Such people will need to develop and examine new meanings. It can help to journal one's thoughts and feelings. Those who are in a more supportive environment usually talk with at least one other person. This could be a therapist, friend, family member, teacher, pastor, mentor, or online acquaintance. Practitioners working with lesbian and gay people on issues of spirituality can encourage bibliotherapy and a search for positive religious or spiritual leaders. Many different kinds of discourse can help validate new meanings (D. L. Levy, 2008).

Rejection by traditional religious institutions can free some lesbian and gay people to create their own personal spirituality (Barret & Barzan, 1996). Spirituality can help people to see their own lives as a source of authority, to develop a greater internal sense of authenticity and integrity, and to make previously rigid positions more flexible. Unhampered by tradition, many people, particularly in larger cities but even in some rural areas, are creating a personal spiritual identity (Barzan, 1995; Barret & Barzan, 1996). There are numerous spiritual pathways including integration of traditional religious practice (Shallenberger, 1998), shamanism, and earth-spirited faiths.

Love et al. (2005) identified three categories of reconciliation with spirituality among students: undeveloped, unreconciled, and reconciled. *Undeveloped* students rejected spirituality. Students who were *unreconciled* engaged in spiritual practice or thought but had not yet reconciled it with their sexual identity. Students displaying *undeveloped and unreconciled* identities abandoned spirituality altogether or were experiencing distress in making connections between their identities. Almost half the participants in the study were in the *reconciled* category. Being reconciled meant that they had integrated their sexual identity with their spirituality. Earlier these students had tended to de-emphasize a conflicting identity (such as gay sexuality) to focus on spiritual development. They reached reconciliation only after long struggles and conflict. But once reconciled, they experienced a strong sense of self-awareness, a strong spiritual identity, separation of religion from spirituality, and integration of their spiritual and sexual identities. They used spirituality as a source of strength and had a relationship with a higher power. Experiences that contributed to the process of reconciliation included having a religious background, attending church camp, experiencing a loving religious environment, having intimate relationships associated with a religious experience, developing reflective self-analysis, working through other difficulties, and working through challenges between religion and sexuality. The ability to more clearly differentiate between religion and spirituality was an important element of reconciliation or integration. Reconciled students still described an important personal relationship with a higher power, but this was not mediated through traditional religious structures or dogma.

Shallenberger (1996, 1998) referred to the process of identity integration as a spiritual journey and identified three key stages: questioning, reintegration, and reclaiming. *Questioning* people engage in an extensive (mostly internal) conversation with themselves. They question their religious beliefs as related to their experiences as lesbian or gay people. In the *reintegration* stage, they attempt to reincorporate their religious identity with their lesbian or gay identity. This is accomplished through reading, talking with loved ones, and identifying and approaching other lesbian and gay people grappling with the same issues. During the *reclaiming* stage they begin to seek out safe spaces where they can reconnect with both their lesbian or gay identity and their religious identity in a community of supportive like-minded people (Shallenberger, 1996).

For lesbian and gay people, moving further into spirituality can help them distance and buffer themselves from the negative, antigay messages received from rejecting-punitive churches (Rodriguez, 1997). Developing a sense of spirituality distinct from formal experiences with their faith groups may also mediate the effect of negative religious experiences on their psychological health (Gage Davidson, 2000; Lease et al., 2005; O'Neill & Ritter, 1992).

Trouble Leaving One's Religion

In a study by Rodriguez and Ouellete (2000a), some participants who had removed themselves entirely from the religion of their parents reported having made peace with that decision. They no longer had a strong personal commitment to their former religious identity. For some, abandoning their religion was easy. For others, however, it was more difficult and done with regret.

Trouble leaving their religion took a psychological toll on some. The pain experienced was sometimes great. Guilt, shame, depression, and rejection may occur after the original conflict between religion and sexual identity is resolved. Isolation resulting from losing one's faith community or from staying closeted within one's faith community may reduce one's support system. Some regained support by seeking out a more affirming faith community, but not everyone had done this (Schuck & Liddle, 2001).

Many may have focused on certain areas of their lives while leaving other areas on the periphery. Others may create flexible ways of expressing the multiple aspects of themselves in diverse settings. They may develop all identities simultaneously or sequentially (Bing, 2004). As clients make their choices, practitioners may need to help them identify the tangible and intangible losses resulting from those choices and to find other ways of meeting their needs (Haldeman, 2004). In this way clients may find individualized and integrative solutions in which benefits are maximized and harms are minimized.

Negotiations in the Outside World

As clients strengthen their sense of worth, identity, and security, more tasks lie ahead. Specifically, they may need help in enhancing acceptance and honesty within their present support systems and making decisions to leave, stay in, or redefine their relationships and associations. Practitioners can help those who have started to self-identify as lesbian or gay to develop decision-making skills about disclosing to others (see Hunter, 2007). For some clients, it may be adaptive to selectively conceal a lesbian or gay identity to maintain key familial, cultural, and economic support, and practitioners can help clients to consider the advantages and disadvantages of disclosure to various people and in various settings (Israel, 2003).

Other clients will need to develop internal and external resources to withstand the loss, fear, and discrimination that often accompany disclosures. Connecting the client with community resources and affirming role models is indispensable. It may also be necessary to support lesbian and gay people from ethnic minorities in finding affirming organizations and support groups that represent their ethnic identities (Loiacano, 1989). One of the most helpful steps is to find a supportive community in which people can feel complete acceptance without having to hide any important aspects of their lives from others. People long to be fully accepted and loved for who they are. This can happen only when the shame of being different or being seen as inferior is removed. This is like finding one's tribe—other people with similar beliefs and values (Burr, 2009).

Gay-Positive, Welcoming, and Gay-Friendly Churches

It is also helpful to refer clients to a reconciling or gay-affirming worship community. For clients with a fundamentalist upbringing, participation in a liberal church can be a drastic change and a significant factor in their ability to integrate their sexual and religious identities. Practitioners should know which congregations in their communities welcome lesbian and gay people and offer them a theology that allows them to integrate their sexual identity with their identity as a person of faith (Haldeman, 2004).

Some affirming congregations have evolved by altering traditional doctrine to make it more inclusive (for example, the Catholic organization Dignity and the Episcopalian organization Integrity). In other cases, new churches have been established specifically to serve the lesbian and gay community—for example, the Metropolitan Community Church, which has focused primarily on lesbian and gay Christians for over 30 years. Within mainline Christian denominations, the United Church of Christ takes a welcoming stance toward lesbian and gay members and clergy (Love et al., 2005). Jewish Renewal is a movement that welcomes same-sex couples. Some lesbian- and gay-affirming Reformed and Reconstructionist Jewish congregations also exist (Frame, 2003; Robinson, 2000). CLOUT, a lesbian-affirming ecumenical Christian movement, has branches in several cities (Christian Lesbians Out Together, n.d.). Unitarian Universalism is also a lesbian and gay affirming organization.

Those who leave their traditional churches have many options to explore, including spiritual and communal life, experimentation with ritual and symbols, and adoption of a new religious family (Bosivert, 2007).

There are over 3,500 reconciling churches in America linked by the desire to provide a place where lesbian and gay people can be reconciled to the church (Burr, 2009; Institute for Welcoming Resources, n.d.). These churches accept lesbian and gay people into their congregations and call on the church to be an inclusive community. They affirm diversity and same-sex sexual orientation (Tigert, 1996). They make it comfortable for lesbian and gay people to attend services and to participate in other church activities. They are also likely to provide social support to lesbian or gay church members. The belief systems of the congregations are more congruent with the social and moral attitudes of their constituents than are the belief systems of nonfriendly churches. This makes it easier to integrate religious beliefs into one's daily thoughts, feelings, and behavior.

Parallels exist between these churches and the lesbian and gay community. Lesbian and gay people are accepted in both. Both have members who support one another in dealing with difficult issues, and both advocate for causes. These opportunities are not offered in or accepted by traditional churches (Chew, 1999).

Churches that welcome gay and lesbian people can be divided into two categories—gay-positive churches that actively address the religious and spiritual needs of lesbian and gay people, and gay-friendly churches that welcome their participation, either implicitly or explicitly, but do not offer any special ministry for them (Rodriguez & Ouellette, 1999).

Another way to integrate sexual identity and religious or spiritual beliefs is to move away from Western religions and seek alternative spiritual paths that are affirming of diverse sexual identities. Developing a non-Western spiritual identity may also buffer the psychological impact of negative religious experiences (Gage Davidson, 2000; Wilson, 1996). Alternative spiritual paths that are affirming of sexual identity include neo-paganism, witchcraft, feminist spirituality, New Age spirituality, Buddhism, Greek and Eastern mythology, and Native American rituals (Gage Davidson, 2000).

Some Latino men studied by D. I. Garcia et al. (2008) joined nontraditional religions or spiritual practices such as Buddhism, Hinduism, and yoga. Most men following this path resided in the San Francisco Bay area, which has a cultural climate more conducive to exploring non-Christian religions and spirituality. Latino lesbian and gay people in San Francisco have been exposed to meditation, spiritual groups, and Eastern religions, which are more widespread there than in other parts of the country. In Chicago and the Midwest, non-Western religions and spiritual practices such as meditation are becoming a trend, but not to the extent as in the San Francisco Bay area. Moreover, fewer participants have family ties in this area compared to those in the Midwest. So they are not pressured to follow a religion because of their families' influence. In addition, all of the people who abandoned the Catholic Church had experienced low or moderate levels of participation and commitment to Catholicism during their childhood. This probably facilitated the transition to another religion in adulthood.

As a result of these and other movements toward greater inclusiveness, some lesbian and gay people may experience little or no conflict between their sexual orientation and their religious or spiritual beliefs. Little or no conflict also may open up discourses for lesbian and gay clients who are struggling with reconciling these identities (Scasta, 1998).

Becoming involved in an open and tolerant church or non-Western religion or spiritual practice can help lesbian and gay people to alleviate the conflict between their religious and sexual identities and increasingly integrate them (Lukenbill, 1998; T. Perry, 1990, Piazza, 1994; Rodriguez & Ouellette, 1999, 2000; White, 1994).

Turning to an inclusive church has been compared to a religious conversion. People who do so must first distance themselves from earlier beliefs and practices, reinterpret specific biblical passages seen as condemning gay and lesbian relations or calling into question their relevance for the modern world and emphasizing biblical values such as love and acceptance. They must then elaborate new meaning, such as the belief that it is God's will for them to be lesbian or gay and Christian. The last phase of this process involves sharing one's conversion with others (Gross, 2008).

Kubicek et al. (2009) found that gay respondents did not always feel comfortable when they first switched to a more accepting church. The switch was particularly challenging for those who had been brought up in a conservative religion. Walking into a church marked with rainbow flags or seeing men sitting with other men could be jarring or shocking (Kubicek et al., 2009). But most were able to move beyond their initial discomfort.

Integration

Not many religious lesbian and gay people report a high degree of success integrating their sexual and religious identities (Dahl & Gallaher, 2009; Sherkat, 2002). When such clients seek out a practitioner, integration is often their ultimate goal. But it is the most complicated option they may take (Rodriguez & Ouellette, 2000a). Conflict and tension due to negative religious messages and organizational intolerance may be a crucial deterrent to identity integration.

If one's goal is integration, one has to redefine one's religious beliefs. Without some kind of adjustment in religious belief, it is almost impossible to fully integrate a lesbian or gay identity with a conservative religious identity (Schuck & Liddle, 2001). Achievement of identity integration means that one holds a positive religious identity and a positive lesbian or gay identity and does not feel conflict between the two (Rodriguez & Ouellette, 2000a). One has to address psychological conflict and distortion when they interfere with this goal and try to find a middle path where no component of the person is violated or disparaged. The ideal integrative solution is to take the view that all aspects of self or identity are worthy of respect and value (Love et al., 2005).

Integration of one's sexual and religious identities can be a lengthy process. Many research respondents studied by Rodriguez (1997) and Rodriguez and Ouellette (2000a) were still involved in a process of integration or had just completed it. Integrated people were significantly older and had attended a gay-positive church for significantly longer periods of time. Another study of students who were integrated found several commonalities, including strong self-awareness, experience with loving religious environments, use of self-reflection, practice working through other difficulties, and a personal relationship with a higher power. Moreover, reconciled people were able to clearly distinguish between religion and spirituality, and held a strong sense of spirituality (Love et al. 2005).

Rodriguez (2006) reported that those taking the integration path were less lonely and less depressed and had more social support, higher self-esteem, and a more positive affect. Being integrated was also related to higher church involvement, church membership, attending more worship services and other church activities, and attending the church for a longer time. Others who reached integration tended to be politically liberal and female. Lesbians were less likely than gay men to report past conflict between their identities and more likely to report being fully integrated. They were more likely to have no Christian religious affiliation or to identify with a personal spirituality or a non-Christian religion. And they were also more likely to describe themselves as theologically liberal (Warner, 1995). Many gay people studied by Kubicek et al. (2009) had investigated other religions and belief systems looking for one in which God would accept them. The journeys of these young men often included exploring other religions such as Islam, Judaism, Christian denominations other than their own, Buddhism, or Hinduism. Eastern religions in particular were seen as attractive as they were perceived to be more liberal.

Some young men who had moved to Los Angeles from another part of the country reported that just being in an environment where they could feel comfortable with their sexuality was helpful to reconciling conflicting beliefs and developing their spirituality. But they mostly found the strength to overcome the conflicts within themselves (Kubicek et al., 2009).

Dahl and Gallaher (2009) studied 105 lesbian, gay, bisexual, queer, and questioning people ages 18 to 24. Many study participants distanced themselves from religious organizations by considering themselves more spiritual than religious (46 percent), reinterpreting religious teachings (42 percent), or no longer identifying with religion (22 percent). These moves helped open the way toward integration. Other factors were also instrumental in integration. The two most frequently reported were accepting oneself and having a sense of completeness (67 percent). Diffusion of tension may have emerged as participants viewed God as making them lesbian or gay. Other factors included reaching new perspectives through biblical or religious readings (49 percent), support from friends in church (31 percent) and from family (30 percent), spiritual reasons (30 percent); affirming religious organizations (17 percent); support from clergy (17 percent); and support from a therapist (13 percent).

Walton (2006) studied a small group of men who identified as gay and as evangelical Christians, who had integrated these identities for at least five years, and who acknowledged both identities in all aspects of their lives. Despite prejudice, the men made decisions and adopted strategies that facilitated a harmonious blending of their identities. Identity integration can result in defiance of those who disapprove and resistance against judgmental moral or political regimes.

Another strategy focused on the issue of choice. Many Christians and others view same-sex attractions as a choice, while many lesbian and gay people say they were born with their attractions. Most of the men studied by Walton (2006) viewed their sexual orientation as a product of God's will and believed that God made certain people lesbian or gay.

Another strategy adopted for identity integration by the men studied by Walton (2006) was *exegesis* or critical (rather than literal) interpretation of biblical text. Exegetical readers consider the social, historical, and political contexts in which the text was written, while literalists do not. Another strategy used by these men was to view inconsistencies between an idealized view of life and one's actual lived experience. A common avenue for this was the recognition of the differences between God and church or between idealized spiritual beliefs and human imperfections. This helped some people move beyond the demand to choose between their gay and Christian identities.

Of Drumm's (2001) Adventist respondents, 23 of 37 successfully integrated their religious and lesbian or gay identities to the point that they were fairly open about their sexual orientation. Factors that helped these respondents integrate their sexual and religious identities included being a member of an accepting congregation or church, working for a non-Adventist employer, and being accepted by their families of origin. R. Phillips (2005) found that better educated, urban, and younger Mormon men were more comfortable embracing a gay identity.

The concept of *sifting* describes a process of selective religious identification or construction of cohesive, nonconflicted identities out of potentially conflicted ones. People can try on different practices and attitudes, evaluate them in terms of personal values, needs, or feelings, and then identity with them or not (Dufour, 2000). They can sift through the practices and attitudes of Christianity and assemble a Christian identity that can be integrated with their lesbian or gay identity. The ability to sift out negative views is critical to resolving the tension between religious and lesbian and gay identities (Wilcox, 2003).

Lesbian and gay people might sift out all aspects of religion that touch on same-sex attractions. They might refuse to accept the negative evaluations of same-sex attractions in scripture or doctrine. They might forge a meta–identity in which their religion's emphasis on a moral and righteous life infuses their intimate relationships with and commitments to others of the same sex (Rosario et al., 2006).

Many other paths to integration are possible, including reading to educate oneself on the issues, talking with others, associating with older and more mature lesbian and gay people, reestablishing a personal relationship with God, and even coping with a life-threatening illness such as HIV/AIDS (Rodriguez, 1997; Rodriguez & Ouellette, 2000). Perhaps one of the main paths is becoming involved with organizations that promote a positive outlook on both same-sex and religious identities. The goal of religious support groups is to deliver both gay-positive and Christian-positive messages and a gay theology that values lesbian and gay Christians and recognizes their spiritual needs. These groups have reinterpreted the Bible in such a way that same-sex relations are viewed in a positive religious light (Englund, 1991; Thumma, 1991). Members hear the message that God loves all people including them.

Rodriguez and Ouellette (2000a) studied identity integration in a church in New York City that ministered especially to the lesbian and gay community and played an important role in helping people achieve integration. The church was the Metropolitan Community Church of New York, a gay-positive Christian church. Rodriguez and Ouellette (1999) described the church as preaching a positive message about same-sex identity and ministering specifically to the lesbian and gay community. They found that three strategies were used to facilitate identity integration: (1) the liturgy enabled its members to recognize the church as a legitimate religious institution that is simultaneously lesbian, gay, and Christian; (2) the pastor provided members a positive way to think about themselves with regard to their sexual identities and their Christianity; and (3) the church provided members with a strong sense of being part of a valued group without creating boundaries that exclude others. Gay-positive churches also emphasize the basic goodness in all people and highlight the value of people regardless of sexual orientation (Gage Davidson, 2000). They celebrate all creation (Struzzo, 1989).

When asked about positive experiences related to faith, spirituality, or religion, most respondents studied by Schuck and Liddle (2001) said such experiences centered on interactions with gay-affirmative congregations, clergy, and religious institutions. Many mentioned good feelings evoked by belonging to a gay-affirmative congregation. Others mentioned attending spiritual institutions run by and for the gay community such as the Metropolitan Community Church, a gay synagogue, or a lesbian and gay Alcoholic Anonymous meeting. Others spoke of attending a gay-affirmative ceremony or event such as a gay-friendly Passover seder or a Gay Pride Day march. Many spoke of support received from heterosexual clergy or congregation members after coming out. Some mentioned lesbian and gay organizations for members of a particular faith as helpful. Other helpful groups included Parents, Families, & Friends of Lesbians and Gays (PFLAG) and other local lesbian and gay support groups or coalitions.

Those who continue to experience conflict between their sexual identity and religion may experience a chronic feeling of not belonging and of being rejected. They may also experience self-denial (denial of their same-sex attractions), religious doubt (the seeming irreconcilability of a lesbian or gay identity and one's religion), and consequent guilt and a sense of unworthiness, loneliness, and fear of disclosure. They are thereby rendered invisible and unacknowledged (Lease et al., 2005). Their attitude is negative. They are more depressed, more lonely, more anxious, and much angrier than lesbian and gay people who have managed to integrate their religious beliefs into their lives or are not in conflict with their religion (Rodriguez, 2006).

Summary

When clients are open to a lesbian or gay identity, practitioners can suggest ways to integrate their sexual and religious identities or other options, such as staying in their church but as openly lesbian or gay people. Practitioners can also help them develop decision-making skills about making disclosures and can connect them with affirming community resources and role models. Affirmative practice is the best approach with these clients. Attending a gay-positive church can provide support that a practitioner cannot. This is one of the best ways to attain integration of one's religious and sexual identities.

❋ **Part IV** ❋

Working with Heterosexist Practitioners

Nine

Conservative Religious Practitioners

Social workers and other practitioners will inevitably encounter lesbian and gay people in their practice and, as discussed in chapter 5, should educate themselves and be ready to work with them and not discriminate against them in any way. This will not always be the case, though, because some social workers and other practitioners have personal values and beliefs about lesbian and gay people that are in conflict with the values and ethics of their profession. Mostly this is due to also being brought up in rejecting–punitive churches. Some practitioners view religion as central to their lives. They are more likely to adhere to religious teachings and have antilesbian and antigay attitudes. But all clients deserve ethical, competent, and effective services from helping agencies (Halpert, Reinhardt, & Toohey, 2007).

The views expressed by practitioners with antilesbian and antigay attitudes are also tied to heterosexism, as noted in chapter 1. The prime reason, however, for their stand against lesbian and gay people is that they heard the same thing in their conservative churches that lesbian and gay people in conflict with their religion heard. Research clearly demonstrates that heterosexism and negative attitudes toward lesbian and gay people correlate with religiosity. But for practitioners, heterosexism translates into not wanting to work with gay and lesbian people, and they may have no desire to transform their values, attitudes, beliefs, or behaviors.

As is the case for some lesbian and gay people, they do not want to separate from the beliefs of their churches.

Some practitioners have a strong religious commitment that includes identification with a particular religious group or denomination and reverence for the authority of its scripture and leaders (Worthington, 1988; Worthington et al., 2003). Religious commitment is the degree of impact on and interpenetration of beliefs and values in one's everyday life. For religiously committed practitioners, religion is the essence of their lives. Dimensions that underlie religious commitment include acceptance of religious tenets, agreement with the tenets, and the importance in their lives of the belief system of their church (Paloutzian, 1996). Some people have moderate to low religious commitment. While they hold religious beliefs and affirm them, they are not highly religiously committed. Therefore, their religious beliefs do not affect their practice with lesbian and gay people. Those with strong religious beliefs and high commitment are more likely to integrate religion into their practice and choose techniques that have associations with or origins in formal religion or ecclesiastical practice. They may guide clients toward religious behavior advocated by rejecting-punitive churches. These practitioners most likely also have a zone of toleration that is narrowly centered on their beliefs. They tolerate few differences in others from their heterosexual orientation and religious beliefs (Worthington, Hook, Wade, Miller, & Sharp, 2006).

Most practitioners have a wide zone of toleration. This is necessary if they are to thrive professionally, given the wide variety of beliefs they encounter among clients. Limits to tolerance mostly arise from religious beliefs and values (Worthington et al., 2006). If the beliefs and values of the practitioner and client are widely discrepant, the relationship will be impaired. The practitioner will not help the client effectively or want to refer him or her to someone who is more value congruent (Worthington, 1988).

Conservative religious orthodox thinking also refuses to consider alternate viewpoints. This is part of the effort to constrain and suppress theological diversity and views on deviation from heterosexuality. Suppression of ideas leads to tunnel vision or being trapped in one way of thinking that rejects alternatives (see chapter 1). In cognitive development, this is the level of dualism or seeing life in narrow terms of good and bad or right and wrong. This is the lowest level of cognitive development. We are supposed to progress to higher levels including relativism, where one understands that there are multiple views on everything rather than holding to one absolutist view of truth. Heterosexist practitioners are stuck in absolutism and dualism. This contributes to their low levels of understanding and acceptance of people, beliefs, and values that are different from what they believe and value (W. G. Perry, 1981).

Almost every social work student, teacher, and supervisor has heard some students and practitioners say, "I will not work with them." This almost always means "I will not work with those sinful, deviant, abominable 'homosexuals.'" Some practitioners say, "I can only work with them if they are willing to change and become heterosexual." Others say "love the sinner, hate the sin." This reflects an attempt to be affirming while maintaining their prejudice against these clients. They are saying that being lesbian or gay is wrong and unacceptable. This contributes to a culture of disrespect and oppression. And this likely does psychological harm or even psychological violence to lesbian and gay clients. Another term for this is hostile heterosexism, and it continues to be documented among social work and human service practitioners and students (Berkman & Zinberg, 1997; Cramer, 1997; Crisp, 2006; Newman, Dannenfelser, & Benishek, 2002).

Historically, hostile heterosexism has been based on ideologies that pathologize "homosexuality." These ideologies come from a number of sources including religious beliefs ("homosexuality" is immoral and sinful) and belief in natural law ("homosexuality" is unnatural). The endorsement of such beliefs has a detrimental impact on lesbian and gay clients. Higher levels of hostile heterosexism have been linked to evaluating same-sex couples as being less emotionally stable, less able to have strong parenting potential, and less able to provide a caring home to adoptive children than opposite-sex couples (Crawford & Solliday, 1996).

Practitioners without affirmative attitudes may minimize or exaggerate the importance of sexual orientation in their clients' lives (Messing, Schoenberg, & Stephens, 1984). Or, they may devalue lived experiences by changing the topic or cutting short clients' discussions of their lives (McHenry & Johnson, 1993).

Crisp (2006) has argued that heterosexist attitudes reduce the effectiveness of services and result in inferior treatment for lesbian, gay, bisexual, and transgender clients. Others have linked such attitudes to causing actual harm to these clients (Ben-Ari, 2001).

Professional codes of ethics were devised primarily to protect the welfare of the public whom practitioners serve. Ethical codes are not about practitioners' personal liberties. They safeguard the public from harm that can be done by practitioners. Our first priority is to avoid harm (A. R. Fisher & DeBord, 2007). Practitioners who have negative views of lesbian and gay people are in conflict with this and other ethical principles (Kawakami, Young, & Dovidio, 2002). They think that any sexuality other than heterosexuality is wrong, immoral, or sinful (A. R. Fisher & DeBord, 2007). Practitioner behaviors that discriminate against lesbian and gay clients violate the codes of ethics of NASW and other helping organizations (Lidderdale, 2002).

The author gives an assignment to social work classes in which students have to state their views on working with selected groups, including lesbian and gay people. Usually a few students state, "I won't work with these sinners and deviants." One student put lesbian and gay people in the same category as murderers. Even using the term "homosexual" shows a prejudicial view, because this term is not acceptable. We should describe people in terms they themselves prefer (Savin-Williams, 2005).

When in compliance with one's code of ethics, one cannot be prejudicial against lesbian and gay clients. This causes them harm. Religious practitioners may claim, however, that emotional and psychological harm is done to them by requiring that they be affirmative with lesbian and gay clients. On the whole, however, this is probably less harmful than the harm that results from prioritizing religious values over lesbian and gay affirmation (A. R. Fisher & DeBord, 2007). Also, the focus here is not on religion per se but on antilesbian and antigay attitudes and behaviors that practitioners justify based on their religious beliefs (see the introduction to this book). Being a stigmatized minority in such an environment can result in chronic stress or psychological violence by being devalued for one's group membership (Root, 1992). When the devaluation is justified on religious grounds, this does psychological harm to lesbian and gay clients (A. R. Fisher & DeBord, 2007). Practitioners are free to believe and value anything they choose in their personal lives as private citizens. As professional practitioners, however, their first priority must be avoidance of harm to all clients (A. R. Fisher & DeBord, 2007).

If students or practitioners state that because of religious beliefs they cannot work with lesbian and gay clients, should they be allowed to remain incompetent in this area? Or should they be allowed to withhold service to members of a population based solely on their group membership? To allow these actions is to approve prejudice and behavioral discrimination. It also creates a hostile practice environment because of the nonaffirming attitudes of these practitioners maintained by their religious beliefs (A. R. Fisher & DeBord, 2007).

Not every value must be equally appreciated. Privileging religious values over lesbian and gay affirmation would be an extension of existing and historical marginalization of lesbian and gay people. We also have to prioritize the principles of nonmaleficence (minimizing harm) and beneficence (doing good) (A. R. Fisher & DeBord, 2007).

Multicultural Values in Social Work

The principle of justice, or protecting the rights of minorities in the face of institutional oppression, is a core principle of the multicultural movement (Okin, Chohen, Howard, & Nussbaum, 1999). All practice can be regarded as multicultural if culture is defined broadly to include race, ethnicity, and nationality, as well as gender, age, social class, disability, and sexual orientation (A. R. Fisher & DeBord, 2007).

According to the multicultural movement, practitioners should be cultur-ally skilled enough to work with a broad range of clients. Requirements for a culturally skilled practitioner for lesbian and gay clients include the following:

- *Awareness of beliefs and attitudes*: Become aware of one's attitudes and beliefs regarding sexual orientation; recognize one's heterosexist assumptions; monitor personal biases; develop a positive view about multiculturalism; and understand how one's values and biases can be an obstacle to helping.

- *Knowledge*: Become knowledgeable and understanding of the world-view of lesbian and gay clients and possess specific knowledge of these clients. Understand their cultural background, the sociopolitical forces that influence them, and the institutional barriers they face. Learn about their minority family structures, values, and beliefs, com-munity characteristics, and resources.

- *Sensitivity*: Be sensitive to lesbian and gay people and respect their partnerships and family structures. Provide a safe, welcoming environ-ment and inclusive services. Use appropriate terminology.

- *Competence*: Develop the skills, interventions, techniques, and strate-gies necessary in serving gay and lesbian clients. (Bidell, 2005; Corey, 2009; Turner, Wilson, & Shirah, 2006)

Practitioners who are uncomfortable with or hostile to lesbian and gay cli-ents most likely got these views from their church. But it is useless to attack their religious views. Their religious affiliation serves as a central, organizing aspect of their identity that they cannot give up. Nor can they step outside of their enmeshment with their religious views to see the power these views have on them. But in order to comply with professional ethics, they have to decide not to let their religion have this power in their practice with lesbian and gay clients.

Given this situation, what can be done? The first thing is to confront such practitioners with the multicultural requirements described above, the ethical standards of their profession, any state codes of conduct for social workers, moral principles, and relevant court rulings.

Social Work *Code of Ethics*

The core values of the profession of social work, described in the NASW (1999) *Code of Ethics,* include service, social justice, recognition of the dignity and worth of each person, the importance of human relationships, integrity, and competence. All social workers licensed to practice must abide by this code of ethics and any other legal standards that govern them when they work with lesbian and gay people. The *Code of Ethics* forbids prejudice and discrimination regarding sexual orientation.

NASW issued its first policy statement of commitment to lesbian and gay clients in 1977 and has reaffirmed and elaborated on this statement many times. In 1996, NASW revised its *Code of Ethics* to clarify and strengthen its ban on discrimination based on sexual orientation with this statement: "Social Workers should act to prevent and eliminate discrimination against any person or group on the basis of...sexual orientation" (NASW, 1996, section 4.02). The *Code of Ethics* also states that "social workers should obtain education about and seek to understand the nature of social diversity and oppression with respect to...sexual orientation" (section 1.04c).

Practitioners are ethically obligated to affirm diversity and not to have any preconceived idea of what a normal person or family is. They also have to know the difference between social workers as private citizens and as professionals. The goal as professionals is neutrality with clients. We are not to judge clients or impose our personal values, attitudes, beliefs, or behaviors on them.

Ethical practice requires that practitioners investigate the values of their culture that are linked to discrimination, social inequality, and harm to clients. The ethical challenge is to understand the beliefs and feelings of clients whose views may be different (Greene, 2007). The highest performance standards are required for social workers and other human services practitioners (Greene, 2004; Haldeman, 2000). Ethical practice requires putting the needs of the client first. This requires that all practitioners examine their beliefs for any bias that might lead them to place their own needs or beliefs ahead of the clients' needs and beliefs. All people are entitled to professional services of equal quality. Practitioners must ensure that their limitations in expertise and competence do not lead to or condone unfair practices (American Psychological Association, 2002). They must eliminate from their professional work any behavior based on bias and prejudice (Greene, 2007). Practitioners must also engage in appropriate training to understand the cultural experiences of lesbian and gay people on the basis of sexual orientation, country of origin, or ethnocultural group.

All ethics codes urge practitioners to be aware of their beliefs, predispositions, and worldviews and how they affect their work. The capacity to step outside of one's own beliefs is critical in practice with ethical professional guidelines that command respect for the dignity of all clients (Greene, 2007). Some of the more powerful codes of ethics indicate that everyone has dignity and worth and everyone has the right to self-determination. No practitioner has the right to exclude some groups from these ethics.

Moral Principles

In addition to the profession's values and codes of ethics, moral principles that are viewed as the foundation for ethical decision-making are also relevant to these situations. They include the following:

- *Autonomy*: This refers to clients' freedom of choice. The social worker or other practitioner should encourage clients to make decisions that are consistent with their values and encourage them to act and think in autonomous ways. This includes being lesbian or gay. Liddle (2003) pointed out that practitioners must temper the desire to make decisions for a client. A practitioner can ask, "Do I understand what this client thinks is the best outcome? Am I willing to help the client toward that goal?"

- *Nonmaleficence*: This is the concept of "do no harm." This moral principle reflects a two-fold concept of not inflicting intentional pain on others and refraining from actions that risk harm to others. Heterosexist actions that harm lesbian and gay people include telling them they are immoral or that they can change if they want to. Some personal values, if acted upon, may be damaging and cause harm. Does the value in question support or require the marginalization or estrangement of one group from others? Does it scapegoat or deem one group less valuable, deserving, or human than others? Does it explicitly devalue people and in so doing cause harm? Invariably the dominant group or groups seek to impose values on subordinate groups and often impose violence on subordinate group members. Reinforcing rather than challenging heterosexism causes lesbian and gay people and their families harm (Greene, 2007). In addition, one must continually think of ways to reduce any potential harm that may come to a client. Finally, it is important to think of ways to encourage clients to think benevolently toward themselves.

- *Beneficence*: This refers to our responsibility to contribute to the welfare of the client by preventing harm and being proactive in attempting to benefit the client (Benoit, 2005). The twin principles of beneficence and nonmaleficence require us seek to benefit clients through our work and to avoid doing harm. Further, these principles require vigilant attention to the possible misuse of one's influence in clients' lives (Benoit, 2005).

- *Justice:* This refers to the principle of providing equal treatment for all clients. This requires that we examine our biases and abilities to ensure that we are acting fairly in our dealings with everyone. Equal treatment extends to lesbian and gay clients (Benoit, 2005).

- *Fidelity:* This refers to honoring commitments to the practice relationship. We must guard the client's trust and therefore not threaten the practice relationship. With lesbian and gay clients, many things can threaten this relationship, both verbal and nonverbal (Benoit, 2005). We must uphold professional roles and obligations, accept responsibility for our behavior, and manage conflicts of interest that could lead to exploitation or harm (Greene, 2007).

- *Integrity:* This refers to accuracy, honesty, and truthfulness in practice with clients (Benoit, 2005).

- *Respect of rights and dignity:* This refers to the dignity and rights of all people and their rights to privacy, confidentiality, and self-determination (Greene, 2007).

Given that extremely heterosexist people do exist in social work schools and agencies, and that they are probably not going to volunteer to leave this profession, is there anything that will get them to modify their negative views of lesbian and gay clients? First, they can be confronted with the ethical and moral principles cited above. If licensed, they have a legal obligation to adhere to their professional code of ethics, and they may be subject to a state code of ethics as well. In addition, a federal court has ruled that a practitioner cannot refuse to work with lesbian and gay clients because of religious beliefs. And the Supreme Court has ruled on lesbian and gay people with relevance to the social work profession.

The *Texas State Board of Social Worker Examiners Code of Conduct* states the following:

> A social worker must observe and comply with the code of conduct and standards of practice set forth in this subchapter. Any violation of the code of ethics or standards of practice will constitute unethical conduct or conduct that discredits or tends to discredit the profession of social work and is grounds for disciplinary action.
>
> (1) A social worker shall not refuse to do or refuse to perform any act or service for which the person is licensed solely on the basis of a client's age, gender, race, color, religion, national origin, disability, sexual orientation, or political affiliation. (Texas Department of State Health Services, 2009)

If a client has as a goal to disclose his or her sexual orientation or to explore sexual identity, is the practitioner who believes these behaviors are a serious sin and violation of the laws of God required by the professional code to work with the client? Does the professional code supersede the personal religious rights of the social worker? Yes, the professional code does supersede. Because the state licensure law in Texas adopts the NASW *Code of Ethics* or parallels it, the practitioner who does not live up to it is violating state law as well as the professional code of ethics. Violation could lead to being reprimanded by the state licensing board or having one's license suspended or revoked.

Many practitioners may find that they cannot suspend their moral or religious judgments about lesbian and gay clients. They see these clients as defective or somehow less deserving because of their sexual orientation (Greene, 2007). People who refuse to work with lesbian and gay people most likely should not be social workers because they are judgmental, condescending, and disrespectful about lesbian and gay people. They are in the most extreme category of heterosexist practitioners: They are overtly prejudiced or hostile toward lesbian and gay people. Others try to hide their prejudice or hostility, but lesbian and gay people pick up on covert attitudes. They have assessed environments all of their lives for signs of prejudice, rejection, hatred, or violence. Bias can be expressed through voice or mannerisms, awkwardness, defensiveness, hesitancy, hostility, distance, disapproval, and contempt. What is worse is that lesbian and gay clients are harmed daily by these heterosexist manifestations in practitioners (Brown, 1989; Pope, 1997). It may be necessary for ethics boards to consider either overt or covert prejudice that results in discrimination when practitioners refuse to work with lesbian and gay clients as a legitimate reason to remove a social worker's license.

Court Rulings

A federal court has ruled on a case in which a practitioner refused to work with lesbian and gay clients because of religious beliefs. In March 2001, the United States Court of Appeals for the Fifth Circuit held that religious beliefs did not justify accommodating a counselor's request to be excused from counseling lesbian and gay clients. Such a refusal by the counselor constitutes illegal discrimination. It is not the client's role to have to adjust to the counselor's values. Counseling is not about the counselor but the needs and values of the client. The court also commented that accommodating a worker's religious beliefs could harm lesbian and gay clients. The counselor wanted to be excused from helping lesbian and gay clients to have better relationships with their partners because their relationships were outside the bounds of marriage. The court stated that being willing to provide counseling only on issues that do not conflict with a counselor's religious beliefs is an inflexible position not protected by the law (*Bruff v. North Mississippi Health Services, Inc.*, 2001; Hermann & Herlihy, 2006).

The court also ruled that an employer can terminate a practitioner who refuses to counsel clients on issues related to the client's sexual orientation, and that settings that allow practitioners to refuse to work with clients on issues related to their sexual orientation are discriminatory and illegal. The states governed by the Fifth Circuit Court of Appeals (Texas, Louisiana, and Mississippi) must follow this ruling (Hermann & Herlihy, 2006).

The Supreme Court has also indicated that discrimination against lesbian and gay people is unconstitutional. In 1966, the Supreme Court held that states violate the equal protection clause of the Fourteenth Amendment if they discriminate on the basis of sexual orientation, even if some of their residents may have personal and religious objections to same-sex relations. This ruling covers practitioners in all states (*Romer v. Evans*, 1996).

More recently, the Supreme Court held on June 26, 2003, in *Lawrence v. Texas* (2003) that state sodomy laws are unconstitutional and struck down all such laws in every state that still had them. Sex between two people of the same sex is not illegal in any state (see http://www.glapn.org/sodomylaws/lawrence/lawrence.htm). One of the bases for this decision was that orthodox religious tradition was not a persuasive enough basis to outweigh the other legal principles that sodomy laws violated.

Clearly, practitioners cannot use their religious beliefs to justify discrimination against clients based on sexual orientation. Practitioners who do so can incur legal liability. Clients can bring a malpractice lawsuit against them because they breached their duty to provide the standard of care of their profession. Most likely the clients would win.

Practitioners who resist working with gay and lesbian clients have a choice. They can reform their views or they can lose their social work license or perhaps be fired or sued. It took legal measures to force people to adapt different views of and behaviors toward African American people during the time of the Civil Rights movement. Nothing else had worked. This same principle is suggested here as the best strategy to use with those in the human services who discriminate against lesbian and gay people.

These practitioners face difficult ethical decisions that the professional codes of ethics can help resolve. Do they aspire to the highest practice standards or not? If not, this is their choice, but there can be ethical and legal troubles ahead. If one loses one's social work license, one can no longer call oneself a social worker or practice in the profession.

School of Social Work Statements

Some schools of social work are asking potential students what they can tolerate before they enroll. The mission statements and other statements of some schools in effect ask if social work is the right major for you? Many schools of social work have as goals appreciation for human diversity, attention to the experiences of marginalized people, and commitment to altering patterns of oppression and discrimination. They want to create an atmosphere that supports the human dignity of all human beings. They will not accept any attitudes or behaviors that reflect the devaluation of any person because of that person's membership in a particular group.

The School of Social Work at the University of Central Florida states the following in its admission requirements on their Web site:

> To be admitted into UCF's undergraduate social work
> program, students must be willing to work directly with and
> on behalf of diverse populations. These include adult men and
> women; persons of African, Asian, Hispanic, or multi-cultural
> descent; children; persons with disabilities; older adults; gay,
> lesbian, bisexual and transgender individuals; or persons
> with HIV/AIDS or other physical, mental conditions and
> economically disadvantaged individuals. (http://www.cohpa.
> ucf.edu/Social/documents/BSWBasicRequirements.pdf)

The mission and goals statements, respectively, of the School of Social Welfare at Stony Brook University in New York are as follows:

> The School of Social Welfare is committed to a more just
> society based on equality, human dignity and social justice.
> We believe that inequality and injustices are deeply embedded
> in society's political and economic structures and ideologies.
> Oppression objectively and subjectively permeates the lives of
> people, resulting in the denial of human dignity, individual and
> cultural diversity, and social and economic justice. Oppression
> is manifest in discrimination on the basis of class, race, ethnicity,
> gender, sexual orientation, religion, age and disability, among
> others. Our purpose is to prepare students for work in
> professional social work practice in the public and non-profit
> sectors of health and social welfare. The School's educational
> process enables people to identify and analyze the nature and
> extent of oppression and engage in social work practice that

affirms people's strengths as a means to create social change in their lives and in society. The school stresses a commitment to the values of human and cultural diversity, human dignity, social and economic justice, and individual and group self-determination. The following goals emerge out of the School's mission statement and guide its educational practice: to develop human relationships that are grounded in social justice, human dignity and mutual respect; to develop new and more just organizational forms; to transform already existing structures to ones which affirm and enhance human dignity and social diversity; and to identify new ways to influence social, economic and political systems to distribute power, resources, rights, and freedom, so as to achieve social justice. (http://www.stonybrookmedicalcenter.org/ssw/mission)

What should happen if some students and practitioners continue with their heterosexist viewpoints and refuse to modify their views of lesbian and gay people in terms of the values and ethics of social work? They should not be in social work, and every social work school and social work agency should refuse to admit or hire them or ask them to leave. Religious beliefs are protected, and each person has a right to his or her own religious beliefs (Kreiglstein, 2003).

But not every person has an automatic right to a social work education or degree or to employment in a social work agency. Social work is not value free; it has a specific set of ethical mandates to which social workers must adhere (Van Soest, 1996). Schools of social work should consider the policies issued by NASW and the Council on Social Education (CSWE) regarding sexual minorities when admitting students. Prospective students should be made aware of these standards, including the statement in the *Code of Ethics* that social workers "should not practice, condone, facilitate, or collaborate with any form of discrimination on the basis of...sexual orientation" (NASW, 1996, section 1.05c) These should be read and signed off on before people are admitted into a school of social work or hired in a social work agency.

Prospective students and practitioners must be made aware of social work's expectations and agree to be open to change regarding their attitudes toward sexual minorities. If students and practitioners know up front about these policies and know their beliefs are in conflict with them, they can make the decision not to seek entrance or a job if they do not wish to question and challenge their beliefs. Asking people to agree to abide by the values and ethics of the profession should not be seen as any more of an infringement on anyone's rights than signing off on policies prohibiting racial discrimination or sexual harassment. Discrimination against any other minority group would not be acceptable within the profession (H. K. Jones, 1996; Van Wormer, Well, & Boes, 2000). If, as a profession, social work admits heterosexist students and practitioners without requiring that they commit to the values of the profession, social work colludes in the perpetuation of heterosexism.

Issues of discrimination can be seen in terms of closed and open societies, or static and dynamic religions, which use authority, goals, rules, and language in entirely different ways. Closed societies are highly authoritarian. They have a static religion. Morality coexists with religion. These societies consider "homosexuality" to be an evil that must be stopped and believe that "homosexuals" must be controlled by moral sanctions and the threat of punishment by God. This maintains the stability of the tribe. In contrast, open societies are liberal. They encourage growth, individuation, autonomy, and difference. They are open to new ways of thinking, being, and living. They create dynamic religions. They encourage opportunities for humans to have greater voice in the development of morality. They have looser interpretations of scripture and customs (Henrickson, 2009). They are more democratic and egalitarian. They support inclusiveness, diversity, and representation. Every society has both closed and open elements (Popper, 1966). Social work is a profession born of an open society. Social workers are dedicated to work for the welfare and self-fulfillment of human beings (International Federation of Social Workers, 2005).

Summary

Most social workers and other practitioners have lesbian and gay clients. But some practitioners refuse to work with these clients because of their religious beliefs. Their zone of toleration is narrow and centered only on their own values. These practitioners have every right to their religious views in their private lives, but not in their practice. They should be confronted with the principles of the multicultural movement, requirements of the NASW *Code of Ethics,* moral principles, and legal requirements for nondiscrimination, and the possible consequences of being out of compliance with these codes.

Those who refuse to work with lesbian and gay clients or discriminate against them are in conflict with all of these codes, principles, state laws, and court rulings. They have a choice between forgoing their religious beliefs when acting in a professional capacity or experiencing consequences such as possibly losing their license to practice. Some schools of social work model through their admissions requirements or mission and goal statements their views that students must be accepting of lesbian and gay people.

Ten

A Program to Transform Heterosexist Practitioners

To move toward affirmative work with lesbian and gay clients, conservative religious practitioners who are not currently affirmative must be transformed. If not, they will continue to violate their profession's code of ethics and other legal standards. The goal of the program presented here is modification of negative attitudes and beliefs about lesbian and gay people (Schreier, 1995)—in other words, changing heterosexism. Effective programs challenge participants to explore how negative attitudes and beliefs limit their personal growth (Schreier & Werden, 2000). The goals are to raise awareness, facilitate change in individual attitudes, and foster change in agencies.

Accessing emotions is one way to facilitate the growth experience (Drum, 1984). Emotions affect the attitude change process. Emotion-based transformation can take varied forms such as eliciting feelings of self-dissatisfaction concerning a given attitude or belief (Rokeach, 1984), appealing to the commonality of emotional experiences (Schreier, 1995), presenting information that suggests that more positive emotional experiences will result from adopting new attitudes or beliefs (Abelson, 1986), and demonstrating the emotional dysfunctionality of targeted attitudes or beliefs (Ajzen & Fishbein, 1980). Self exploration is also a required part of this training. This includes exploration of internal beliefs and values (Iasenza, 1989; B. C. Murphy, 1991; J. Phillips, 2000).

B. C. Murphy (1991) proposed that professionals can acquire and strengthen lesbian- and gay-affirmative qualities through socialization. It is hoped that group participants will, through socialization, internalize new values and beliefs and be able to impart affirmative views of lesbian and gay people.

The instructor facilitates participation and group development and also teaches. He or she also discusses the potential risks of participation, such as when change in beliefs and attitudes influence relationships outside of the course (Lidderdale, 2002).

The program has a number of interventions, so it will take several weeks to complete. Extensive empirical work is needed on interventions. Unfortunately, there is little empirical work on what interventions might bring transformation about.

The suggestions presented here follow a stage approach. If practitioners seriously address the various steps in this program, they will most likely have different views at the end of the program, especially if they are open to change. What is needed are interventions that strongly challenge practitioners to identify biases in themselves and to work to modify them. Ideas are presented in nonadversarial ways. Program participants must feel respected, heard, and nurtured to derive benefits from the program (Whitehead & Nokes, 1990).

The program will start with the information presented here. The program also makes it clear to the participants who they are regarding lesbian and gay clients and where they need to be. It also points out several barriers to change that have to be overcome.

Introduction for Participants

This transformation program is mandatory for anyone with prejudicial attitudes toward lesbian and gay people, and full participation is expected. Some of you will be more open to the program than others and perhaps even eager to change. Some of you will resist change. The program is intense, however, and may bring some resisters along. If it does, you will join the many heterosexual practitioners who are affirmative with lesbian and gay clients. And you will be out of harm's way in terms of your code of ethics and other requirements to keep your license.

Everyone, including practitioners and clients, grew up in a heterosexist culture. You display heterosexist or biased views in your practice with lesbian and gay clients. This can happen without your awareness because of the embeddedness of the heterosexist ideology in everyone. Recently there has been resistance to same-sex marriage initiatives and a higher visibility of lesbian and gay people who are social activists. This may have led you to feel more comfortable in overtly expressing your negative bias toward them (Greene, 2007).

You can share the world with heterosexual clients who grew up in a conservative religion and heterosexist culture. Your view of lesbian and gay clients, however, is distorted by your internalized heterosexism and religious views of them (Greene, 2007). You must transform your belief system so you can work effectively with these clients. Internalized heterosexism and your religious beliefs distort your view of lesbian and gay clients and their dilemma. It also influences your choice of interventions with these clients.

This program will not be easy, as human nature prefers repetitive patterns. It is more comfortable to stick with the status quo. A sense of harmony is highly valued by most people, so beliefs and attitudes are fairly resistant to change (Quackenbush, 1989). And our brains will override new ideas that challenge our ways of thinking. This explains why it is so difficult to change our minds once we have taken a position. If we have a religion that works for us, then how will we be able to assimilate new ideas and challenges that push the boundaries of traditional belief?

Nevertheless, this program focuses on change in both heterosexism and religious beliefs that influence you to have negative views of lesbian and gay people. Most likely your behaviors toward lesbian and gay clients include silence or deliberately ignoring matters of sexual orientation, not reacting to derogatory remarks made about them, thinking of them in a negative way, behaving differently toward anyone you think is lesbian or gay, and offering religious guidance to them (Kahn, 2006). If you are practitioners in social work or another human service profession with an ethical code, you must change to become more affirmative with lesbian and gay clients or face consequences based on your ethical code and other requirements.

You must first examine your own internal, often unconscious, biases towards sexual minorities (Barret & Barzan, 1996). Most of you probably think you do no harm to clients. But the fact is that everyone has harmful internal biases and prejudices (Rudolph, 1992).

Understanding that heterosexism permeates most social institutions and may be influencing your attitudes, you must have a vigilant sensitivity to avoid projecting these attitudes onto lesbian and gay clients (Barret & Barzan, 1996). Of course, simply being aware of biases influenced by heterosexism is not sufficient.

Ethical practice requires that you presume that you harbor heterosexist bias and that you actively work to understand it and disengage from it (Greene, 2007). An overarching principle of practice is to do no harm and to guard against misuse of professional influence. Ethical practice requires putting the needs of the client first. This requires you to examine your beliefs for any bias that might lead you to place your needs or beliefs ahead of the client's needs and beliefs. Justice urges you to practice in ways that recognize all people as entitled to professional services of equal quality and also to take care to ensure that any limitations of yours in expertise and competence do not lead to or condone unfair practices. Respect of rights and dignity will challenge you to be aware of cultural distinctions that include sexual orientation and to eliminate from your professional work any behavior based on bias and prejudice about those distinctions (Greene, 2007).

You must also be mindful of your vocabulary. Call lesbian and gay people what they want to be called. Do not use the term "homosexual." Do not use the words "unnatural" and "abnormal." No one can be recruited to a lesbian or gay sexual orientation. Lesbian and gay people do not have a lifestyle—they have a life, just as you do, and in most ways their lives are very similar to yours. The only "gay agenda" is to be treated with respect and equality. Gay people are not asking for special rights for themselves, but for equal rights for every person.

You need to help clients address religion and spirituality in ways that are affirmative rather than condemning of them (Ritter & Terndrup, 2002). But if you do not seem able to do this, I must ask: Why do you want to remain incompetent in this area (A. R. Fisher & DeBord, 2007)? Do you realize that when you refer a lesbian or gay client to someone else, it sends a negative message—"I disapprove of you"? Your practitioner role is conflated with your personal beliefs and system of values. This institutionalizes a prejudiced world view that results in harm to lesbian and gay clients.

Kohlberg said that the dominant stage of moral reasoning in American adults is stage 4, the law and order stage. It is not until the mid 20s or early 30s that a few people reach stage 5, where they begin to wrestle with ideas of justice that may supersede the norms of their society (Crain, 1985; Kohlberg, Levine, & Hewer, 1983; Kohlberg & Lickona, 1976). The capacity to step outside of your beliefs is critical to reaching a higher moral reasoning stage and the ability to practice in accordance with ethical professional guidelines that urge respect for the dignity of all clients. Many of you may find that you cannot suspend your own moral or religious judgments about these clients. If you are unable to see lesbian and gay clients as people who are not defective or somehow less deserving, you should not be in your professional practice (Greene, 2007).

Competencies needed to work effectively with lesbian and gay clients have been identified (Bieschke et al., 2007; Israel, Ketz, Detrie, Burke, & Shulman, 2003). The top three are: absence of any strong personal convictions that same-sex attractions are immoral, wrong, or evil, or should be changed; a nonheterosexist attitude; and comfort with and acceptance of same-sex intimacy. You must also be explicit in your affirmation of gay and lesbian people. The environment where services are provided must also be affirmative (Matthews, Selvidge, & Fisher 2005).

Transformation Stages

We will follow the stage model developed by Prochaska and DiClemente (1986) and addressed by Tyler, Jackman-Wheitner, Strader, and Lenox (1997) and others. The four stages are (1) precontemplative, (2) contemplation, (3) action, and (4) maintenance. According to Prochaska and DiClemente, the important factor in whether interventions will affect you is your readiness to change.

While some of you are prepared to change, others are at the precontemplative stage and unaware of a need to change. If you are one of these people, you do not understand or acknowledge that your current behavior and attitudes have a negative impact on people who are not heterosexual. You do not experience emotional reactions to the negative aspects of your attitudes and behaviors. You are, therefore, not motivated to make any attempts to change your attitudes and behaviors. For those of you who are open to change at this stage, you may be most impacted by your experiences here. The goal is for all of you to modify the perspective that supports your current heterosexist attitudes and behaviors and to shift to a new perspective. This is a task of growth and development.

Each session will take about two hours. The format will include information given by the facilitator on various topics. Experiential activities are the major activity and will take place in most sessions. Discussion will be asked for after each informational presentation and activity, as well as at the beginning of each session. You will fill out a pre- and post-evaluation, and you will be asked to give your reaction to each session.

Questions to Answer at the Beginning and End of the Program

You will be asked to answer a set of questions at the beginning of the training and again at the end. The questions include the following: Are there a variety of equally acceptable alternatives regarding sexual orientation? Is heterosexuality preferable? Do you place limits on those who do not identify as heterosexual? Limits could include careers, parenting, or other areas in which lesbian and gay people have been discriminated against. Do you fully embrace removal of "homosexuality" as a mental illness by the American Psychiatric Association and your profession, or do you still think lesbian and gay people are mentally ill or unstable? Do you think being lesbian or gay is shameful or sinful (Matthews, 2007)?

Reaction Papers

You will also be asked to turn in a reaction paper at the beginning of each session starting with the second session. You are asked to respond to the following questions:

- ❧ *Fact*: What did the session say to you?

- ❧ *Meaning*: What did it mean to you?

- ❧ *Concretizing*: Give concrete examples of how you could apply the ideas or principles in your work setting.

- ❧ *Congruence*: How did the session fit with your beliefs, feelings, and values—your view of the world? It is disconfirming or confirming information? Explain.

- ❧ *Response*: What was of most importance to you in the session? What actions do you want to take?

At the beginning of sessions 1–5, reaction papers will be read to the group.

In addition between each session (1–5) perform an "I intend" behavior. On a blank sheet of paper, write one lesbian- and gay-affirmative action you promise to take before the next session (Finkel, Storaasli, Bandele, & Schaefer, 2003). You will be asked to report during the next session on what you did and how it felt to do it.

Session 1

This session focuses on your beliefs and attitudes about lesbian and gay people. It is critical to perform an honest self-examination of your attitudes and beliefs regarding sexual orientation (Haldeman & Buhrke, 2000). The Riddle (1996) Homophobia Scale will show you where you line up in terms of your beliefs about lesbian and gay people. Check the category you are in. Discuss with the group how you think you got to the place on the scale you are at and where you would like to move to and why.

Riddle Homophobia Scale

1. *Repulsion:* At this level, "homosexuality" is seen as a crime against nature. Lesbian and gay people are seen as sick, crazy, immoral, sinful, and wicked. Anything is considered justified to change them: prison, hospitalization, behavior therapy, violence, etc.

2. *Pity:* At this level, people consider heterosexuality more mature and certainly preferable. They believe that any possibility of becoming heterosexual should be reinforced and that those who say they were born lesbian or gay should be pitied.

3. *Tolerance:* At this level, "homosexuality" is considered to be just a phase of adolescent development that many people go through and most people grow out of. Thus, lesbian and gay people are considered less mature than heterosexuals and treated with the protectiveness and indulgence one uses with a child. They are not considered appropriate candidates for positions of authority because they are seen as still working through immature behavior.

4. *Acceptance:* People at this level work to accept lesbian and gay people and may make statements such as "you're not a lesbian, you're a person," "what you do is your own business," or "it's fine with me, just don't flaunt it."

5. *Support:* At this level, people work to safeguard the rights of lesbian and gay people. They may be uncomfortable personally with lesbian and gay people, but they are aware of the heterosexist climate and irrational unfairness lesbian and gay people face.

6. *Admiration:* At this level, people acknowledge that being lesbian or gay in our society takes strength. They are willing to truly examine their heterosexist attitudes, values, and behaviors.

7. *Appreciation:* People at this level value human diversity and see lesbian and gay people as a valid part of that diversity. They are willing to combat heterosexism in themselves and others.

8. *Nurturance:* At this level, people assume that lesbian and gay people are indispensable in our society. They view them with genuine affection and delight and are willing to be allies and advocates for them.

Questions

What are your beliefs and attitudes about lesbian and gay people? What are your beliefs and attitudes about developing lesbian- and gay-affirmative beliefs, emotions, and behaviors (Dillon et al., 2004)? Discuss your answers with the group.

Fears and Wants

Here is a blank card. Write the word "fears" on one side and "wants" on the other side. Write down three fears you have about working with lesbian and gay clients and three things you want regarding lesbian and gay clients. The cards will be redistributed around the room randomly. Then each of you will introduce yourself and read out loud what is written on the card you received. The responses will be recorded on the blackboard or on large sheets of paper under the two headings. We will then discuss the fears and wants you have when working with lesbian and gay clients (adapted from Blumenfeld, 1992).

How You Arrived at Your Beliefs about Lesbian and Gay People

Record the history of your beliefs and feelings toward same-sex sexual identities. Describe how you felt when you first became aware of your attitudes toward lesbian and gay people. When did you first become aware of terms such as "queer," "fag," "homo," and "dyke"? When and how did you first meet a lesbian or gay person? What was your reaction? What do you think were the sources of your feelings and beliefs? What messages about lesbian and gay people do you recall hearing from parents, teachers, peers, religious leaders, and others in your community? Share your histories with each other in a discussion. This can help us understand how cultural values influence individual attitudes (American Psychological Association Task Force, 1998).

At the end of every session, these questions will be asked of the participants:

- ❧ What have you learned so far?

- ❧ What questions do you have?

- ❧ What do you want to change? (Zuckerman & Simons, 1996)

- ❧ What did you notice?

- ❧ What did you think or feel? (Kocarek & Pelling, 2003)

- ❧ What were your reactions to intellectual, emotional, and physical experiences during this session? (Lidderdale, 2002)

Session 2

This session also includes early learning about lesbian and gay people and comments they have heard about these people. In addition it focuses on stereotypes, myths, and biases.

Read reaction papers and I intend papers to the group. Discuss.

One-Minute Answers to Questions

Divide into pairs. Ask one of the following questions, and then take turns answering the question in one minute while the other person listens. Find another partner and repeat the process.

- ❧ How did you learn that you were expected to be heterosexual?

- ❧ What is the first time you learned that there was a sexual orientation other than heterosexual?

- ❧ What do you remember about the time when you first learned about lesbian and gay people?

- ❧ What did you hear about lesbian and gay people?

- ❧ From what sources did you learn about lesbian and gay people?

List on the board what students learned from each other regarding their early learning about lesbian and gay people, sources of the learning, and ways they were taught they should be heterosexual.

Other Enquiries

Name and write all the words (positive, negative, or neutral) you have heard to describe anyone considered to be lesbian or gay.

Talk about and write down some of the statements and comments you have heard about lesbian and gay people at school or college, on television, in other media, at work, or in other places.

Describe what lesbian and gay people have in common with you (Foreman & Quinlan, 2008).

Stereotypes

Examples of stereotypes about gay and lesbian people include that they are child molesters; that lesbians want to be men and gay men want to be women; that same-sex relationships never last; and that a good sexual experience with a heterosexual can turn lesbian and gay people into heterosexuals (Chen-Hayes, 1997).

What are your reactions to this list of stereotypes? Which are the most familiar to you? What do you know about how you learned these stereotypes? Do you now question any of them? Did any of you know lesbian or gay people while growing up? What did you learn from them that counters these stereotypes?

Add additional stereotypes that you have heard to this list.

What did you learn from this exercise about stereotypes and how we are socialized into our beliefs about sexual identity? What did you learn about what you think is acceptable or not acceptable to think about lesbian and gay people? Have you learned anything that dispels any of the stereotypes that you previously learned (Blumenfeld, 1992; Griffin & Harro, 1997)?

Myths about Lesbian and Gay People

Myths, or falsehoods and misconceptions, about lesbian and gay people include the following:

- Lesbian and gay people can be identified by their mannerisms or physical characteristics.

- Lesbian and gay people have made a conscious decision to be nonheterosexual.

- Being lesbian or gay is a psychological disorder that can be cured by psychotherapy.

- In lesbian and gay relationships, one partner usually plays the husband or "butch" role and the other plays the wife or "femme" role.

- Lesbian and gay people are bad parents.

- Lesbian and gay people are obsessed with sex and sexually compulsive.

- Being lesbian or gay means you have mental health problems.

Every one of these myths is false. What else have you heard that you know to be untrue about lesbian and gay people (Foreman & Quinlan, 2008)?

Biases

What words and images do you have when you hear the words "lesbian" and "gay"? Reflect on situations in which you have experienced biases from others about you. How did this make you feel? How did it affect your interaction with the other person (Turner et al., 2006)?

What are some ways you can overcome stereotypes, myths, and biases? Ask these questions for participant response.

- ❀ What have you learned so far?

- ❀ What questions do you have?

- ❀ What do you want to change? (Zuckerman & Simons, 1996)

- ❀ What did you notice?

- ❀ What did you think or feel? (Kocarek & Pelling, 2003)

- ❀ What were your reactions to intellectual, emotional, and physical experiences during this session? (Lidderdale, 2002)

Session 3

The goal in this session is to establish an accurate picture of the complexity of sexual identity. This may be done by using multidimensional assessments of the degrees of emotional and erotic attractions toward men and women; the range of sexual fantasies, behaviors, values, gender roles, and identity preferences; and the duration and changes in intensities of these experiences over time (Beckstead & Israel, 2007). The facilitator will discuss how complex human sexual identity is compared to the either/or categories that we learned. How does the material contradict what you have learned? In addition, there will be a speaker's panel of lesbian and gay people, and role playing of lesbian and gay people

Read reaction papers and I intend papers to the group. Discuss.

Kinsey Continuum of Sexual Identity

Hand out a copy of the Kinsey Continuum of Sexual Identity. Ask participants: Place yourself on the continuum, considering fantasies, dreams, thoughts, sexual activity, and emotions or feelings. Reflect on the fact that rarely do individuals fit into either end of the continuum. Kinsey's continuum model of sexuality was one of the first challenges to the idea that there were two clear-cut categories of people: heterosexual or homosexual (Parker 2007). Kinsey's work questioned the notion that individuals were exclusively heterosexual or "homosexual" by creating a classification system that placed individuals along a continuum.

Kinsey Continuum of Sexual Identity

Psychologically responds and behaves:

0 exclusively toward other gender

1 predominantly toward other gender; incidentally toward same gender

2 predominantly toward other gender; more than incidentally toward same gender

3 equally toward other and same gender

4 predominantly toward same gender

5 predominantly toward same gender; incidentally toward other gender

6 exclusively toward same gender (Kinsey, Pomeroy, & Martin, 1948)

Klein Grid

Introduce the Klein Grid (Klein, Sepekoff, & Wolf, 1985), which was developed after Kinsey's work and contains more dimensions. (This widely used tool is readily available online [see, for example, http://kleingridonline.com/].)

The Klein Grid takes in seven dimensions:

1. sexual attraction

2. sexual behavior

3. sexual fantasies

4. emotional preference

5. social preference

6. lifestyle preference, and

7. self-identification.

Respondents provide information about themselves in all categories for three time periods:

1. the past,

2. the present, and

3. the ideal (a transtemporal category comprising what a respondent would most prefer).

Ask participants to identify themselves on the seven dimensions over three time periods.

Then ask:

- ❦ What did you learn from the Kinsey Continuum and the Klein Grid?

- ❦ How does it confirm or contradict your understanding of sexual identity?

- ❦ How does it affect how you now understand sexual identity?

(In addition to online sources and Klein et al., 1985, the Klein Grid can be found in Griffin & Harro, 1997.)

Speakers Panel

A panel of lesbian and gay people will ask you to see the world from their perspective. They will invite you to listen to them and interact with them. They will talk about their experiences such as coming out and making disclosures (Kahn, 2006).

Role-Playing

You are asked to assume the roles of lesbian and gay people in various scenarios. The purpose is to press you to identify with the struggles and prejudices that lesbian and gay people face daily in a heterosexist society. During this role play, you may consider for the first time how prejudice and discrimination affects them. Among many role-play possibilities are various forms of victimization such as name-calling and rejecting someone who has made a disclosure. Participants could also role-play situations that have come up in practice with lesbian and gay clients (Hunter, 1998; Lidderdale, 2002).

Ask these questions for participant response.

- ❦ What have you learned so far?

- ❦ What questions do you have?

- ❦ What do you want to change? (Zuckerman & Simons, 1996)

- ❦ What did you notice?

- ❦ What did you think or feel? (Kocarek & Pelling, 2003)

- ❦ What were your reactions to intellectual, emotional, and physical experiences during this session? (Lidderdale, 2002)

Session 4

This session focuses on developing empathy with lesbian and gay people. Read reaction papers and I intend papers to the group. Discuss.

Guided Imagery

Emert and Milburn (1997) provided an example of a guided imagery experience. Imagine yourselves waking up one morning as a lesbian or gay person. Imagine the fears that arise as a result of this discovery. Explore situations such as an incident of overt discrimination, interacting in a social setting, or making disclosures. The goals of guided imagery activities are empathy and sensitivity. A second guided imagery exercise involves imagining having a same-sex relationship. What does the person look like? How does he or she respond? What is it like to experience a sexual relationship with this person?

Walk a Mile in My Shoes

Coming out can result in the loss of significant relationships, social affiliations, career position, and financial standing (Rotheram-Borus & Fernandez, 1995). Most of us have experienced loss in one form or another. Tear a sheet of paper into 16 equal pieces. Divide them into four piles representing people, roles, possessions, and activities. Write down on the separate pieces of paper the names of four people you care about, four life roles, four possessions, and four activities that are special and central to your current life.

Turn the papers over. Pick one paper from each group and crumple it and throw it to the floor without looking at it. Don't turn the other papers over. When you act on heterosexist beliefs you are unaware of the devastation it creates.

Move among participants and take some papers. Take all the papers from some participants, a few from others, and none at all from others. Return to one from whom you have not taken anything, and take all of that person's papers. Crumple them and throw them on the floor (Schreier & Werden, 2000). Discuss what this exercise shows about loss. Ask: What do you feel about the losses that lesbian and gay people experience?

Empathy Development

Have participants close their eyes. Read a number of scenarios in which they are asked to imagine they are a lesbian or gay person (Turner et al., 2006).

Reverse Questionnaire

Imagine how your immediate environment would be different if heterosexuals were the minority group. This will help you understand the breadth and depth of our heterosexual culture and its pervasive influence on all aspects of our lives. It also prompts you to begin thinking about the kind of questions that are frequently asked of lesbian and gay people that are not asked of heterosexual people. Examples of such questions are: What do you think caused your heterosexuality? Is it possible that your heterosexuality is a phase you will grow out of? If you never slept with a person of the same sex, it is possible that all you need is a good lesbian or gay lover? To whom have your disclosed your heterosexual tendencies? Why do you insist on flaunting your heterosexuality? Why do heterosexuals place so much emphasis on sex (Obear, 1989)? Discuss with the group your reactions to this exercise.

Are You or Aren't You?

Here are facedown cards that read gay, lesbian, or heterosexual. Take one, and assume that identity. Divide into pairs. For two minutes, discuss imaginary weekend activities you participated in. Do not mention the sex or name of any significant other with whom you shared the weekend. After two minutes, switch to a new partner and repeat the exercise. In each round, note the names of the person with whom you talk, whether you thought the identity that person assumed was lesbian, gay, or heterosexual, and why.

After several rounds, assemble the group, ask participants to share what they noted during the exercise, and record this information on the board. Lead a discussion about how stereotypes and faulty beliefs influence interpersonal interactions. Ask: What did you discover about your own beliefs and attitudes and how they affect others? What changes do you perceive in your beliefs and attitudes as a result of this experience? What changes do you want to make (Schreier & Werden, 2000)?

Ask these questions for participant response.

- What have you learned so far?

- What questions do you have?

- What do you want to change? (Zuckerman & Simons, 1996)

- What did you notice?

- What did you think or feel? (Kocarek & Pelling, 2003)

- What were your reactions to intellectual, emotional, and physical experiences during this session? (Lidderdale, 2002)

Session 5

This session also has some empathy exercises and ones on how one thinks about lesbian and gay people. One is challenged to think about how their behaviors and attitude create problems for lesbian and gay people and what are they willing to do about this.

Read reaction papers and I intend statements to the group. Discuss.

Contemplative Stage

At this stage, you should be aware of a problem situation and you may be willing to consider your behaviors and attitudes in relation to the problem. Here the need to question yourself becomes increasingly important. This is the stage we referred to at the beginning of this training as the contemplative stage.

Are you aware of how your behaviors and attitudes create a problem for lesbian and gay clients? How does it do this? What do you want to do about it?

Continuum Activity

Using cardboard pieces with numbers written on them, lay out a scale of 1 to 10 on the floor of the room. Consider your personal reactions to a series of questions and rate your response on a scale of 1 (very little) to 10 (very much). Move to that number on the floor and comment briefly on your choice. An example of a question is: How much do you value having friends of varying sexual orientations?

Prompted by different questions, people will likely move to different places on the scale. It is helpful to begin with questions that require an evaluation of one's values and beliefs and later move to questions that evaluate specific behaviors (Hunter, 1998).

Four Corners

Post a sign in each corner of the room stating "strongly agree," "agree," "disagree," and "strongly disagree." Read statements about lesbian and gay people and ask group members to stand in the corner that represents their response.

Examples of statements include "I want to be friends with a lesbian or gay person" and "My thinking about lesbian and gay people is getting more positive." Ask groups in each corner to argue for their statement and listen to the arguments from the other groups.

Repeat with several statements (Turner et al., 2006).

Modified Think-Aloud Protocol

This activity involves reading a brief vignette that describes a situation that a lesbian or gay person might encounter. Quickly write down the thoughts you had during the reading. Then evaluate your responses as evaluative, information seeking, or emotional. This activity clarifies automatic thoughts that may not be in awareness. Open the process to group discussion (Hunter, 1998).

Ask these questions for participant response.

- ❧ What have you learned so far?

- ❧ What questions do you have?

- ❧ What do you want to change? (Zuckerman & Simons, 1996)

- ❧ What did you notice?

- ❧ What did you think or feel? (Kocarek & Pelling, 2003)

- ❧ What were your reactions to intellectual, emotional, and physical experiences during this session? (Lidderdale, 2002)

Session 6

The stage is probably the most difficult, because it involves attempts at new behaviors and attitudes and commitments to action. Meaningful change can occur only in your life outside of the program experience. The components essential to change can be developed, however, even though what happens later may not be observed except in human services jobs.

Action Stage

First, identify specific changes you desire in your personal thoughts and behaviors or changes in your work environment. Then develop action plans for follow-up practice. You can work in a group with similar goals (Prochaska & DiClemente,1986).

Part of this strategy is to identify your desired behaviors; environmental factors that will support your new behaviors, such as being allies with and advocates for lesbian and gay people; and environmental factors that will obstruct the new behaviors, such as pressure from family members, colleagues, or others to maintain old attitudes and behaviors (Prochaska & DiClemente,1986).

Maintenance Stage

Gaining a sense that behaviors, thoughts, and feelings are more congruent is important in the maintenance stage (Prochaska, Norcross, & DiClemente, 1994). In addition, it is crucial that you experience a personal sense that you are developing into the kind of person you want to be. This leads to an increased sense of personal value and of being valued by others. Support for maintaining new attitudes and behaviors can be found in community groups such as PFLAG and Metropolitan Community Church congregations. There are also many opportunities for volunteer work. Within the social work profession, you can attend meetings of the lesbian and gay committees of NASW and CSWE.

Tyler et al. (1997) emphasized that it is important for you to engage yourselves in an ongoing evaluation process where you compare earlier beliefs, values, and actions related to lesbian and gay people with where you are now. Awareness of successful growth experiences tends to generate an ongoing growth process. You should track changes in the statements you make about lesbian and gay people, and in your thoughts, feelings, and behaviors.

Answer Questions Given at the Beginning of the Training

Answer again the set of questions you answered at the beginning of the training. Your answers will be compared to the answers you gave then. The questions include the following: Are there a variety of equally acceptable alternatives regarding sexual orientation? Is heterosexuality preferable? Do you place limits on those who do not identify as heterosexual? Limits could include careers, parenting or other areas in which lesbian and gay people have been discriminated against. Do you fully embrace removal of "homosexuality" as a mental illness by the American Psychiatric Association and your profession, or do you still think lesbian and gay people are mentally ill or unstable? Or, do you think being lesbian or gay is shameful or sinful (Matthews, 2007)?

Differences among people at the various stages are useful in selecting interventions, but it may also be possible to address participants who are at different stages as a group. Self-reflective activity, or self-evaluation, which is part of the maintenance level, may also benefit people at earlier stages. Similarly, people at all levels can develop action plans, although they will contain different goals.

This model is dynamic and cyclical. Participants may move through all of the stages many times or you may be asked to repeat the stages if progress has not been satisfactory. You will be provided with resources, such as organizations, Web sites, and articles, that you can consult to help you better serve your lesbian and gay clients with regard to coming out, forming clubs, addressing harassment, and finding support (Kahn, 2006). Practitioners also need opportunities to practice skills through additional role-playing (Kocarek & Pelling, 2003).

Other Assignments for the Maintenance Stage

Becoming an Ally: Write a short paper to turn in on how you can develop as an ally of lesbian and gay people (Lidderdale, 2007).

Promise Statement: Write down and sign a promise that you will not use any derogatory language toward sexual minorities and that you will affirm the identities of lesbian and gay people; provide resources that help them accept their sexual orientation rather than try to change it; and keep negative heterosexist and religious beliefs out of your interactions with them (Kahn, 2006). Describe your goals in becoming an affirmative practitioner and how you will know when you have reached them.

Maintenance Through One's Supervisor

Follow-up activities with group participants are necessary, along with cooperation from supervisors at their jobs to help them integrate their new views at their agency (Turner et al., 2006).

Supervisors must be supportive and create a safe environment for those in their agency who went through the training, just as, during the training, the facilitator must model respect for all participants. The supervisor should create an affirmative environment for discussion of attitudes and biases. This requires a thorough understanding of lesbian and gay issues and self-exploration. The supervisor's openness about his or her own self-exploration and understanding of affirmative practice allows supervisees to be open in discussing their views. They can also talk about the preparation they went through for work with lesbian and gay clients in which they had to explore their biases.

Participants' supervisors can continue to advise them after the training ends on how to be culturally competent practitioners. They can assess practitioners and their skills and competencies in working with lesbian and gay clients, as well as deficits and areas where growth is needed. The goal is to provide sensitive affirmative practice. Affirmative supervision plays a key role in preparing practitioners who have had this training and others at the agency to become culturally competent with lesbian and gay clients (Halpert et al., 2007).

Affirmative Agency Environment

Environments both for lesbian and gay clients and for service providers should also be affirmative. Participants should encourage their agencies to develop agency policies and procedures to challenge heterosexism. The organizational climate should also change, as the climate in which practitioners work is predictive of the degree to which individual practitioners practice affirmatively (Bieschke & Matthews, 1996). Individual practitioners can help to create such a climate. It should convey affirmation to all clients regardless of how they identify themselves.

An office can say a lot to lesbian and gay clients. Something as simple as a rainbow button pinned to a bulletin board can tell the client looking for signs of safety that the practitioner has made a conscious effort to communicate affirmation. Agencies can create a climate that communicates affirmation through policies and practices (Eldridge & Barnett, 1991). Forms should reflect that some clients may be in permanent relationships that do not legally qualify as marriages. Reading material in the waiting room should include publications of interest to the lesbian and gay population. Practitioners should know resources in the community and should have materials specific to each group within the lesbian and gay community as well as on the community as a whole (Matthews, 2007). The books on practitioners' shelves tell visitors something about the areas in which they have sought to educate themselves and whether they have taken time to learn something about their clients' experiences (Matthews, 2007).

Practitioners should also communicate affirmation within their relationships with clients. Use language that does not assume heterosexuality. Allow clients to define themselves and discuss what the definition means to them. In some cultural contexts, clients do not identify as gay even if their sexual relations are exclusively with people of the same sex. This is not denial but reflects a cultural context. To become better able to grasp nuances, read books, watch movies, and visit the lesbian and gay community and its events. Become involved with a local lesbian and gay community center or agency (Matthews, 2007).

Research on Interventions with Practitioners

Israel and Hackett (2004) did a rare study using an experimental design involving two types of training: provision of information and attitude exploration. The design established four conditions: attitude exploration only, information only, combined training (both information and attitude exploration), and a control condition (no information or attitude exploration). This design allowed for the evaluation of the separate and unique effects of providing information and exploring attitudes as well as the effect of combining the two.

The participants who received information only were more knowledgeable at posttest than were participants who did not receive information, even after only one session. The results of attitude exploration were opposite of the expected results: Participants who underwent the attitude exploration reported more negative cognitive attitudes afterward than participants who did not undergo this training. A likely explanation for this is that those in the attitude-exploration group were challenged to assess their actual feelings about lesbian, gay, and bisexual people. They may have experienced some discomfort in having their attitudes challenged, whereas those in the information-only and control groups were not challenged and remained positive. Those undergoing attitude exploration may have gone beyond surface responses and recognized the underlying negative attitudes that they held. Perhaps this is a necessary step toward more meaningful exploration of change in attitudes, but this study did not shed light on this hypothesis.

In-depth training may be necessary to have an impact on attitudes. Future studies could compare the effects of different information content or different approaches to attitude change on knowledge, attitudes, and practitioner development qualitatively; studies that are longer or use multiple training interventions could also help identify the conditions necessary for changes in attitudes. In addition, a behavioral evaluation of practitioner competence could capture in future studies what is not evident from paper-and-pencil attitude measures. Such endeavors can contribute to the creation of empirically sound training models for practitioners and consequently more effective and affirmative services for lesbian and gay clients.

In the training described in this chapter, practitioners were challenged to assess their attitudes toward lesbian and gay people, and that probably does cause discomfort. The purpose of bombarding the participants with many attitude exercises is to get them to identify their negative views and the effects of those views on lesbian and gay clients. The training takes about six weeks, so participants have time to process what they are going through. How they answered questions at the end of each stage and in the action stage lets trainers know if progress is being made. The before and after questions, as well as answers to questions turned in each week, are useful to assess changes.

Measures of programming efficacy should achieve two primary goals (Drum, 1984). The first is validating the extent to which intended outcomes were obtained. The second is identifying what elements of the program contributed to the achievement of intended outcomes. For example, did heterosexist beliefs change, and if so, what aspects of the program contributed to those changes? On an individual level, variables can be measured to determine successful outcomes.

A systemic-level impact on policies, procedures, and incidents of heterosexism can be assessed. Self-report measures can be highly effective in measuring pre- and postprogramming attitudes and beliefs and overall satisfaction with the program (Lennon, Maloney, Miller, Wright, & Chambliss, 1997). Various scales are available for this. For example, for assessing levels of heterosexist attitudes and beliefs, one can use the Modified Attitudes toward Homosexuality Scale (Price, 1982) and the Affective Reactions to Homosexuality Scale (Innala & Ernulf, 1987).

Clearly, there is a need for more research on the use of programming such as that described in this chapter (Garnets & D'Augelli, 1994).

Summary

This chapter focused on transforming practitioners with negative views toward lesbian and gay people. Some will not want to participate because they see nothing wrong with their views, but participation is mandatory. Those open to change are invited to move further. Participants go through various exercises. Sessions before reaching the maintenance stage are the longest, with many exercises that focus on identifying attitudes, biases, myths, and stereotypes and developing empathy. The last session focuses on action plans and maintenance. At the core of this session is an assessment of what kind of person participants now want to be. They are encouraged to continue to track their changes in their agencies and to work on making the agency and their office more affirmative and inviting for lesbian and gay clients.

Few studies have identified what works to change attitudes. It appears that addressing attitudes, although uncomfortable, is necessary. This training does that. The length of this program allows participants time to think about what they have been through and where they want to go during the training and afterward.

References

Abelson, R. P. (1986). Beliefs are like possessions. *Journal for the Theory of Social Behavior, 16,* 223–250.

Ajzen, I., & Fishbein, M. (1980). *Understanding attitudes and predicting social behavior.* Englewood Cliffs, NJ: Prentice-Hall.

Allen, D. J., & Oleson, T. (1999). Shame and internalized homophobia in gay men. *Journal of Homosexuality, 37,* 33–43.

Almazan, E. P. (2007). *Sexual orientation, social structure, and adolescent mental health.* Unpublished doctoral dissertation, Indiana University, Bloomington.

Altemeyer, B. (2003). Why do religious fundamentalists tend to be prejudiced? *International Journal of Psychology of Religion, 13,* 17–28.

Altemeyer, B., & Hunsberger, B. (1992). Authoritarianism, religious fundamentalism, quest, and prejudice. *International Journal of Psychology of Religion, 2,* 113–133.

American Psychiatric Association. (1973). *Diagnostic and statistical manual of mental disorders* (2nd ed.). Washington, DC: Author.

American Psychiatric Association. (1980). *Diagnostic and statistical manual of mental disorders* (3rd ed.). Washington, DC: Author.

American Psychiatric Association. (1987). *Diagnostic and statistical manual of mental disorders* (3rd ed., rev). Washington, DC: Author.

American Psychiatric Association. (1994). *Diagnostic and statistical manual of mental disorders* (4th ed.). Washington, DC: Author.

American Psychiatric Association. (2000). *Diagnostic and statistical manual of mental disorders* (4th ed., text rev.). Washington, DC: Author.

American Psychiatric Association. (2000). *Therapies focused on attempts to change sexual orientation (reparative or conversion therapies).* Retrieved from http://www.psych.org/Departments/EDU/Library/APAOfficialDocumentsandRelated/PositionStatements/200001.aspx

American Psychological Association. (1998). Appropriate therapeutic responses to sexual orientation. *American Psychologist, 53,* 882–939.

American Psychological Association. (2002). Ethical principles of psychologists and code of conduct. *American Psychologist, 57,* 1060–1073.

American Psychological Association Task Force. (1998, April). American Psychological Association's Task Force on Diversity Issues at the Precolleage and Undergraduate Levels of Education in Psychology. *Monitor on Psychology, 29,* 39.

Anderson, D. A. (1994). Lesbian and gay adolescents: Social and developmental considerations. *High School Journal, 77,* 13–19.

Androutsopoulou, A. (2001a). Fiction as an aid to therapy: A narrative and family rationale for practice. *Journal of Family Therapy, 23,* 278–295.

Androutsopoulou, A. (2001b). The self-characterization as a narrative tool: Applications in therapy with individuals and families. *Family Process, 40,* 79–94.

Atkinson, D. R., & Hackett, G. (1998). *Counseling diverse populations* (2nd ed.). Boston: McGraw-Hill.

Barret, R., & Barzan, R. (1996). Spiritual experiences of gay men and lesbians. *Counseling and Values, 41,* 4–15.

Barzan, B. (1995). Reinhabiting: Finding love in nature. In B. Barzan (Ed.), *Sex and spirit: Exploring gay men's spirituality* (pp. 123–129). San Francisco: White Crane.

Bassett, R. L., Baldwin, D., Tammaro, J., Mackmer, D., Mundig, C., Wareing, A., & Tschorke, D. (2001). Reconsidering intrinsic religion as a source of universal compassion. *Journal of Psychology and Theology, 30,* 131–143.

Batson, C. D., Floyd, R. B., Meyer, J. M., & Winner, A. L. (1999). And who is my neighbor? Intrinsic religion as a source of universal compassion. *Journal for the Scientific Study of Religion, 38,* 445–458.

Baumgartner, L. M., (2001). An update on transformational learning. *New Directions for Adult and Continuing Education, 89,* 15–24.

Beck, A. T., & Alford, B. A. (2008). *Depression: Causes and treatment* (2nd ed.). Philadelphia: University of Pennsylvania Press.

Becker, R., & Knox, H. (2009, December/2010, January). Mormon Church backs anti-discrimination laws. *Empty Closet,* 8A.

Beckstead, A. L. (2002). Cures versus choices: Agendas in sexual reorientation therapy. *Journal of Gay & Lesbian Psychotherapy, 5,* 87–115.

Beckstead, A. L., & Israel, T. (2007). Affirmative counseling and psychotherapy focused on issues related to sexual orientation conflicts. In K. J. Bieschke, R. M. Perez, & K. A. DeBord (Eds.), *Handbook of counseling and psychotherapy with lesbian, gay, bisexual, and transgender clients* (pp. 221–224). Washington, DC: American Psychological Association.

Beckstead, A. L., & Morrow, S. L. (2004). Mormon clients' experiences of conversion therapy: The need for a new treatment approach. *Counseling Psychologist, 32,* 651–669.

Beckwith, H. D. (2007). Risky behavior in college students: The influence of religiosity and spirituality. *Dissertation Abstracts International 67* (10), 6045B.

Ben-Ari, A. T. (2001). Homosexuality and heterosexism—Views from academics in the helping professions. *British Journal of Social Work, 31,* 119–131.

Bennett, L. (1998). *Mixed blessings: Organized religion and gay and lesbian Americans in 1998.* Washington, DC: Human Rights Campaign Foundation.

Benoit, M. (2005). Conflict between religious commitment and same-sex attraction: Possibilities for virtuous response. *Ethics and Behavior, 15,* 309–325.

Berger, B. M. (1981). *The survival of a counterculture: Ideological work and everyday life among rural communards.* Berkley: University of California Press.

Berger, P. (1967). *The sacred canopy: Elements of a sociological theory of religion.* New York: Anchor Books.

Bergin, A. E. (1991). Values and religious issues in psychotherapy and mental health. *American Psychologist, 46,* 394–404.

Berkman, C., & Zinberg, J. G. (1997). Homophobia and heterosexism in social workers. *Social Work, 42,* 319–331.

Berzon, B. (1988). *Permanent partners: Building gay and lesbian relationships that last.* New York: E. P. Dutton.

Besen, W. R. (2003). *Anything but straight: Unmasking the scandals and lies behind the ex-gay myth.* Binghamton, NY: Harrington Park Press.

Bhurga, D. (1997). Coming out by South Asian gay men in the United Kingdom. *Archives of Sexual Behavior, 26,* 547–557.

Bidell, M. P. (2005). Counselor preparation: The Sexual Orientation Counselor Competency Scale: Assessing attitudes, skills, and knowledge of counselors working with lesbian, gay, and bisexual clients. *Counselor Education & Supervision, 44,* 267–279.

Bieschke, K. J., & Matthews, C. R. (1996). Career counselor attitudes and behaviors toward gay, lesbian, and bisexual clients. *Journal of Vocational Behavior, 48,* 243–255.

Bieschke, K. J., Paul, P. L., & Blasko, K. A. (2007). Review of empirical counseling and psychotherapy. In K. J. Bieschke, R. M. Perez, & K. A. DeBord (Eds.), *Handbook of counseling and psychotherapy with lesbian, gay, bisexual, and transgender clients* (2nd ed., pp. 293–315). Washington, DC: American Psychological Association.

Bing, V. M. (2004). Out of the closet but still in hiding: Conflicts and identity issues for a black–white biracial lesbian. *Women & Therapy, 27,* 185–201.

Blumenfeld, W. J. (1992). Conducting anti-heterosexism workshops: A sample. In W. J. Blumenfeld (Ed.), *Homophobia: How we all pay the price* (pp. 273–302). Boston: Beacon Press.

Boatwright. K. J., Gilbert, M. S., Forrest, L., & Ketzenberger, K. (1996). Impact of sexual identity development on career trajectory: Listening to the voices of lesbian women. *Journal of Vocational Behavior, 48,* 210–228.

Bohan, J. S. (1996). *Psychology and sexual orientation*. New York: Routledge.

Boisvert, D. (2007). Homosexuality and spirituality. In J. S. Siker (Ed.), *Homosexuality and religion: An encyclopedia* (pp. 32–44). Westport, CT: Greenwood Press.

Boswell, J. (1980). *Christianity, social tolerance and homosexuality: Gay people in western Europe from the beginning of the Christian era to the fourteenth century.* Chicago: University of Chicago Press.

Bradford, J., Ryan, C., & Rothblum, E. D. (1994). National Lesbian Health Care Survey: Implications for mental health care. *Journal of Consulting and Clinical Psychology, 62,* 228–242.

Brady, S., & Busse, W. J. (1994). The Gay Identity Questionnaire: A brief measure of homosexual identity formation. *Journal of Homosexuality, 26,* 1–22.

Brammer, R. (2004). *Diversity in counseling: Exploring gender and ethnic differences.* Pacific Grove, CA: Brooks/Cole.

Bringaze, T. B. (1998). *Factors contributing to success in the coming out process: A national survey of leaders in the lesbian community.* Unpublished doctoral dissertation, Department of Educational Psychology and Special Education, Southern Illinois University, Carbondale.

Brown, L. S. (1986). Confronting internalized oppression in sex therapy with lesbians. *Journal of Homosexuality, 12,* 99–107.

Brown, L. S. (1989). New voices, new visions: Toward a lesbian/gay paradigm for psychology. *Psychology of Women, 13,* 445–458.

Brown, L. S. (1995). Therapy with same-sex couples: An introduction. In N. S. Jacobson & A. S. Guttman (Eds.), *Clinical handbook of couple therapy* (pp. 274–291). New York: Guilford Press.

Brown, L. S. (1996). Ethical concerns with sexual minority patients. In R. P. Cabaj & T. S. Stein (Eds.), *Textbook of homosexuality and mental health* (pp. 897–916). Washington, DC: American Psychiatric Press.

Brown-Taylor, B. (2000). *Speaking of sin: The lost language of salvation.* Cambridge MA: Cowley Publications.

Bruff v. North Mississippi Health Services, Inc., 244 F.3d 495 (5th Cir. 2001).

Buchanan, M., Dzelme, K., Harris, D., & Hecker, L. (2001). Challenges of being simultaneously gay or lesbian and spiritual and/or religious: A narrative perspective. *American Journal of Family Therapy, 29,* 435–449.

Buisson-Fenet, H. (1999). *De la dissonance à l'esprit critique: Surquelques façons d' être clerc et homosexuel. Social Compass, 46,* 75–84.

Burdette, A. M., Ellison, C. G., & Hill, T. D. (2005). Conservative Protestantism and tolerance toward homosexuals: An examination of potential mechanisms. *Sociological Inquiry, 75,* 177–219.

Burns, D. (1990). *The feeling good handbook.* New York: Plume.

Burr, K. A. (2009). *Coming out, coming home: Making room for gay spirituality in therapy.* New York: Routledge.

Calhoun-Brown, A. (1996). African American churches and political mobilization: The psychological impact of organizational resources. *Journal of Politics, 58,* 935–953.

Cass, V. C. (1984). Homosexual identity formation: Testing a theoretical model. *Journal of Sex Research, 20,* 143–167.

Cass, V. C. (1996). Sexual orientation identity formation: A western phenomenon. In R. P. Cabaj & T. S. Stein (Eds.), *Textbook of homosexuality and mental health* (pp. 227–351). Washington, DC: American Psychiatric Press.

Chan, C. S. (1989). Issues of identity development among Asian-American lesbians and gay men. *Journal of Counseling and Development, 68,* 16–20.

Chan, C. S. (1992). Don't ask, don't tell, don't know: The formation of a homosexual identity and sexual expression among Asian American lesbians. In B. Greene (Ed.), *Ethnic and cultural diversity among lesbians and gay men* (pp. 240–248). Thousand Oaks, CA: Sage Publications.

Chen-Hayes, S. (1997). Counseling lesbian, bisexual, and gay persons in couple and family relationships: Overcoming the stereotypes. *Family Journal: Counseling and Therapy for Couples and Families, 5,* 236–240.

Chew, C. M. (1999). The relationship between religion and psychological adjustment in gay men and lesbians. *Dissertation Abstracts International, 60* (08), 4208B. (UMI No. 9942759)

Christian Lesbians Out Together. (n.d.). Retrieved from http://www.cloutsisters.org/home/

Church of Christ. (2008). *What does the word of God say about homosexuality?* Retrieved from http://church-of-christ.org/homosexuality.htm

Church of Jesus Christ of Latter-Day Saints. (n.d.). *Same-gender attraction.* Retrieved from http://new.lds.org/study/topics/same-gender-attraction?lang=eg

Clark, J. M. (1987). Special considerations in pastoral care of gay persons with AIDS. *Journal of Pastoral Counseling, 22,* 32–45.

Clark, J. M., Brown, J. C., & Hochstein, L. M. (1990). Institutional religion and gay/lesbian oppression. In F. W. Bozett & M. B. Sussman (Eds.), *Homosexuality and family relations* (pp. 265–284). Binghamton, NY: Haworth Press.

Cody, P. J., & Welch, P. L. (1997). Rural gay men in northern New England: Life experiences and coping styles. *Journal of Homosexuality, 33,* 51–67.

Cohler, B. J., Galatzer-Levy, R. M., Boxer, A., & Irvin, E. (2000). Adolescence and youth: Realizing gay and lesbian sexual identity. In *The course of gay and lesbian lives: Social and psychoanalytic perspectives* (pp. 144–192). Chicago: University of Chicago Press.

Conan, N. (2007). *The Episcopal Church and the rift over homosexuality* [Transcript]. Washington, DC: National Public Radio.

Cooper, J., & Fazio, R. (1984). A new look at cognitive dissonance theory. *Advances in Experimental Social Psychology, 17,* 299–265.

Corey, G. (2009). *Theory and practice of counseling and psychotherapy.* Belmont, CA: Thompson–Brooks/Cole.

Corey, G., Corey, M. S., & Callanan, P. (1998). *Issues and ethics in the helping professions* (4th ed.). Pacific Grove, CA: Brooks/Cole.

Crain, W. C. (1985). *Kohlberg's stage of moral development, theories of development.* New York: Prentice-Hall.

Cramer, E. P. (1997). Strategies for reducing social work student's homophobia. In J. T. Sears & W. L. Williams (Eds.), *Overcoming heterosexism and homophobia: Strategies that work* (pp. 287–298). New York: Columbia University Press.

Crawford, I., & Solliday, E. (1996). The attitudes of undergraduate college students toward gay parenting. *Journal of Homosexuality, 30,* 63–77.

Crisp, C. (2006). Correlates of homophobia and use of gay affirmative practice among social workers. *Journal of Human Behavior in the Social Environment, 14,* 119–143.

Crocker, J. (1995). Stigma. In A. Manstead & M. Hewstone (Eds.), *The Blackwell encyclopedia of social psychology* (pp. 633–634). Cambridge, MA: Blackwell.

Crocker, J., & Major, B. (1989). Social stigma and self-esteem: The self-protective properties of stigma. *Psychological Review, 96,* 608–630.

Croteau, J. M., & Kusek, M. T. (1992). Gay and lesbian speaker panels: Implementation and research. *Journal of Counseling and Development, 70,* 396–400.

Cummings, N. A., & Cummings, J. L. (2009). Psychology's war on Protestants is a one size fits all. In N. A. Cummings, W. T. O'Donohue, & J. L. Cummings (Eds.), *Psychology's war on religion* (pp. 47–171). Phoenix, AR: Zeig, Tucker & Theisen.

Cummings, N. A., O'Donohue, W. T., & Cummings, J. L. (Eds.) (2009). *Psychology's war on religion.* Phoenix, AZ: Zeig, Tucker & Theisen.

Cutts, R. N., & Parks, C. W. (2009). Religious involvement among black men self-labeling as gay. *Journal of Gay & Lesbian Social Services, 21,* 232–246.

Dahl, A. L., & Gallaher, R. V. (2009). LGBQQ young adult experiences of religion and sexual identity integration. *Journal of LGBT Issues in Counseling, 3,* 92–112.

D'Augelli, A. R. (1992). Teaching lesbian and gay development: From oppression to exceptionality. *Journal of Homosexuality, 22,* 213–227.

Davie, G. (1994). The religious factor in the emergence of Europe as a global region. *Social Compass, 41,* 95–112.

Decker, L. R. (1993). The role of trauma in spiritual development. *Journal of Humanistic Psychology, 33,* 33–44.

Deutsch, M., Coleman, P. T., & Marcus, E. C. (2006). *The handbook of conflict resolution: Theory and practice* (2nd ed.). San Francisco: Jossey-Bass.

Diamond, L. M. (2003). Was it a phase? Young women's relinquishment of lesbian/bisexual identities over a 5-year period. *Journal of Personality and Social Psychology, 84,* 352–364.

Diamond, S. (1998). *Not by politics alone: The enduring influence of the Christian right*. New York: Guilford Press.

Dillon, F. R., Worthington, R. L., Savoy, H. B., Rooney, S. C., Becker-Schutte, A., & Guerra, R. M. (2004). On becoming allies: A qualitative study of lesbian-, gay-, and bisexual-affirmative counselor training. *Counselor Education and Supervision, 43,* 162–178.

Divine Links. (2008). Retrieved from http://divine-links.net/NorthAmerica.aspx

Donnelly, S. (2001). *Building a new moral, religious, or spiritual identity: Perspective transformation in lesbian women.* Unpublished doctoral dissertation, Texas A&M University, College Station.

Dove, B. (2000). *Mormon Church won't budge on homosexuality.* Retrieved from http://www.beliefnet.com/Faiths/2001/01/Mormon-Church-Wont-Budge-On-Homosexuality.aspx?p=3

Drescher, J. (1998). I'm your handyman: A history of reparative therapies. *Journal of Homosexuality, 36,* 19–42.

Drum, D. J. (1984). Implementing theme-focused prevention: A challenge for the 1980's. *Personnel and Guidance Journal, 62,* 509–514.

Drumm, R. D. (2001). Gay and lesbian Seventh-Day Adventists: Strategies and outcomes of resisting homosexuality. *Social Work and Christianity: Journal of the National Association of Christians in Social Work, 28,* 124–140.

Duck, R. J., & Hunsberger, B. (1999). Religious orientation and prejudice: The role of religious proscription, right-wing authoritarianism and social desirability. *International Journal for the Psychology of Religion, 9,* 157–179.

Dufour, L. R. (2000). Sifting through tradition: The creation of Jewish feminist identities. *Journal of the Scientific Study of Religion, 39,* 90–106.

Dworkin, S. W. (1997). Female, lesbian and Jewish: Complex and invisible. In B. Greene (Ed.), *Ethnic and cultural diversity among lesbians and gay men* (pp. 63–87). Thousand Oaks, CA: Sage Publications.

Eldridge, N. J., & Barnett, D. C. (1991). Counseling gay and lesbian students. In N. J. Evans & V. A. Wall (Eds.), *Beyond tolerance: Gays, lesbians, and bisexual on campus* (pp. 147–178). Alexandria, VA: American College Personnel Association.

Emert, T., & Milburn, L. (1997). Sensitive supervisors, prepared practicum, and "queer" clients: A training model for beginning counselors. In J. T. Sears & W. L. Williams (Eds.), *Overcoming heterosexism and homophobia* (pp. 272–286). New York: Columbia University Press.

Emsberger, D. J., & Monaster, G. L. (1981). Moral development, intrinsic/extrinsic religious orientation, and denominational teaching. *Genetic Psychology Monographs, 104,* 23–41.

Endsjo, D. O. (2005). Lesbian, gay, bisexual, and transgender rights and the religious relativism of human rights. *Human Rights Review, 6,* 102–110.

English, F. (1996). The lure of fundamentalism. *Transactional Analysis, 26,* 23–30.

Englund, M. E. (1991). *The Bible and homosexuality*. Gaithersburg, MD: Chi Rho Press.

Enron, L. J. (1993). Homosexuality and Judaism. In A. Swindler (Ed.), *Homosexuality and world religions* (pp. 103–134). Valley Forge, PA: Trinity.

Evangelical Lutheran Church in America. (n.d.). *Lutheran roots in America: The historical origins of the Evangelical Lutheran Church in America*. Retrieved from http://www.elca.org/Who-We-Are/History/Lutheran-Roots-in-America.aspx

Fassinger, R. E. (2000). Applying counseling theories to lesbian, gay, and bisexual clients: Possibilities and pitfalls. In R. Perez, K. DeBord, & K. Bieschke (Eds.), *Handbook of counseling and psychotherapy with lesbians, gays, and bisexual clients* (pp. 107–132). Washington, DC: American Psychological Association.

Fassinger, R. E., & Richie, B. S. (1997). Sex matters: Gender and sexual orientation in training for multicultural counseling competence. In D. B. Pope-Davis & B. S. Richie (Eds.), *Multicultural counseling competencies: Assessment, education, training, and supervision* (pp. 83–110). Thousand Oaks, CA: Sage Publications.

Fellows of Research Institute. (2005, June 15). *Homosexuality: Your questions answered*. Retrieved from http://erlc.com/article/homosexuality-your-questions-answered/

Fellows, W. (1996). *Farm boys: Lives of gay men from the rural Midwest*. Madison: University of Wisconsin Press.

Fernandez, E. (1990, February 4). The ministry works to put gays straight. *San Francisco Examiner*, p. A1.

Festinger, L. (1957). *A theory of cognitive dissonance*. Stanford, CA: Stanford University Press.

Fetner, T. (2005). Ex-gay rhetoric and the politics of sexuality: The Christian antigay/profamily movement's "Truth in Love" ad campaign. *Journal of Homosexuality, 50,* 71–89.

Finkel, M. J., Storaasli, R. D., Bandele, A., & Schaefer, V. (2003). Diversity training in graduate school: An exploratory evaluation of the Safe Zone Project. *Professional Psychology: Research and Practice, 34,* 555–561.

Finlay, B. & Walther, C. S. (2003). The relation of religious affiliation, service attendance, and other factors to homophobic attitudes among university students. *Review of Religious Research, 44,* 370–393.

Fisher, A. R. & DeBord, K. A. (2007). Perceived conflicts between affirmation of religious diversity and affirmation of sexual diversity: That's perceived. In K. J. Bieschke, R. M. Perez, & K. A. DeBord (Eds.), *Handbook of counseling and psychotherapy with lesbian, gay, bisexual and transgender clients* (2nd ed., pp. 317–339). Washington, DC: American Psychological Association.

Fisher, R. D., Derison, D., Polley, C. F., III, Cadman, J., & Johnston, D. (1994). Religiousness, religious orientation, and attitudes toward gays and lesbians. *Journal of Applied Social Psychology, 24,* 614–630.

Folayan, A. (1992). African-American issues: The soul of it. In B. Berzon (Ed.), *Positively gay: New approaches to gay and lesbian life* (pp. 235–239). Berkeley, CA: Celestial Arts.

Foreman, M., & Quinlan, M. (2008). Increasing social work students' awareness of heterosexism and homophobia—A partnership between a community gay health project and a school of social work. *Social Work Education, 27,* 152–158.

Foucault, M. (1965). *Madness and civilization: A history of insanity in the age of reason.* New York: Random House.

Foucault, M. (1980). *Power/knowledge: Selected interviews and other writings.* New York: Pantheon Books.

Fowler, J. W. (1981). *Stages of faith: The psychology of human development and the quest for meaning.* San Francisco: Harper & Row.

Fowler, J. W. (1996). Pluralism and oneness in religious experience: William James, faith development theory, and clinical practice. In E. P. Shafranske (Ed.), *Religion and the clinical practice of psychology* (pp. 165–186). Washington, DC: American Psychological Association.

Frame, M. W. (2003). *Integrating religion and spirituality into counseling: A comprehensive approach.* Pacific Grove, CA: Brooks/Cole.

Francis, L. E. (1997). Ideology and interpersonal emotion management: Redefining identity in two support groups. *Social Psychology Quarterly, 60,* 153–171.

Freedman, J., & Combs, G. (1995, September). *Questions for exploring political issues in therapy.* Paper presented at the annual conference of the American Association for Marriage and Family Therapy, Baltimore.

Friedman, R. C., & Downey, J. (1994). Special article: Homosexuality. *New England Journal of Medicine, 331,* 923–930.

Fulton, A. S., Gorsuch, R. L., & Maynard, E. A. (1999). Religious orientation, antihomosexual sentiment, and fundamentalism among Christians. *Journal for the Scientific Study of Religion, 38,* 14–22.

Fuss, D. (1989). *Essentially speaking: Feminism, nature and difference.* New York: Routledge.

Gage Davidson, M. (2000). Religion and spirituality. In R. M. Perez, K. A. DeBord, & K. J. Bieschke (Eds.), *Handbook of counseling and psychotherapy with lesbian, gay, and bisexual clients* (pp. 409–433). Washington, DC: American Psychological Association.

Garcia, D. I., Gray-Stanley, J., & Ramirez-Valles, J. (2008). "The priest obviously doesn't know that I'm gay": The religious and spiritual journeys of Latino gay men. *Journal of Homosexuality, 55,* 411–436.

Garcia, E. (2007). *Addressing religious conflicts with adolescents who experience same-sex attraction.* Unpublished doctoral dissertation, Regent University, Virginia Beach, VA.

Garnets, L., & D'Augelli, A. R. (1994). Empowering lesbian and gay communities: A call for collaboration with community psychology. *American Journal of Community Psychology, 22,* 447–470.

Garnets, L., Hancock, K. A., Cochran, S. D., Goodchilds, J., & Peplau, L. A. (1991). Issues in psychotherapy with lesbians and gay men: A survey of psychologists. *American Psychologist, 46,* 964–972.

Garnets, L., Herek, G. M., & Levy, B. (1990). Violence and victimization of lesbians and gay men: Mental health consequences. *Journal of Interpersonal Violence, 5,* 366–383.

George, L. K., Larson, D., Koenig, H., & McCullough, M. (2000). Spirituality and health: What we know and what we need to know. *Journal of Social and Clinical Psychology, 19,* 102–116.

Glock, T. (1992). Asian-Pacific Islander issues: Identity integration and pride. In B. Berzon (Ed.), *Positively gay: New approaches to gay and lesbian life* (pp. 334–341). Berkeley, CA: Celestial Arts.

Goffman, E. (1963). *Stigma: Notes on the management of a spoiled identity.* New York: Simon & Schuster.

Goldenberg, I., & Goldenberg, H. (2004). *Family therapy: An overview* (6th ed.). Pacific Grove CA: Brooks/Cole.

Gonsiorek, J. C. (1982a). Introduction: Present and future direction in gay and lesbian mental health. *Journal of Homosexuality, 7,* 5–20.

Gonsiorek, J. C. (1982b). Introduction to mental health issues and homosexuality. *American Behavioral Scientist, 25,* 267–382.

Gonsiorek, J. C. (1993). Mental health issues of gay and lesbian adolescents. In L. G. Garnets & D. C. Kimmel (Eds.), *Psychological perspectives on lesbian and gay male experience* (pp. 469–485). New York: Columbia University Press.

Gonsiorek, J. C. (1995). Gay male identities: Concepts and issues. In A. R. D'Augelli & C. J. Patterson (Eds.), *Lesbian, gay, and bisexual identities over the lifespan: Psychological perspectives* (pp. 24–47). New York: Oxford University Press.

Gonsiorek, J. C. (1996). Mental health and sexual orientation. In R. C. Savin-Williams & K. M. Cohen (Eds.), *The lives of lesbians, gay men, and bisexuals: Children to adults* (pp. 462–478). Fort Worth, TX: Harcourt Brace.

Gorski, E. (2009, December 20). *Evangelical church opens doors fully to gays.* Retrieved from the *Middletown Journal* Web site: http://www.middletown journal.com/lifestyle/ohio-churches-religion-faith/evangelical-church-opens-doors-fully-to-gays-457019.html

Gorsuch, R. L. (1988). Psychology of religion. *Annual Review of Psychology, 39,* 201–221.

Gove, C., Bimbi, D. S., Nani'n, J. E., & Parsons, J. T. (2006). Race, ethnicity, gender, and generational factors associated with the coming out process among gay, lesbian, and bisexual individuals. *Journal of Sex Research, 43,* 115–121.

Greenberg, D. F., & Bystryn, M. H. (1982). Christian intolerance of homosexuality. *American Journal of Sociology, 88,* 515–548.

Greene, B. (2003). What difference does a difference make? Societal privilege, disadvantage, and discord in human relationships. In J. Robinson & L. James (Eds.), *Diversity in human interactions: The tapestry of America* (pp. 3–20). New York: Oxford University Press.

Greene, B. (2004). African American lesbians and other culturally diverse people in psychodynamic psychotherapies: Useful paradigms or oxymoron? *Journal of Lesbian Studies, 8,* 57–77.

Greene, B. (2007). Delivering ethical psychological services to lesbian, gay, and bisexual clients. In K. J. Bieschke, R. M. Perez, & K. A. DeBord, *Handbook of counseling and psychotherapy with lesbian, gay, bisexual, and transgender clients* (pp. 181–199). Washington, DC: American Psychological Association.

Griffin, P., & Harro, B. (1997). Heterosexism: Curriculum design. In M. Adams, L. A. Bell, & P. Griffin (Eds.), *Teaching for diversity and social justice* (pp. 141–158). New York: Routledge.

Groeneman, S., & Tobin, G. (2004). *The decline of religious identity in the United States.* San Francisco: Institute for Jewish & Community Research.

Gross, M. (2008). To be Christian and homosexual: From shame to identity-based claims. *Nova Religio: The Journal of Alternative & Emergent Religion, 11,* 77–101.

Grossman, C. (2002, March 7). Charting the unchurched in America. *USA Today.* Retrieved from http://usatoday.com/life/2002/2002-03-07-no-religion.htm

Haan, N., Smith, B., & Block, J. (1968). Moral reasoning of young adults. *Journal of Personality and Social Psychology, 10,* 183–201.

Haldeman, D. C. (1991). Sexual orientation conversion therapy for gay men and lesbians: A scientific examination. In J. C. Gonsiorek and J. D. Weinrich (Eds.), *Homosexuality: Research implications for public policy* (pp. 149–160). Newbury Park, CA: Sage.

Haldeman, D. C. (1994). The practice and ethics of sexual orientation conversion therapy. *Journal of Consulting and Clinical Psychology, 62,* 221–227.

Haldeman, D. C. (1995, April). Sexual orientation conversion therapy update. *Division 44 Newsletter* (Society for the Psychological Study of Lesbian and Gay Issues, American Psychological Association), 4–6.

Haldeman, D. C. (1996). Spirituality and religion in the lives of lesbians and gay men. In R. P. Cabaj & T. S. Stein (Eds.), *Textbook of homosexuality and mental health* (pp. 881–896). Washington, DC: American Psychiatric Press.

Haldeman, D. C. (1998). Ceremonies and religion in same-sex marriages. In R. P. Cabaj & D. W. Purcell (Eds.), *On the road to same-sex marriage* (pp. 141–164). San Francisco: Jossey-Bass.

Haldeman, D. C. (2000, August). Gay rights, patient rights: The implications of sexual orientation conversion therapy. Paper presented at the 108th Annual Convention of the American Psychological Association, Washington, DC.

Haldeman, D. C. (2001). Therapeutic antidotes: Helping gay and bisexual men recover from conversion therapies. *Journal of Gay and Lesbian Psychotherapy, 5,* 117–130.

Haldeman, D. C. (2002). Gay rights, patient rights: The implications of sexual orientation conversion therapy. *Professional Psychology: Research and Practice, 33,* 260–264.

Haldeman, D. C. (2004). When sexual and religious orientations collide: Considerations in working with conflicted same-sex attracted male clients. *Counseling Psychologist, 32,* 691–715.

Haldeman, D. C., & Buhrke, R. A. (2000). Under a rainbow flag. In J. D. Robinson & L. C. James (Eds.), *Diversity in human interactions: The tapestry of America* (pp. 145–156). New York: Oxford University Press.

Halpert, S. C., Reinhardt, B., & Toohey, M. J. (2007). In K. J. Bieschke, R. M. Perez, K. A. DeBord (Eds.), *Affirmative clinical supervision: Handbook of counseling and psychotherapy with lesbian, gay, bisexual, and transgender clients* (2nd ed., pp. 341–358). Washington, DC: American Psychological Association.

Hancock, K. A. (2000). Lesbian, gay, and bisexual lives: Basic issues in psychotherapy training and practice. In B. Greene & G. L. Groom (Eds.), *Education, research, and practice in lesbian, gay, bisexual, and transgendered psychology: A resource manual* (pp. 91–130). Thousand Oaks, CA: Sage Publications.

Harris, J. I. (2001). *Religious variables relevant to internalized homophobia and sexual identity development.* Unpublished doctoral dissertation, Texas Tech University, Lubbock.

Harris, J. I., Cook, S. W., & Kashubeck-West, S. (2008). Religious attitudes, internalized homophobia, and identity in gay and lesbian adults. *Journal of Gay & Lesbian Mental Health, 12,* 205–225.

Harris, J. I., Schoneman, S. W., & Carrera, S. R. (2002). Religiosity and anxiety among college students. *Mental Health, Religion & Culture, 5,* 253–265.

Heermann, M., Wiggins, M. I., & Rutter, P. A. (2007). Creating a space for spiritual practice: Pastoral possibilities with sexual minorities. *Pastoral Psychology, 55,* 711–721.

Helminiak, D. A. (1994). *What the Bible really says about homosexuality.* San Francisco: Alamo Square Press.

Henrickson, M. (2009). Sexuality, religion, and authority: Toward reframing estrangement. *Journal of Religion & Spirituality in Social Work: Social Thought, 28,* 48–62.

Herdt, G. H., & Boxer, A. (1993). *Children of the horizons: How gay and lesbian teens are leading a way out of the closet.* Boston: Beacon Press.

Herek, G. M. (1987). Religious orientation and prejudice: A comparison of racial and sexual attitudes. *Personality and Social Psychology Bulletin, 13,* 34–44.

Herek, G. M. (1992). Homophobia. In W. R. Dynes (Ed.), *Encyclopedia of homosexuality* (552–555). New York: Garland.

Herek, G. M. (1995). Psychological heterosexism in the United States. In A. R. D'Augelli & C. J. Patterson (Eds.), *Lesbian, gay, and bisexual identities over the lifespan: Psychological perspectives* (pp. 321–346). New York: Oxford University Press.

Hermann, M. A., & Herlihy, B. R. (2006). Legal and ethical implications of refusing to counsel homosexual clients. *Journal of Counseling & Development, 84,* 414–418.

Hetrick, E. S., & Martin, A. D. (1984). Ego-dystonic homosexuality: A developmental view. In E. S. Hetrick & T. S. Stein (Eds.), *Innovations in psychotherapy with homosexuals* (pp. 2–21). Washington, DC: American Psychiatric Press.

Heyward, C. (1984). *Our passion for justice: Images of power, sexuality and liberation.* Cleveland: Pilgrim Press.

Hodge, D. R. (2005). Epistemological frameworks, homosexuality and religion: How people of faith understand the intersection between homosexuality and religion. *Social Work, 50,* 207–218.

Hodge, D. R., & McGrew, C. C. (2006). Spirituality, religion, and the interrelationship: A nationally representative study. *Journal of Social Work Education, 42,* 637–654.

Hogge, J., & Friedman, S. T. (1967). The Scriptural Literalism Scale: A preliminary report. *Journal of Psychology, 66,* 275–279.

Horne, S. G., & Noffsinger-Frazier, N. (2003). Reconciling religion/spirituality with sexual identity. In J. Whitman (Ed.), *The therapists' notebook for lesbian, gay, and bisexual clients* (pp. 202–209). Binghamton, NY: Haworth Press.

Horowitz, J. L., & Newcomb, M. D. (2001). A multidimensional approach to homosexual identity. *Journal of Homosexuality, 42,* 1–19.

House, R., & Holloway, E. (1992). Empowering the counseling professional to work with gay and lesbian clients. In S. Dworkin & F. Gutierrez (Eds.), *Counseling gay men and lesbians: Journey to the end of the rainbow* (pp. 307–324). Alexandria, VA: American Counseling Association.

Houts, A. C. (2009). Reformed theology is a resource in conflicts between psychology and religious faith. In Cummings, N. A., O'Donohue, W. T., & Cummings, J. L. *Psychology's war on religion* (pp. 257–306). Phoenix, AZ: Zeit, Tucker & Theisen.

Human Rights Campaign. (n.d.). *Stances of faiths on LGBT issues: Judaism.* Retrieved from http://www.hrc.org/issues/5013.htm

Hunsberger, B. (1996). Religious fundamentalism, right-wing authoritarianism, and hostility toward homosexuals in non-Christian religious groups. *International Journal for the Psychology of Religion, 6,* 39–49.

Hunsberger, B., & Jackson, L. M. (2005). Religion, meaning and prejudice. *Journal of Social Issues, 61,* 807–826.

Hunsberger, B., Pratt, M., & Prancer, S. (1994). Religious fundamentalism and religious doubts: Content, connection, and complexity of thinking. *International Journal for the Psychology of Religion, 33,* 335–346.

Hunter, S. (1998). *Lesbian, gay, and transgendered youth*. Arlington: Judith Granger Birmingham Center for Child Welfare, University of Texas at Arlington.

Hunter, S. (2007). *Coming out and disclosures: LGBT persons across the life course*. Binghamton, NY: Haworth Press.

Iasenza, S. (1989). Some challenges of integrating sexual orientation into counselor education training and research. *Journal of Counseling and Development, 68*, 73–76.

Innala, S. M., & Ernulf, K. E. (1987). The relationship between affective and cognitive components of homophobic reaction: Three cross-national replications. *Archives of Sexual Behavior, 16*, 501–509.

Institute for Welcoming Resources. (n.d.). Retrieved from http://www.welcomingresources.org

International Federation of Social Workers. (2005). *About the IFSW: Introduction*. Retrieved from http://ifsw.org/en/p380000002.html

Ironson, G. (2006). An increase in religiousness/spirituality occurs after HIV diagnosis and predicts slower disease progression over 1 year in people with HIV. *Journal of General Internal Medicine, 21*, 62–68.

Isay, R. A. (1990). *Being homosexual: Gay men and their development*. New York: Farrar, Straus and Giroux.

Israel, T. (2003). What counselors need to know about working with sexual minority clients. In D. R. Atkinson & G. Hackett (Eds), *Counseling diverse populations* (pp. 347–364). New York: McGraw-Hill.

Israel, T., & Hackett, G. (2004). Counselor education on lesbian, gay, and bisexual issues: Comparing information and attitude-exploration. *Counselor Education and Supervision, 43*, 179–191.

Israel, T., Ketz, K., Detrie, P. M., Burke, M. C., & Shulman, J. L. (2003). Identifying counselor competencies for working with lesbian, gay, and bisexual clients. *Journal of Gay & Lesbian Psychotherapy, 7*, 3–21.

Israel, T., & Selvidge, M.M.D. (2003). Contributions of multicultural counseling to counselor competency with lesbian, gay, and bisexual clients. *Journal of Multicultural Counseling and Development, 31*, 99–112.

Jimenez, J. (2006). Epistemological frameworks, homosexuality, and religion: A response to Hodge. *Social Work, 51*, 185–187.

Johnson, T. R. (1995). The significance of religion for aging well. *American Behavioral Scientist, 39*, 186–208.

Johnson, W. B. (2001). To dispute or not to dispute: Ethical REBT with religious clients. *Cognitive & Behavioral Practice, 8*, 39–47.

Johnson, W. B. (2004). Rational emotive behavior therapy for disturbance about sexual orientation. In P. S. Richards & A. E. Bergin (Eds.), *Casebook for a spiritual strategy in counseling and psychotherapy* (pp. 247–266). Washington, DC: American Psychological Association.

Johnston, L. B., & Jenkins, D. (2006). Lesbians and gay men embrace their sexual orientation after conversion therapy and ex-gay ministries: A qualitative study. *Social Work in Mental Health, 4,* 61–82.

Jones, H. K. (1996). *Toward a Christian understanding of the homosexual.* New York: Association Press.

Jones, R. P., & Cox, D. (2009, July 1). *Episcopal Church walks with American clergy on gay and lesbian equality.* Retrieved from http://www.religiondispatches. org/archive/sexandgender/1689/episcopal_church_walks_with_ameri can_clergy_on_gay_and_lesbian_equality

Jordan, K. M., & Deluty, R. H. (1995). Clinical interventions by psychologists with lesbians and gay men. *Journal of Clinical Psychology, 51,* 448–456.

Jordan, M. (2007). Religion trouble. *GLQ: A Journal of Lesbian and Gay Studies, 13,* 563–575.

Judge. (2006, July). *Jehovah's Witnesses and homosexuality.* Retrieved from http:// ulcseminary.org/forum/index.php?showtopic=11229

Kahn, M. M. (2006). Conservative Christian teachers: Possible consequences for lesbian, gay, and bisexual youth. *Intercultural Education, 17,* 359–371.

Kaiser Family Foundation. (2001). *Inside-out: A report on the experiences of lesbians, gays, and bisexuals in America and the public's view on issues and politics related to sexual orientation.* Retrieved from http://www.kff.org/kaiserpolls/upload/ New-Surveys-on-Experiences-of-Lesbians-Gays-and-Bisexuals-and-the- Public-s-Views-Related-to-Sexual-Orientation-Report.pdf

Karp, D. A. (1992). Illness ambiguity and the search for meaning: A case study of a self-help group for affective disorders. *Journal of Contemporary Ethnography, 21,* 139–169.

Kawakami, K., Young, H., & Dovidio, J. F. (2002). Automatic stereotyping: Category, trait, and behavioral activations. *Personality and Social Psychology Bulletin, 28,* 3–15.

Kelly, E. W. (1994). The role of religion and spirituality in counselor education: A national survey. *Counselor Education & Supervision, 33,* 227–237.

Kinsey, A. C., Pomeroy, W. B., & Martin, C. E. (1948). *Sexual behavior in the human male.* Philadelphia: W. B. Saunders.

Kitzinger, C. (1991). Lesbian and gay men in the workplace: Psychosocial issues. In M. J. Davidson & J. Earnshaw (Eds.), *Vulnerable workers: Psychosocial and legal issues* (pp. 223–257). New York: John Wiley & Sons.

Klein, F., Sepekoff, B., & Wolf, T. J. (1985). Sexual orientation: A multivariable dynamic process. *Journal of Homosexuality, 11,* 35–49.

Kocarek, C. E., & Pelling, N. J. (2003). Beyond knowledge and awareness: Enhancing counselor skills for work with gay, lesbian, and bisexual clients. *Journal of Multicultural Counseling and Development, 31,* 99–112.

Koenig, H. G. (1993). Religion and aging. *Reviews in Clinical Gerontology, 3,* 195–203.

Koenig, H. G., McCullough, M. E., Larson, D. B. (2001). *Handbook of religion and health*. New York: Oxford University Press.

Kohlberg, L., Levine, C., & Hewer, A. (1983). *Moral stages: A current formulation and a response to critics*. Basel, Switzerland: Karger.

Kohlberg, L., & Lickona, T. (Eds.). (1976). *Moral development and behavior: Theory, research and social issues*. New York: Holt, Rinehart and Winston.

Kosmin, B. A., Mayer, E., & Keysar, A. (2001). *American religious identification survey*. Unpublished report, City University of New York Graduate School and University Center.

Krajeski, J. P., Myers, M. F., Valgemae, A., Pattison, E. M., & Mansell, E. (1981). "Ex-gays": Religious abuse of psychiatry? *American Journal of Psychiatry, 138,* 852–853.

Kreiglstein, M. (2003). Heterosexism and social work: An ethical issue. *Journal of Human Behavior in the Social Environment, 8,* 75–91.

Kubicek, K., McDavitt, B., Carpineto, J., Weiss, G., Iverson, E. F., & Kipke, M. D. (2009). God made me gay for a reason: Young men who have sex with men's resiliency in resolving internalized homophobia from religious sources. *Journal of Adolescent Research, 24,* 601–633.

Kus, R. J. (1992). Spirituality in everyday life: Experiences of gay men of Alcoholics Anonymous. *Journal of Chemical Dependency Treatment, 5,* 49–66.

Langdridge, D. (2008). Are you angry or are you heterosexual? A queer critique of lesbian and gay models of identity development. In L. Moon (Ed.), *Feeling queer or queer feelings? Radical approaches to counseling sex, sexualities and genders* (pp. 23–35). New York: Routledge.

Lasser, J. S., & Gottlieb, M. C. (2004). Treating patients distressed regarding their sexual orientation: Clinical and ethical alternatives. *Professional Psychology: Research and Practice, 35,* 194–200.

Laumann, E. D., Gagnon, J. H., Michael, R. T., & Michaels, S. (1994). *The social organization of sexuality: Sexual practices in the United States*. Chicago: University of Chicago Press.

Lawrence v. Texas, 539 U.S. 558 (2003).

Laythe, B., Finkel, D., & Kirkpatrick, L. A. (2001). Predicting prejudice from religious fundamentalism and right-wing authoritarianism: A multiple-regression approach. *Journal for the Scientific Study of Religion, 40,* 1–10.

Lazarus, R. S. (1991). *Emotion and adaptation*. New York: Oxford University Press.

Lazarus, R. S., & Folkman, S. (1984). *Stress, appraisal, and coping*. New York: Springer.

Leaders to allow more gays in clergy. (2009, August 22). *Dallas Morning News,* p. 8A.

Lease, S. H., Horne, S. G., & Noffsinger-Frazier, N. (2005). Affirming faith experiences and psychological health for Caucasian lesbian, gay and bisexual individuals. *Journal of Counseling Psychology, 52,* 378–388.

Lease, S. H., & Shulman, J. S. (2003). A preliminary investigation of the role of religion for family members of lesbian, gay male, or bisexual male and female individuals. *Counseling and Values, 47,* 195–209.

Lee, K. G., & Busto, R. (1991, Fall). When the spirit moves us. *OUT/LOOK, 14,* 83–85.

Lennon, L., Maloney, C., Miller, J., Wright, C., & Chambliss, C. (1997). *The challenges of evaluating formal parental programming.* Collegeville, PA: Ursinus College. (ERIC Document Reproduction Service No. ED 410514)

Leong, P. (2006). Religion, flesh, and blood: Re-creating religious culture in the context of HIV/AIDS. *Sociology of Religion, 67,* 295–311.

LeVay, S. (1996). *Queer science: The use and abuse of research into homosexuality.* Cambridge, MA: MIT Press.

Levy, D. L. (2008). *Gay, lesbian, and queer individuals with a Christian upbringing exploring the process of resolving conflict between sexual identity and religious beliefs.* Unpublished doctoral dissertation, University of Georgia, Athens.

Levy, E. F. (1995). Feminist social work practice with lesbian and gay clients. In N. Van Den Bergh (Ed.), *Feminist practice in the 21st century* (pp. 278–294). Washington, DC: NASW Press.

Lewin, E. (1993). *Lesbian mothers: Accounts of gender in American culture.* Ithaca, NY: Cornell University Press.

Library of Congress. (1998). *Religion and the founding of the American republic.* Retrieved from http://www.loc.gov/exhibits/religion/

Lidderdale, M. A. (2002). Practitioner training for counseling lesbian, gay, and bisexual clients. *Journal of Lesbian Studies, 6,* 111–120.

Liddle, B. J. (2003, Spring). Editor's note: How shall we meet the needs of conflicted clients who are not yet ready to consider a positive LGB Identity? *Division 44 Newsletter* (Society for the Psychological Study of Lesbian and Gay Issues, American Psychological Association), 3.

Loiacano, D. K. (1989). Gay identity issues among black Americans: Racism, homophobia, and the need for validation. *Journal of Counseling and Development, 68,* 21–25.

Love, P. (1997). Contradiction and paradox: Attempting to change the culture of sexual orientation at a small Catholic college. *Review of Higher Education, 20,* 381–398.

Love, P., Bock, M., Jannarone, A., & Richardson, R. (2005). Identity interaction: Exploring the spiritual experiences of lesbian and gay college students. *Journal of College Student Development, 46,* 193–209.

Lukenbill, B. W. (1998). Observations on the corporate culture of a gay and lesbian congregation. *Journal for the Scientific Study of Religion, 37,* 440–452.

Mahaffy, K. A. (1996). Cognitive dissonance and its resolution: A study of lesbian Christians. *Journal for the Scientific Study of Religion, 35,* 392–402.

Mallon, G. (1998). Knowledge for practice with gay and lesbian persons. In G. P. Mallon (Ed.), *Foundations of social work practice with lesbian and gay persons* (pp. 1–30). Binghamton, NY: Haworth Press.

Malyon, A. K. (1982). Psychotherapeutic implications of internalized homophobia in gay men. *Journal of Homosexuality, 7,* 59–69.

Mancini, T., & Rzeznik, F. M. (1993). *One nation under God* [Video]. Retrieved from http://www.imdb.com/title/tt0107748

Markowitz, L. M. (1998). Dangerous practice: Inside the conversionist therapy controversy. *In the Family, 4,* 10–13, 25.

Marsden, G. M. (2006). *Fundamentalism and American culture* (2nd ed). New York: Oxford University Press.

Marszalek, J. F., III, & Cashwell, C. S. (1998). The gay and lesbian affirmative development (GLAD) model: Facilitating positive gay identity development. *Adultspan Journal, 1,* 13–31.

Marszalek, J. F., III, Cashwell, C. S., Dunn, M. S., & Jones, K. H. (2004). Comparing gay identity development theory to cognitive development: An empirical study. *Journal of Homosexuality, 48,* 103–123.

Martin, A. (1984). The emperor's new clothes: Modern attempts to change sexual orientation. In T. Stein & E. Hetrick (Eds.), *Innovations in psychotherapy with homosexuals* (pp. 24–57). Washington, DC: American Psychiatric Press.

Matteson, D. R. (1996). Counseling and psychotherapy with bisexual and exploring clients. In B. A. Firestein (Ed.), *Bisexuality: The psychology and politics of an invisible minority* (pp. 185–213). Thousand Oaks, CA: Sage Publications.

Matthews, C. (2007). Affirmative lesbian, gay, and bisexual counseling with all clients. In K. J. Bieschke, R. M. Perez, & K. A. DeBord (Eds.), *Handbook of counseling and psychotherapy with lesbian, gay, bisexual, and transgender clients* (pp. 201–219). Washington, DC: American Psychological Association.

Matthews, C., Selvidge, M.M.D., & Fisher, K. (2005). Addiction counselors' attitudes and behaviors toward lesbian, gay, and bisexual clients. *Journal of Counseling and Development, 83,* 57–65.

McCarn, S. R., & Fassinger, R. E. (1996). Revisioning sexual minority identity formation: A new model of lesbian identity and its implications for counseling and research. *Counseling Psychologist, 24,* 508–534.

McClatchy. (2009, February 2). *Mormons admit larger role in California's Prop. 8 campaign.* Retrieved from http://www.mcclatchydc.com/2009/02/02/61260/mormons-admit-larger-role-in-californias.html

McGrady, M. L., & McDonnell, K. A. (2006). Helping lesbian and gay clients work toward positive spiritual health. In K. B. Helmeke & C. F. Sori (Eds.), *The therapist's notebook for integrating spirituality in counseling: Homework, handouts, and activities for use in psychotherapy* (pp. 163–175). Binghamton, NY: Haworth Press.

McHenry, S., & Johnson, J. (1993). Homophobia in the therapies and gay or lesbian client: Conscious and unconscious collusion in self-hate. *Psychotherapy, 30,* 141–151.

McKenna, K.Y.A., & Bargh, J. A. (1998). Coming out in the age of the Internet: Identity "demarginalization" through virtual group participation. *Journal of Personality, 75,* 681–694.

McLean, R., & Marini, I. (2008). Working with gay men from a narrative counseling perspective: A case study. *Journal of LGBT Issues in Counseling, 2,* 243–257.

McNaught, B. (1988). *On being gay: Thoughts on family, faith, and love.* New York: St. Martins Press.

McQueeney, K. (2009). "We are God's children, y'all": Race, gender, and sexuality in lesbian-and gay-affirming congregations. *Social Problems, 56,* 151–173.

Meara, N. M., Schmidt, L. D., & Day, J. D. (1996). Principles and virtues: A foundation for ethical decisions, policies, and character. *Counseling Psychologist, 24,* 4–77.

Melendez, M. P., & LaSala, M. C. (2006). Who's oppressing whom? Homosexuality, Christianity, and social work. *Social Work, 51,* 371–376.

Melton, J. G. (1991). *The church speaks on: Homosexuality.* Detroit, MI: Gale Research.

Merriam, S. B., Caffarella, R. S., & Baumgartner, L. M. (2007). Transformational learning. In *Learning in adulthood: A comprehensive guide* (3rd ed., pp. 130–158). San Francisco: Jossey-Bass.

Messing, A. E., Schoenberg, R., & Stephens, R. K. (1984). Confronting homophobia in health care settings: Guidelines for social work practice. *Journal of Social Work & Human Sexuality, 2,* 65–74.

Meyer, I. H. (1995). Minority stress and mental health in gay men. *Journal of Health and Social Behavior, 7,* 9–25.

Meyer, I. H., & Dean, L. (1998). Internalized homophobia, intimacy, and sexual behavior among gay and bisexual men. In G. M. Herek (Ed.), *Stigma and sexual orientation: Understanding prejudice against lesbians, gay men, and bisexuals* (pp. 160–186). Thousand Oaks, CA: Sage Publications.

Mezirow, J. (1997). Transformative learning: Theory to practice. *New Directions for Adult and Continuing Education, 74,* 5–12.

Miceli, M. S. (2005). Morality politics vs. identity politics: Framing processes and competition among Christian Right and gay social movement organizations. *Sociological Forum, 20,* 589–594.

Miller, M. (2000, May 8). As a pious churchgoer, Stuart Matis prayed and worked to change his sexual orientation. He died trying. *Newsweek,* 38–39.

Minton, H. L., & McDonald, G. J. (1985). Homosexual identity formation as a developmental process. *Journal of Homosexuality, 9,* 91–104.

Mondimore, F. M. (1996). *A natural history of homosexuality.* Baltimore: Johns Hopkins University Press.

Morin, S. F. (1977). Heterosexual bias in research on lesbianism and male homosexuality. *American Psychologist, 32,* 629–637.

Morris, P. (2002). *Redemptive therapy: The science of Christian counseling.* Retrieved from http://christiantherapist.com/News/111902_02.htm

Morrow, D. R. (2003). Cast into the wilderness: The impact of institutionalized religion on lesbians. *Journal of Lesbian Studies, 7,* 109–123.

Morrow, D. R., & Tyson, B. (2006). Religion and spirituality. In D. F. Morrow & L. Messinger (Eds.), *Sexual orientation and gender expression in social work practice* (pp. 384–404). New York: Columbia University Press.

Morrow, S. L., & Beckstead, A. L. (2004). Conversion therapies for same-sex attracted clients in religious conflict: Context, predisposing factors, experiences, and implications for therapy. *Counseling Psychologist, 32,* 641–650.

Murphy, B. C. (1991). Educating mental health professionals about gay and lesbian issues. *Journal of Homosexuality, 22,* 229–246.

Murphy, T. F. (1992). Redirecting sexual orientation: Techniques and justifications. *Journal of Sex Research, 29,* 501–523.

Murphy, T. F. (1997). *Gay science: The ethics of sexual orientation research.* New York: Columbia University Press.

National Association of Social Workers. (1996). *Code of ethics.* Washington, DC: Author.

National Association of Social Workers. (1999). *Code of ethics of the National Association of Social Workers.* Retrieved from http://www.socialworkers.org/pubs/codenew/code.asp

National Association of Social Workers (2003). *"Reparative" and "conversion" therapies for lesbians and gay men: Position statement.* Retrieved from https://www.socialworkers.org/diversity/lgb/reparative.asp?back=yes

Neisen, J. H. (1990). Heterosexism: Redefining homophobia for the 1990's. *Journal of Gay & Lesbian Psychotherapy, 1,* 21–35.

Nelson, J. (1982). *Psychology, religion, and spirituality.* New York: Springer.

Newman, B. S., Dannenfelser, P. I., & Benishek, L. (2002). Assessing beginning social work and counseling students' acceptance of lesbians and gay men. *Journal of Social Work Education, 38,* 273–288.

Nicolosi, J. (1991). *Reparative therapy of male homosexuality.* Northvale, NJ: Jason Aronoson.

Noll, M. (1992). *A history of Christianity in the United States and Canada.* Grand Rapids, MI: W.M.B. Erdmans.

Nugent, R., & Gramick, J. (1989). Homosexuality: Protestant, Catholic, and Jewish issues: A fishbone tale. In R. Hasbany (Ed.), *Homosexuality and religion* (pp. 7–46). Binghamton, NY: Harrington Park Press.

Nungesser, L. (1983). *Homosexual acts, actors and identities.* New York: Praeger.

Obear, K. (1989, March). *Opening doors to understanding and acceptance: Facilitating workshops on lesbian, gay, and bisexual issues.* Workshop presented at the meeting of the American College Personnel Association, Washington, DC.

Okin, S. M., Chohen, J., Howard, M. & Nussbaum, M. C. (1999). *Is multiculturalism bad for women?* Princeton, NJ: Princeton University Press.

Olson, L., & Cadge, W. (2002). Talking about homosexuality: The views of mainline Protestant clergy. *Journal for the Scientific Study of Religion, 41,* 153–167.

O'Neill, C., & Ritter, K. (1992). *Coming out within: stages of spiritual awakening for lesbians and gay men.* San Francisco: Harper.

Osanna, S. M., Helms, J. E., & Leonard, M. M. (1992). Do "womanist" identity attitudes influence college women's self-esteem and perception of environmental bias? *Journal of Counseling and Development, 70,* 402–408.

Otis, M. D., & Skinner, W. F. (1996). The prevalence of victimization and its effects on mental well-being among lesbian and gay people. *Journal of Homosexuality, 30,* 93–121.

Pachankis, J., & Goldfried, M. (2004). Clinical issues in working with lesbian, gay, and bisexual clients. *Psychotherapy: Theory, Research, Practice, Training, 41,* 227–246.

Painter, K. (1998, August 15). Conversion of gays: Morality or bigotry? *USA Today,* p. 1D.

Paloutzian, R. F. (1996). *Invitation to the psychology of religion* (2nd ed.). Boston: Allyn & Bacon.

Pargament, K. I. (1997). *The psychology of religion and coping.* New York: Guilford Press.

Parker, B. A. (2007). Orientations: GLBTQ. In M. S. Tepper & A. F. Owens (Eds.), *Sexual health, Vol. 1: Psychological foundations* (pp. 231–262). Westport, CT: Praeger.

Parks, C. (1999). Lesbian identity development: An examination of differences across generations. *American Journal of Orthopsychiatry, 69,* 347361.

Patterson, C. J. (1995). Sexual orientation and human development: An overview. *Developmental Psychology, 31,* 3–11.

Pattison, E. M., & Pattison, M. L. (1980). Ex-gays: Religiously mediated change in homosexuals. *American Journal of Psychiatry, 137,* 1553–1562.

Perlstein, M. (1996). Integrating a gay, lesbian, or bisexual person's religious and spiritual needs and choices into psychotherapy. In C. J. Alexander (Ed.), *Gay and lesbian mental health: A sourcebook for practitioners* (pp. 173–188). Binghamton, NY: Harrington Park Press.

Perry, T. (1990). *Don't be afraid anymore: The story of Reverend Troy Perry and the Metropolitan Community Churches.* New York: St. Martin's Press.

Perry, W. G., Jr. (1981). Cognitive and ethical growth: The making of meaning. In Arthur W. Chickering and Associates, *The modern American college* (pp. 76–116). San Francisco: Jossey-Bass.

Pew Forum. (2008). *U.S. religious landscape survey.* Washington, DC: Pew Forum on Religion and Public life. Retrieved from http://religions.pewforum.org/

Phellas, C. N. (1999). Sexual and ethnic identities of Anglo-Cypriot men resident in London who have sex with men. *Dissertation Abstracts International, 60,* 559C–560C.

Phillips, J. (2000). Training issues and considerations. In R. M. Perez, K. A. DeBord, & K. J. Bieschke (Eds.), *Handbook of counseling and psychotherapy with lesbian, gay, and bisexual clients* (pp. 337–358). Washington, DC: American Psychological Association.

Phillips, R. (2005). *Conservative Christian identity and same-sex orientation: The case of gay Mormons.* New York: Peter Lang.

Piazza, M. S. (1994). *Holy homosexuals: The truth about being gay or lesbian and Christian.* Dallas: Sources of Hope.

Plante, T. G., & Boccaccini, M. (1997). Reliability and validity of the Santa Clara Strength of Religious Faith Questionnaire. *Pastoral Psychology, 45,* 429–437.

Ponticelli, C. M. (1999). Crafting stories of sexual identity reconstruction. *Social Psychology Quarterly, 62,* 157–172.

Pope, M. (1997). Sexual issues for older lesbians and gays. *Topics in Geriatric Rehabilitation, 12,* 53–60.

Popper, K. R. (1966). *The open society and its enemies* (5th ed.). London: Routledge and Kegan Paul.

Price, J. H. (1982). High school students' attitudes toward homosexuality. *Journal of School Health, 52,* 469–474.

Prochaska, J. O., & DiClemente, C. C. (1986). The transtheoretical approach. In J. Norcross (Ed.), *Handbook of eclectic psychotherapy* (pp. 163–199). New York: Brunner/Mazel.

Prochaska, J. O., Norcross, J. C., & DiClemente, C. C. (1994). *Changing for good: The revolutionary program that explains the six stages of change and teaches you how to free yourself from bad habits.* New York: Wm. Morrow.

Purcell, D. W., Camos, P. F., & Perrilla, J. L. (1996). Therapy with lesbians and gay men: A cognitive behavioral perspective. *Cognitive and Behavioral Practice, 3,* 391–415.

Quackenbush, R. H. (1989). Comparison and contrast between belief system and cognitive theory. *Journal of Psychology, 123,* 315–328.

Ratzinger, J. (1986). *Letter to the bishops of the Catholic church on the pastoral care of homosexual persons.* Rome: Vatican Congregation for the Doctrine of the Faith.

Raw Story. (2009, December 2). *Gays "will never go to heaven": Cardinal.* Retrieved from http://rawstory.com/news/afp/Gays_will_never_go_to_heaven_cardin_12022009.htm#

Ream, G. L. (2001, August). *Intrinsic religion and internalized homophobia in sexual minority youth.* Paper presented at the Annual Conference of the American Psychological Association, San Francisco.

Ream, G. L., & Savin-Williams, R. C. (2005). Reconciling Christianity and posi-tive non-heterosexual identity in adolescences, with implications for psycho-logical well-being. *Journal of Gay and Lesbian Issues in Education, 2,* 19–36.

Reid, J. E. (1995). Development in late life: Older lesbian and gay lives. In A. R. D'Augelli & C. J. Patterson (Eds.), *Lesbian, gay, and bisexual identities over the lifes-pan: Psychological perspectives* (pp. 215– 241). New York: Oxford University Press.

Riddle, D. (1996). Riddle Homophobia Scale. In M. Adams, P. Brigham, P. Dalpes, & L. Marchesani (Eds.), *Social diversity and social justice: Gay, lesbian and bisexual oppression* (p. 31). Dubuque, IA: Kendall/Hunt.

Right Wing Watch. (2009). *People for the American Way.* Retrieved from http://www.rightwingwatch.org/category/individuals/steven-l-anderson

Ritter, K. Y., & O'Neill, C. W. (1989). Moving through loss: The spiritual journey of gay men and lesbian women. *Journal of Counseling and Development, 68,* 9–15.

Ritter, K. Y., & O'Neill, C. W. (1995). Moving through loss: The spiritual jour-ney of gay men and lesbian women. In M. T. Burke & J. G. Miranti (Eds.), *Counseling: The spiritual dimension* (pp. 127–142). Alexandria, VA: American Counseling Association.

Ritter, K. Y., & Terndrup, A. I. (2002). *Handbook of affirmative psychotherapy with lesbians and gay men.* New York: Guilford Press.

Robinson, B. A. (2001). *Religious identification in the U.S.: How American adults view themselves.* Retrieved from http://www.religioustolerance.org/chr_prac2.htm

Rodriguez, E. M. (1997). *Gay and lesbian Christians: Conflict and integration between religious and homosexual identities.* Unpublished master's thesis, City University of New York Graduate Center.

Rodriguez, E. M. (2006). *At the intersection of church and gay: Religion, spirituality, conflict, and integration in gay, lesbian, and bisexual people of faith.* Unpublished doctoral dissertation, City University of New York Graduate Center.

Rodriguez, E. M., & Ouellette, S. C. (1999). The Metropolitan Community Church of New York: A gay and lesbian community. *Community Psychologist, 32,* 24–29.

Rodriguez, E. M., & Ouellette, S. C. (2000). Gay and lesbian Christians: Homo-sexual and religious identity integration in the members and participants of a gay-positive church. *Journal for Scientific Study of Religions, 39,* 333–347.

Rokeach, M. (1984). A belief system theory of stability and change. In S. J. Ball Rokeach, M. Rokeach, & J. W. Grube (Eds.), *The great American values test: Influencing behavior and belief through television* (pp. 17–38). New York: Free Press.

Romer v. Evans, 517 U.S. 620 (1996).

Root, M. P. P. (1992). Reconstructing the impact of trauma on personality. In L. S. Brown & M. Ballou (Eds.), *Personality and psychopathology: Feminist reappraisals* (pp. 229–265). New York: Guilford Press.

Rosario, M., Yali, A. M., Hunter, J., & Gwadz, M. V. (2006). Religion and health among lesbian, gay and bisexual youths: An empirical investigation and theoretical explanation. In A. M. Omoto & H. S. Kurzman (Eds.), *Sexual orientation and mental health: Examining identity and development in lesbian, gay and bisexual people* (pp. 117–140). Washington, DC: American Psychological Association.

Rosenberg, K. P. (1994). Notes and comments: Biology and homosexuality. *Journal of Sex & Marital Therapy, 20,* 147–151.

Rosik, C. H. (2003). Motivational, ethical, and epistemological foundations in the treatment of unwanted homoerotic attraction. *Journal of Marital and Family Therapy, 29,* 13–28.

Ross, M. W., & Rosser, B. R. (1996). Measurement and correlates of internalized homophobia: A factor analytic study. *Journal of Clinical Psychology, 52,* 15–21.

Rostosky, S. S., Riggle, E.D.B., Gray, B. E., & Hatton, R. L. (2007). Minority stress experiences in committed couple relationships. *Professional Psychology: Research and Practice, 38,* 392–400.

Roth, S., & Epston, D. (1996). Developing externalizing conversation: An exercise. *Journal of Systemic Therapies, 15,* 5–12.

Rothblum, E. D. (1989). Introduction: Lesbianism as a model of a positive lifestyle for women. In E. D. Rothblum & E. Cole (Eds.), *Lesbianism: Affirming nontraditional roles* (pp. 1–12). Binghamton, NY: Haworth Press.

Rotheram-Borus, M. J., & Fernandez, M. I. (1995). Sexual orientation and developmental challenges experienced by gay and lesbian youths. *Suicide and Life-Threatening Behavior, 25,* 26–34.

Rostosky, S. S., Riggle, E.D.B., Gray, B. E., & Hatton, R. L. (2007). Minority stress experiences in committed same-sex couple relationships. *Professional Psychology: Research and Practice, 38,* 392–400.

Rudolph, J. (1992). The impact of contemporary ideology and AIDS on the counseling of gay clients. In M. T. Burke & J. Miranti (Eds.), *Ethical and spiritual values in counseling* (pp. 143–154). Alexandria, VA: American Counseling Association.

Rust, P. C. (2003). Finding a sexual identity and community: Therapeutic implications and cultural assumptions in scientific models of coming out. In L. D. Garnets & D. C. Kimmel (Eds.), *Psychological perspectives on lesbian, gay and bisexual experiences* (2nd ed., pp. 227–269). New York: Columbia University Press.

Sands, K. M. (2007). Homosexuality, religion, and the law. In J. S. Siker (Ed.), *Homosexuality and religion: An encyclopedia* (pp. 3–18). Westport, CN: Greenwood Press.

Savin-Williams, R. C. (1990). *Gay and lesbian youth: Expressions of identity.* New York: Hemisphere.

Savin-Williams, R. C. (2005). *The new gay teenager.* Cambridge, MA: Harvard University Press.

Savin-Williams, R. C. (2009). How many gays are there? It depends. In D. A. Hope (Ed.), *Contemporary perspectives on lesbian, gay, and bisexual identities* (pp. 5–41). New York: Springer.

Scasta, D. (1998). Issues in helping people come out. *Journal of Gay & Lesbian Psychotherapy, 2,* 87–98.

Schaeffer, K. W., Hyde, R. A., Kroencke, T., McCormick, B., & Nottebaum, L. (2000). Religiously motivated sexual orientation change. *Journal of Psychology and Christianity, 19,* 61–70.

Schested, K. (1999). Biblical fidelity and sexual orientation. In W. Wink (Ed.), *Homosexuality and Christian faith: Questions of conscience for the churches* (pp. 50–60). Minneapolis: Fortress.

Schreier, B. A. (1995). Moving beyond tolerance: A new paradigm for programming about homophobia/biphobia and heterosexism. *Journal of College Student Development, 36,* 19–26.

Schreier, B. A. (1995). Moving beyond tolerance: A new paradigm for programming about homophobia/biphobia and heterosexism. *Journal of College Student Development, 36,* 19–26.

Schreier, B. A., & Werden, D. L. (2000). Psychoeducational programming: Creating a context of mental health for people who are lesbian, gay, or bisexual. In R. M. Perez, K. A. Debord, & K. J. Bieschke (Eds.), *Handbook of counseling and psychotherapy with lesbian, gay and bisexual clients* (pp. 359–382). Washington, DC: American Psychological Association.

Schuck, K. D., & Liddle, B. J. (2001). Religious conflicts experienced by lesbian, gay, and bisexual individuals. *Journal of Gay & Lesbian Psychotherapy, 5,* 63–82.

Schwalbe, M. L., & Mason-Schrock, D. (1996). Identity work as group process. In B. Markovsky, M. Lovaglia, & R. Simon (Eds.), *Group processes* (Vol. 13, pp. 113–147). Greenwich, CT: JAI Press.

Schwartz, J. P., & Lindley, L. D. (2005). Religious fundamentalism and attachment: Prediction of homophobia. *International Journal for the Psychology of Religion, 15,* 145–157.

Shafranske, E. P. (1966). *Religion and the clinical practice of psychology.* Washington, DC: American Psychological Association.

Shallenberger, D. (1996). Reclaiming the spirit: The journeys of gay men and lesbian women toward integration. *Qualitative Sociology, 19,* 195–215.

Shallenberger, D. (1998). *Reclaiming the spirit: Gay men and lesbians come to terms with religion.* New Brunswick, NJ: Rutgers University Press.

Shannon, J. W., & Woods, W. J. (1991). Affirmative psychotherapy for gay men. *Counseling Psychologist, 19,* 197–215.

Shapiro, V. (1996). Subjugated knowledge and the working alliance: The narratives of Russian Jewish immigrants. *In Session: Psychotherapy in Practice, 1,* 9–22.

Sherkat, D. E. (2002). Sexuality and religious commitment in the United States: An empirical examination. *Journal for the Scientific Study of Religion, 41*, 313–323.

Sherkat, D. E., & Ellison, C. G., (1997). The cognitive structure of a moral crusade: Conservative Protestantism and opposition to pornography. *Social Forces, 75*, 957–980.

Shidlo, A. (1994). Internalized homophobia: Conceptual and empirical issues in measurement. In B. Greene and G. Herek (Eds.), *Lesbian and gay psychology: Theory, research and clinical applications* (pp. 176–205). Thousand Oaks, CA: Sage.

Shidlo, A., & Schroeder, M. (2002). Changing sexual orientation: A consumer's report. *Professional Psychology: Research and Practice, 33*, 249–259.

Smith, J. (1988). Psychotherapy, homosexuality, and homophobia. *Journal of Homosexuality, 5*, 59–74.

Snow, D. A., Rochford, E. B., Worden, S. K., & Benford, R. D. (1986). Frame alignment processes, micromobilization and movement participation. *American Sociological Review, 51*, 464–481.

Socarides, C. (1992). Sexual politics and scientific logic: The issue of homosexuality. *Journal of Psychohistory, 19*, 307–329.

Socarides, C. (1995). *Homosexuality: A freedom too far.* Phoenix, AZ: Adam Margrave.

Stein, T. S. (1988). Theoretical considerations in psychotherapy with gay men and lesbians. *Journal of Homosexuality, 17*, 45–55.

Stein, T. S. (1993). Overview of new developments in understanding homosexuality. *Review of Psychiatry, 12*, 9–40.

Stein, T. S. (1996). A critique of approaches to changing sexual orientation. In R. P. Cabaj & T. S. Stein (Eds.), *Textbook of homosexuality and mental health* (pp. 525–537). Washington, DC: American Psychiatric Press.

Stein, T. S., & Cohen, C. J. (1984). Psychotherapy with gay men and lesbian: Examination of homophobia, coming-out, and identity. In E. S. Hetrick & T. S. Stein (Eds.), *Innovations in psychotherapy with homosexuals* (pp. 60–73). Washington, DC: American Psychiatric Press.

Struzzo, J. A. (1989). Pastoral counseling and homosexuality. *Journal of Homosexuality, 18*, 195–222.

Svensson, T. K. (2003). *A bioethical analysis of sexual reorientation interventions: The ethics of conversion therapy.* Parkland, FL: Brown Walker Press.

Tan, P. P. (2005). The importance of spirituality among gay and lesbian individuals. *Journal of Homosexuality, 49*, 135–144.

Taylor, T. S. (2000). Is God good for you, good for your neighbor? The influence of religious orientation on demoralization and attitudes toward lesbians and gay men. *Dissertation Abstracts International, 60* (12), 4472A.

Texas Department of State Health Services. (2009). *Texas State Board of Social Worker Examiners Code of Conduct.* Retrieved from http://www.dshs.state.tx.us/SocialWork/sw_conduct.shtm

Throckmorton, W., & Yarhouse, M. A. (2006). *Sexual identity therapy: Practice guidelines for managing sexual identity conflicts.* Unpublished manuscript.

Thumma, S. (1991). Negotiating a religious identity: The case of the gay evangelical. *Sociological Analysis, 52,* 333–347.

Thyer, B. A., & Myers, L. L. (2009). Religious discrimination in social work academic programs: Whither social justice? *Journal of Religion & Spirituality in Social Work, 28,* 144–160.

Tigert, L. M. (1996). *Coming out while staying in: Struggles and celebrations of lesbians, gays, bisexuals in the church.* Cleveland: Pilgrim Press.

Tolbert, M. A. (2002). *Homoeroticism in the biblical world: Biblical texts in historical context.* Retrieved from http://www.clgs.org/homoeroticism-biblical-world -biblical-texts-historical-contexts

Tozer, E. E., & Hayes, J. A. (2004). Why do individuals seek conversion therapy? The role of religiosity, internalized homonegativity, and identity development. *Counseling Psychologist, 32,* 716–740.

Tozer, E. E., & McClanahan, M. K. (1999). Treating the purple menace: Ethical considerations of conversion therapy and affirmative alternatives. *Counseling Psychologist, 27,* 722–742.

Turner, K. L., Wilson, W. L., & Shirah, M. K. (2006). Lesbian, gay, bisexual, and transgender cultural competency for public health practitioners. In M. D. Shankle (Ed.), *The handbook of lesbian, gay, bisexual, and transgender public health: A practitioner's guide to service* (pp. 59–83). Binghamton, NY: Harrington Park Press.

Tyler, J. M., Jackman-Wheitner, L., Strader, S., & Lenox, R. (1997). A change-model approach to raising awareness of gay, lesbian, and bisexual issues among graduate students in counseling. *Journal of Sex Education, 22,* 37–43.

Unitarian Universalist Association of Congregations. (2008). *Beliefs within our faith.* Retrieved from http://www.uua.org/visitors/beliefswithin/index.shtml

Unitarian Universalist Association of Congregations. (2009). *UU perspectives.* Retrieved from http://www.uua.org/visitors/uuperspectives/index.shtml

Unitarian Universalist Association of Congregations. (2010). *Our history.* Retrieved from http://www.uua.org/visitors/ourhistory/index.shtml

United Church of Christ National Bodies. (n.d.). *Social policy statements on LGBT concerns.* Retrieved from http://www.ucc.org/lgbt/statements.html

United Methodist Church. (2004). *What is the denomination's position on homosexuality?* Retrieved from http://archives.umc.org/interior.asp?mid=1324

United States Constitution, Amendment 1. Retrieved from http://www.archives. gov/exhibits/charters/bill_of_rights_transcript.html

Vance, L. A. (2008). Converging on the heterosexual dyad: Changing Mormon and Adventist sexual norms and implications for gay and lesbian adherents. *Nova Religio: The Journal of Alternative and Emergent Religion, 11,* 56–76.

Van Soest, D. (1996). The influence of competing ideologies about homosexuality on nondiscrimination policy: Implications for social work education. *Journal of Social Work Education, 32*, 53–64.

Van Wormer, K., Well, J., & Boes, M. (2000). *Social work with lesbians, gays, and bisexuals: A strengths perspective.* Boston: Allyn & Bacon.

Veenvliet, S. G., & Esses, V. M. (2007). *Religious fundamentalism, zero-sum beliefs, and negative attitudes toward same-sex marriage: An attitude function analysis.* Manuscript in preparation.

Vincke, J., De Rycke, L., & Bolton, R. (1999). Gay identity and the experience of gay social stress. *Journal of Applied Social Psychology, 29*, 1316–1331.

Violence against LGBT people. (n.d.). Retrieved from Wikipedia: http://en.wikipedia.org/wiki/Violence_against_LGBT_people

Wagner, G., Brandolo, E., & Rabkin, J. (1996). Internalized homophobia in a sample of HIV+ gay men and its relationship to psychological distress, coping and illness progression. *Journal of Homosexuality, 32*, 91–106.

Wagner, G., Serafini, J., Rabkin, J., Remien, R., & Williams, J. (1994). Integration of one's religion and homosexuality: A weapon against internalized homophobia? *Journal of Homosexuality, 26*, 91–110.

Wallace, B., Carter, R., Nani'n, J., Keller, R., & Alleyne, V. (2002). Identity development for "diverse and different others": Integrating stages of change, motivational interviewing, and identity theories for race, people of color, sexual orientation, and disability. In B. Wallace and R. Carter (Eds.), *Understanding and dealing with violence: A multicultural approach* (pp. 41–91). Thousand Oaks, CA: Sage Publications.

Walters, K. L., & Simoni, J. M. (1993). Lesbian and gay male group identity and self-esteem: Implications for counseling. *Journal of Counseling Psychology, 40*, 94–99.

Walton, G. (2006). "Fag church": Men who integrate gay and Christian identities. *Journal of Homosexuality, 51*, 1–17.

Warner, R. S. (1995). The metropolitan community churches and the gay agenda: Power of Pentecostalism and essentialism. In D. G. Bromley, M. J. Neitz, and M. S. Goldman (Eds.), *Religion and the social order: Sex, lies, and sanctity: Religion and deviance in contemporary North America* (pp. 81–108). Greenwich, CT: JAI Press.

Webster, A. (1998). Queer to be religious: Lesbian adventures beyond the Christian/post-Christian dichotomy. *Theology & Sexuality, 8*, 27–39.

White, M. (1993). Deconstruction and therapy. In S. Gilligan & R. Price (Eds.), *Therapeutic conversation* (pp. 22–61). New York: W. W. Norton.

White, M. (1994). *Stranger at the gate: To be gay and Christian in America.* New York: Simon and Shuster.

White, M. (1995). *Reauthoring lives: Interviews and essays.* Adelaide, South Australia: Dulwich Centre Publications.

White, M., & Epston, D. (1990). *Narrative means to therapeutic ends.* New York: W. W. Norton.

Whitehead, M. M., & Nokes, K. M. (1990). An examination of demographic variables, nurturance, and empathy among homosexual and heterosexual Big Brother/Big Sister volunteers. *Journal of Homosexuality, 19,* 89–101.

Wig, N. N. (1999). Mental health and spiritual values: A view from the East. *International Review of Psychiatry, 11,* 92–96.

Wilcox, M. M. (2002). When Sheila's a lesbian: Religious individualism among lesbian, gay, bisexual, and transgender Christians. *Sociology of Religion, 63,* 497–513.

Wilcox, M. M. (2003). *Coming out in Christianity: Religion, identity, and community.* Bloomington: Indiana University Press.

Wilkinson, W. W. (2004). Religiosity, authoritarianism, and homophobia: A multidimensional approach. *International Journal for the Psychology of Religion, 14,* 55–67.

Wilkinson, W. W., & Roys, A. C. (2005). The components of sexual orientation, religiosity, and heterosexuals' impressions of gay men and lesbians. *Journal of Social Psychology, 145,* 65–83.

Williams, W. (1999). The abominable sin: The Spanish campaign against "sodomy," and its results in modern Latin America. In L. Gross & J. D. Woods (Eds.), *The Columbia reader on lesbians and gay men in media, society, and politics* (pp. 125–134). New York: Columbia University Press.

Wilson, A. (1996). How we find ourselves: Identity development and two-spirit people. *Harvard Educational Review, 66,* 303–317.

Winslade, J. M., & Monk, G. D. (1999). *Narrative counseling in schools: Powerful and brief* (2nd ed.). Thousand Oaks, CA: Corwin Press.

Wolkomir, M. (2001). Emotion work, commitment and the authentication of the self: The case of gay and ex-gay Christian support groups. *Journal of Contemporary Ethnography, 30,* 305–334.

Wood, M. E. (2000). How we got this way: The science of homosexuality and the Christian Right. *Journal of Homosexuality, 38,* 19–40.

Wooden, Q. A., Kawasaki, H., & Mayeda, R. (1983). Lifestyles and identity management among gay Japanese-American males. *Alternate Lifestyles, 5,* 236–243.

Woodman, N. J., & Lenna, H. R. (1980). *Counseling with gay men and women: A guide for facilitating positive lifestyles.* San Francisco: Jossey-Bass.

Worthington, E. L. (1988). Understanding the values of religious clients: A model and its application to counseling. *Journal of Counseling Psychology, 35,* 166–174.

Worthington, E. L., Hight, T. L., Ripley, J. S., McCullough, M. E., Berry, J. W., & Schmitt, M. M. (2003). The religious commitment inventory: Development, refinement, and validation of a brief scale for research and counseling. *Journal of Counseling Psychology, 50,* 84–96.

Worthington, E. L., Hook, J. M., Wade, N. G., Miller, A. J., & Sharp, C. B. (2008). The effects of a therapist's religion on the marriage therapist and marriage counseling. In O. J. Duba (Ed.), *The role of religion in marriage and family counseling* (pp. 17–34). New York: Routledge.

Yakushko, O. (2005). Influence of social support, existential well-being, and stress over sexual orientation on self esteem of gay, lesbian, and bisexual individuals. *International Journal for the Advancement of Counseling, 27,* 131–143.

Yarhouse, M. A. (2001). Sexual identity development: The influence of valuative frameworks on identity synthesis. *Psychotherapy, 38,* 331–341.

Yarhouse, M. A. (2009). The battle regarding sexuality. In N. A. Cummings, W. T. O'Donohue, & J. L. Cummings (Eds.), *Psychology's war on religion* (pp. 63–93). Phoenix, AZ: Zeig, Tucker & Theisen.

Yarhouse, M.A., & Burkett, L.A. (2002). An inclusive response to LGB and conservative religious persons: The case of same-sex attraction and behavior. *Professional Psychology: Research and Practice, 33,* 235–241.

Yarhouse, M. A., & Tan, E.S.N. (2004). *Sexual identity synthesis: Attributions, meaning-making and the search for congruence.* Lanham, MD: University Press of America.

Yep, G. A. (2002). From homophobia and heterosexism to heteronormativity: Toward the development of a model of queer interventions in the university classroom. In E. Cramer (Ed.), *Addressing homophobia and heterosexism on college campuses* (pp. 163–176). Binghamton, NY: Harrington Park Press.

Yip, A.K.T. (1997a). Attacking the attacker: Gay Christians talk back. *British Journal of Sociology, 48,* 113–127.

Yip, A.K.T. (1997b). Dare to differ: Gay and lesbian Catholics' assessment of official Catholic positions on sexuality. *Sociology of Religion, 58,* 165–180.

Yip, A.K.T. (1998). Gay male Christians' perceptions of the Christian community in relation to their sexuality. *Theology & Sexuality, 8,* 40–51.

Yip, A.K.T. (2000). Leaving the church to keep my faith: The lived experiences of non-heterosexual Christians. In L. Francis & Y. Kata (Eds.), *Joining and leaving religion: Research perspectives* (pp. 129–145). Leominster, England: Gracewing.

Yip, A.K.T. (2002). The persistence of faith among nonheterosexual Christians: Evidence for the neo-secularization thesis of religious transformation. *Journal for the Scientific Study of Religion, 41,* 199–212.

Yip, A.K.T. (2003). Spirituality and sexuality: An exploration of the religious beliefs of non-heterosexual Christians in Great Britain. *Theology & Sexuality, 9,* 137–154.

Yip, A.K.T. (2005). Queering religious texts: An exploration of British non-heterosexual Christians' and Muslims' strategy of constructing sexuality-affirming hermeneutics. *Sociology, 39,* 47–65.

Yip, A.K.T. (2007). Sexual orientation discrimination in religious communities. In M.V. L. Badgett & J. Frank (Eds.), *Sexual orientation discrimination: An international perspective* (pp. 209–224). New York: Routledge.

Zinnbauer, B. J., Pargament, K. I., Cole, B., Rey, M. S., Butter, E. M., Belavich, T. G., Hipp, K. M., Scott, A. B., & Kadar, J. L. (1997). Religion and spirituality: Unfuzzying the fuzzy. *Journal for the Scientific Study of Religion, 36,* 549–564.

Zuckerman, A. J., & Simons, G. F. (1996). *Sexual orientation in the workplace: Gay men, lesbians, bisexuals, and heterosexuals working together.* Thousand Oaks, CA: Sage Publications.

Index

A

Abelson, R. P., 127

abomination, 13, 16, 19, 26, 52

abstinence. *See* celibacy

Accept, 48–49

acceptance, 19, 36, 50, 55–56, 75, 82, 103, 105, 130. *See also under* sexual identity

activism, 34–35, 47, 88, 129

Affective Reactions to Homosexuality Scale, 148

affirmation, 22, 82–83, 116

affirmative agency environment, 146

affirmative practice, 68, 71, 97–99, 109, 145–146

affirmative religion, 46, 49–51, 74–75, 83, 94–95, 100, 103–105, 107, 108

affirming theological literature, 88, 95

African American stigmatization, 27–28

AIDS, 108, 123

Ajsen, I., 127

Alcoholics Anonymous, 109

Alford, B. A., 89

alienation, 5, 28, 31–33, 35, 56

Allen, D. J., 28

Alleyne, V. 37

Almazan, E. P., 28

Altemeyer, B., 5, 8

alternative religions, 22, 55, 100, 104–105, 106

American Academy of Pediatrics, 67

American Counseling Association, 67

American Medical Association, 67

American Psychiatric Association, 60, 62, 63, 64, 66, 131, 144

   position statement on SRT Web site, 66

American Psychological Association, 60, 66–67

   code of ethics, 66, 118

Task Force, 134

Anderson, D. A., 93

Androutsopoulou, A., 91

Anglican Communion, 21

Asian American stigmatization, 27–28

Atkinson, D. R., 66

authoritarianism, 9

autonomy, 119, 125

B

Baldwin, D., 7

Bandele, A., 132

Baptist Church, 8, 15, 17, 51

Bargh, J. A., 34

Barnett, D. C., 146

Barret, R., 7, 20, 25, 26, 27, 54, 57, 72, 86, 94, 100, 101, 129

Barzan, R., 7, 20, 25, 26, 27, 54, 57, 72, 81, 86, 94, 100, 101, 129

Bassett, R. L., 7

Derison, D., 5
De Rycke, L., 29
Detrie, P. M., 130
Deutsch, M., 8
devaluation, 34, 73, 93, 115, 116, 123
Diamond, L. M., 73
Diamond, S., 23
DiClemente, C. C., 143–144
Dignity (organization), 19–20, 103
dignity, 118, 123
Dillon, F. R., 134
disclosure. *See under* sexual identity
discrimination, 5–6, 67, 115, 144
    by practitioner, 116, 118, 121–
        122, 124
    prevention, 3, 18, 19, 22, 88, 115, 118,
        123, 125
    religious, 8, 9, 12, 17, 100
    societal, 4, 34, 103, 123, 125,
        131, 138
Donnelly, S., 21
Dove, B., 18
Dovidio, J. F., 115
Downey, J., 9
Drescher, J., 64
drug and alcohol abuse, 5, 39, 47, 80
Drum, D. J., 127, 147
Drumm, R. D., 45, 108
Duck, R. J., 5, 9
Dufour, L. R., 108
Dunn, M. S., 31, 33, 34–35
Dworkin, S. W., 7, 20
Dzelme, K., 8, 76, 91, 92

E

Eastern religions, 100, 104, 106, 107. *See*
    also specific religions
Eldridge, N. J., 146
Ellison, C. G., 5, 49
Emert, T., 140
Emsberger, D. J., 53
English, F., 9

Englund, M. E., 108
Enron, L. J., 14
Episcopal Church, 21. *See also* Integrity
Epston, D., 90, 91
equality, 21, 120, 123, 130
Ernulf, K. E., 148
essentialism, 44, 54, 106–108
    defined, 57
Esses, V. M., 5
evangelical groups, 8, 14, 108
Evangelical Lutheran Church in
    America, 15, 21–22
    Missouri Synod of, 15
Evangelicals Concerned, 94
Evergreen International, 65
Exodus Movement, 65

F

faith development, 53
family conflicts, 25, 27–28, 31. *See also*
    under rejection
Fassinger, R. E., 72, 80, 87
Fazio, R., 44
fear of disclosure, 82, 88, 103, 109
fear of rejection, 31, 32, 35, 48, 63, 82,
    by church, 26–27, 29, 46, 48, 60,
        66, 76
Feeling Good Handbook, The
    (Burns), 94
Fellows of Research Institute, 64
Fellows, W., 47, 95
Fernandez, E., 64
Fernandez, M. I., 140
Festinger, L., 44
Fetner, T., 65
Finkel, M. J., 132
Fishbein, M., 127
Fisher, A. R., 7, 115, 116, 130
Fisher, K., 130
Fisher, R. D., 5
Florida, 123
Floyd, R. B., 5, 6

Folkman, S., 79
Foreman, M., 135
Forrest, L., 5
Foucault, M., 90
Fourteenth Amendment, 122
Fowler, J. W., 53
Frame, M. W., 55, 72, 94, 104
Francis, L. E., 50
Freedman, J., 91
Friedman, R. C., 9
Friedman, S. T., 9
Friends (Quakers), 23
fundamentalist beliefs and groups. *See*
 conservative beliefs and groups
Fuss, D., 54

G

Gage Davidson, M., 7, 28, 29, 56, 71, 82,
 102, 104, 109
Gagnon, J. H., 64
Gallaher, R. V., 106, 107
Garcia, D. I., 46–47, 100, 105
Garcia, E., 76, 77–79
Garnets, L., 35, 73, 148
Gay Christian Movement, 88
gay-friendly churches, 20, 103–105
 defined, 104
"Gay Identity Issues Among Black
 Americans: Racism, Homophobia,
 and the Need for Validation"
 (Loiacano), 94
gay marriage
 opposition to, 3, 18, 128
 support for, 17, 19
gay-positive churches, 106, 108–109
 defined, 104
Gay Pride Day, 109
Gilbert, M. S., 5
Glock, T., 80
Goffman, E., 36, 53
Goldenberg, H., 91, 92
Goldenberg, I., 91, 92

Goldfried, M., 71, 82
Gonsiorek, J. C., 5, 28, 35, 36, 65, 66
Goodchilds, J., 73
Gorski, E., 20
Gottlieb, M. C., 72, 74
Gove, C., 37
Gramick, J., 5, 6, 7, 13, 19, 20,
 23, 59
Gray, B. E., 115
Gray-Stanley, J., 46–47
Greenberg, D. F., 6
Greene, B., 9, 28, 61, 63, 93, 118,
 119–120, 121, 129–130
Griffin, P., 136
Gross, M., 27, 45, 46, 105
group therapy, 87–88
Guerra, R. M., 134
guilt, 5, 26–27, 31, 32, 39, 53, 54, 60, 76,
 80, 109
Gwadz, M. V., 44, 46, 47, 108

H

Haan, N., 53
Hackett, G., 66, 146
Haldeman, D. C., 7, 35, 61, 64, 65, 66, 71,
 73, 74, 76, 81, 82, 85, 86, 87, 95, 99,
 100, 102, 103, 118, 132
Halpert, S. C., 113, 145
Hancock, K. A., 29, 73
Harris, D., 8, 76, 91, 92, 93
Harris, J. I., 5, 53
Harro, B., 136
Hatton, R. L., 115
Hayes, J. A., 32, 60, 61
Hecker, L., 8, 76, 91, 92
Heerman, M., 83, 89
Helminiak, D. A., 94
Henrickson, M., 88, 125
Herdt, G. H., 30, 36
Herek, G. M., 3, 4, 35
Herlihy, B. R., 122
Hermann, M. A., 122

heterosexism
    anger toward, 34–35, 38, 99
    as a barrier to the coming-out
        process, 29–31, 34, 39
    defined, 3
    hostile, 115, 121
    internalized by gays and lesbians, 5, 7,
        35–36, 49–50, 53, 60, 71, 79, 82,
        93, 95, 99, 129
    in practitioners, 60–65, 72–73,
        111–116, 120–121, 125
    religious, 5–6, 8–14, 27, 49, 52
    societal, 3–5, 34, 57, 98, 128, 129, 138
Hetrick, E. S., 36
Hewer, A., 130
Heyward, C., 71
Highland Church, 20
Hight, T. L., 76, 114
Hill, T. D., 5
Hinduism, 22, 105, 107
Hipp, K. M., 56
HIV/AIDS, 108, 123
Hochstein, L. M., 6, 15
Hodge, D. R., 13, 55
Hogge, J., 8
Holloway, E., 73
Homosexuals Anonymous, 65
Hook, J. M., 114
Horne, S. G., 6, 13, 28, 32, 56, 83, 94,
    102, 109
Horowitz, J. L., 37
hostility toward church, 35, 37, 57
House, R., 73
Houts, A. C., 8, 12
Howard, M., 116
Human Rights Campaign, 19
Hunsberger, B., 5, 8, 9
Hunter, J., 44, 46, 47, 108
Hunter, S., 103, 139, 143
Huntington Park, California, 22
Hyde, R. A., 61
hypocrisy, 10, 52

I

Iasenza, S., 127
identity
    acceptance, 34
    comparison, 32–33
    confusion, 30–32
    foreclosure, 31, 32, 33, 34
    oppositional, 50–51
    pride, 34–35
    synthesis, 35–36
    tolerance, 33–34
    See also integration; sexual identity
inerrancy of the Bible, 8–9
informed consent, 83
Innala, S. M., 148
Institute for Welcoming Resources, 104
integration, 30, 35, 88, 97, 99, 106–109
    stages, 101–102
    strategies, 107, 108
Integrity (organization), 103
integrity, 82, 101, 120
International Federation of Social
    Workers, 125
intervention, 75, 86–89, 93, 117,
    128–129, 144, 146–147
intolerance, 48, 60, 106
Isay, R. A., 66
Islam, 6, 13, 26, 107
Israel, T., 59, 72, 73, 74, 76, 78, 79, 80,
    81, 86, 87, 88, 93, 99, 103, 130,
    137, 146
"Issues of Identity Development Among
    Asian-American Lesbians and Gay
    Men" (Chan), 94
Iverson, E. F., 27, 52, 53, 54, 55, 56, 105

J

Jackman-Wheitner, L., 131, 144
Jackson, L. M., 5
Jannarone, A., 56, 101, 104, 106
Jehovah's Witnesses, 16
Jenkins, D., 60

Polley, C. F., III, 5
Pomeroy, W. B., 138
Ponticelli, C. M., 50
Pope Benedict XVI, 20
Pope John Paul II, 19
Pope, M., 121
Popper, K. R., 125
postconventional religious reasoning, 53, 93
practitioner
  assessment of client, 75–81
  conservative religious, 113–116, 127
  court rulings regarding, 121–122
  discrimination by, 116, 118, 121–122, 124
  ethics, 62, 63, 64, 65, 66, 67, 68, 74, 95, 113–118, 120–122, 124, 128–129
  goal identification, 81–83
  heterosexism, 60–65, 111–116, 120–121, 125
  internalized heterosexism, 72–73, 83
  intervention by, 75, 86–89, 93, 117
  legal obligations, 120–122, 125
  moral principles, 119–121, 125
  negative views by, 72, 115, 120, 129, 147–148
  power of, 68, 72, 73
  preparation, 71–75, 86–87, 93, 98, 101, 109, 117
  requirements, 117–118, 128–129, 148
  tolerance, 114, 123, 125
  See also affirmative practice; transformation
Prancer, S., 9
Pratt, M., 9
prayer, 26, 37–39, 45, 64, 65, 68
prejudice
  practitioner, 66, 72, 115, 116, 118, 121, 128, 130, 138
  religious, 7, 9, 107
  societal, 4, 34, 35
Presbyterian Church, 15

Price, J. H., 148
Prochaska, J. O., 131, 143
Protestant churches, 6, 8, 14, 15, 107. See also specific religions
Purcell, D. W., 5

Q

Quackenbush, R. H., 129
Quakers (Friends), 23, 24
queer spirituality, 56–57
queer theory, 36–37
quest identity, 61
Quinlan, M., 39, 135, 136

R

Rabkhi, J., 5, 28
Rabkin, 86
Ramirez-Valles, J., 46–47
rational–emotive behavioral therapy, 89–94
  bibliotherapy, 94, 101
  countering misinformation, 93–94
  independent thinking, 92–93
  narrative perspective, 90–92
Ratzinger, J., 20. See also Pope Benedict XVI
Raw Story, 20
Ream, G. L., 5
Redding, California, 4
Reid, J. E., 31
Reinhardt, B., 113, 145
rejecting-punitive religion See under religious views
rejection
  by church, 6–7, 26, 60, 100, 101
  by family, 27, 75, 81
  by society, 36, 51, 139
rejection of church, 26, 39, 44–47, 55, 56, 85, 95, 99, 100, 102
rejection of sexual identity, 7, 28, 85–87
religion, separation from spirituality. See spirituality

Strader, S., 131
Stranger at the Gate (White), 75
Struzzo, 71, 82, 109
suicidal ideation and behavior, 5, 27, 28,
    33, 39, 44, 45, 50, 80
support groups, 38, 48–49, 61, 82, 88,
    94–95, 101–104, 107, 108, 109, 144
Supreme Court, 120, 122
Svensson, T. K., 67

T
Tammaro, J., 7
Tan, E.S.N., 71, 75, 77, 78
Tan, P. P., 56
Taylor, T. S., 9, 95
Terndrup, A. I., 29, 130
Texas Department of State Health
    Services, 120
Texas licensure law, 121
Texas State Board of Social Worker
    Examiners Code of Conduct, 120
Throckmorton, W., 74, 83
Thumma, S., 43, 44, 45, 46, 47, 50,
    86, 108
Tigert, L. M., 23, 24, 103
Tolbert, M. A., 14
Toohey, M. J., 113, 145
Tozer, E. E., 32, 60, 61, 67, 68, 73, 78, 80,
    87, 98, 99
transformation, 127–148
    affirmative, 127–130, 145
    affirmative supervision in, 145
    biases in, 137
    competencies, 130
    empathy development in, 140–142
    guided imagery in, 140
    heterosexism, 129, 140
        disengagement from, 129–130,
            145–147
    history of beliefs about same-sex
        identities in, 134–135
    interventions, 128, 131, 144, 146–147

research on, 128, 146–148
language use in, 130, 135, 146
negativity in, 125, 129–131
Promise Statement, 145
questions, 131, 134–135, 141–145
reaction papers, 132
religious beliefs in, 129
reverse questionnaire, 141
role-playing, 138–139, 141
self-examination in, 127, 129,
    132–144, 147
stages, 131
    action, 143, 147
    contemplative, 142
    maintenance, 144–145
    precontemplative, 131–141
stereotypes in, 136
transformational learning theory, 95
trauma, 79, 80
Tschorke, D., 7
Turner, K. L., 117, 137, 140, 142, 145
Tyler, J. M., 131, 144
Tyson, B., 10, 79

U
Unitarian Universalist Association of
    Congregations, 22, 24, 103
    Web site, 22
United Church of Christ National
    Bodies, 16–17, 103
    Human Resource Campaign 2010, 17
    Web site, 17
United Methodist Church, 15, 20–21
United States Constitution, 122
United States Court of Appeals for the
    Fifth Circuit, 121–122
USA Today, 65

V
Valgemae, A., 93–94
validation, 39, 73
Van Soest, D., 123